I0820494

History's Greatest Philosophers

History's Greatest Philosophers

Classical Wisdom for Modern Times

Jamie Ryder

First published in Great Britain in 2025 by
Pen & Sword History
An imprint of Pen & Sword Books Limited
Yorkshire – Philadelphia

ISBN 978 1 03610 704 8

A CIP catalogue record for this book is
available from the British Library.

Typeset by Mac Style
Printed in the UK by CPI Group (UK) Ltd, Croydon, CR0 4YY.

The Publisher's authorised representative in the EU for product
safety is Authorised Rep Compliance Ltd., Ground Floor,
71 Lower Baggot Street, Dublin D02 P593, Ireland.
www.arccompliance.com

For a complete list of Pen & Sword titles please contact

PEN & SWORD BOOKS LIMITED
47 Church Street, Barnsley, South Yorkshire, S70 2AS, England
E-mail: enquiries@pen-and-sword.co.uk
Website: www.pen-and-sword.co.uk
or
PEN AND SWORD BOOKS
1950 Lawrence Road, Havertown, PA 19083, USA
E-mail: uspen-and-sword@casematepublishers.com
Website: www.penandswordbooks.com

Contents

Acknowledgements		vi
Introduction		viii
Chapter 1	The Stoic Emperor and Resilient Leadership	1
Chapter 2	The Philosophical Orator and the Slippery Slope of Pride	15
Chapter 3	The Roman Socrates and Compassionate Living	25
Chapter 4	The Old Master and Going With the Flow	34
Chapter 5	The Architect of the City of Ladies and Defying Expectations	40
Chapter 6	The Prince of Politics and Making Your Own Luck	48
Chapter 7	The Everyman Philosopher and Not Knowing Anything	61
Chapter 8	The Foremother of Feminism and the Vindication to Live	73
Chapter 9	The Art Critic and the Architecture of the World	81
Chapter 10	The Philosophical Writer and the Absurdity of Life	91
Chapter 11	The Outsider and the Philosophy of Otherness	102
Chapter 12	The Lady of Truth and the Fight for Freedom	116
Chapter 13	The Philosopher of Signs and the Mythology of Pop Culture	124
Interviews		131
Notes		170
Bibliography		177
Index		182

Acknowledgements

The creation of this book wouldn't be possible without the encouragement and diligence of several people. Thank you to my parents and my partner Kim for always supporting me with my writing endeavours. Thank you to Pen & Sword Books and my commissioning editor Sarah-Beth Watkins for hearing out my idea and taking a chance on this project. Thank you to Chris Cocks, a copy editor with the kind of eye for detail that turns raw work into finished products. Thank you to all the academics, scholars and philosophers whose work is generously accessible and who helped me with creating the profiles of the people in this book. In particular, the work of Donald Robertson and Ryan Holiday was a spark that lit the match and sent me on a philosophical journey that I'll be walking for the rest of my days.

I'd also like to personally thank everyone who agreed to be interviewed and share your thoughts about what philosophy means to you in life and business. Thank you to Britanny Polat for your wonderful insights into how Stoicism can be applied to women and men. Thank you to Ben Wilber-Force Ritchie and Dr Brennan Jacoby for showing me how philosophy can be applied realistically to the working world. Thank you to fellow traveller Anya Leonard for your tireless pursuit of making philosophy fun. Thank you to Glenn Fisher for the reminder that philosophy can't exist in a vacuum and to think anything otherwise is downright waffy. Thank you to Sam McNernry for your perspective on historical data and how it shapes lives. Thank you to Tyler Paytas for your command of technical concepts and for helping me make sense of them. Thank you to Rachael and Vikas Shah for the enlightening conversations on sustainability and ethics.

I'd like to mention the people who've been integral to improving the book with feedback. Thank you to David Williams for all the nights we debated philosophy and mental health over rum and other drinks. Thank you to James Richardson for your honest critiques of LGBT perspectives and experiences. Thank you to Andy Hall for having the bravery to live and breathe your own principles and inspiring me to live mine. Thank you to Nelchael Antoine for the positivity about sharing life paths that are worlds away from my own. Thank you to Jack Leigh for the reminder that life without laughter isn't worth a damn thing.

And thank you for reading the book.

Introduction

March 2020. The world went into lockdown and I remember feeling so many things all at once. Crippling uncertainty. A bottomless pit of anxiety in my stomach. Frustration at being trapped in place without any answers. As the days turned into weeks and the weeks turned into months, isolation and loneliness set in. I was bouncing off the walls of my one-bedroom flat, cut off from my family and partner, still without any answers from a UK government that felt like it was getting off on changing the rules at a whim.

But as bad as all that loneliness and anxiety felt, there was a part of me that wanted to find answers. To find meaning among the chaos, doom scrolling and death of the COVID-19 pandemic. That purpose came through philosophy. I began listening to podcasts on schools of thought like Stoicism and Epicureanism. I watched YouTube videos about Eastern philosophies like Taoism. I devoured books for days and then re-read them to look for points I'd missed the first and second time around. I journaled every day, wrestling with the new lessons I was learning, discarding old thought patterns, rethinking what I wanted for my future.

Over the course of six months, I reflected on the change philosophy had brought to my life. I felt more present, more content to slow down and appreciate the small details of the everyday. Sure, anxiety and uncertainty were still with me, like two black dogs keeping pace with every step I took forward. But I noticed I was better at dealing with the feelings and addressing them. I had a toolkit of philosophical practices that helped guide my decisions. I realised my entire perception of philosophy had been transformed. Where once I'd thought it dry and academic, the stuff of classrooms and armchair conversations, it'd become crystallised as action. Practical philosophy that changed my perception of who I believed I was. It helped me feel more confident and engaged with my environment.

Most of all, it provided more questions than answers. It made me wonder what philosophy is and how it can be applied across different aspects of life.

Because the topic isn't just one belief system, school of thought or perspective. It's the very essence of life that we experience, no matter our backgrounds. Or it's the pursuit of wanting to be better. Maybe it's an attitude that becomes a guiding principle. Perhaps it's having a laugh with your mates at the pub, setting the world to rights over a good glass and good company. Or to go back to the original meaning of the word 'philosopher' it's to simply be a lover of wisdom.

So, if you're looking for an academic book about philosophy then you should stop reading now. *History's Greatest Philosophers: Classical Wisdom for Modern Times* is about practical philosophy. The kind that shows the subject as a way of life through leaders, rebels, renegades, politicians and creatives who changed the status quo and brought radical new ideas to life. People who were brought to rock bottom, climbed to the greatest heights of society and lived somewhere in between. Great statesmen like the Stoic emperor Marcus Aurelius. Savvy politicos who lived for court intrigues like Niccolo Machiavelli and those who preferred to spend time playing with their pets and questioning everything like Michel de Montaigne. Revolutionary women like Sojourner Truth who broke the gender mould and flipped societal expectations upside down.

The lives of these philosophers are captured through essays, anecdotes and short stories. You'll see the mistakes they made. The flaws that rubbed people the wrong way. The moments of vulnerability that brought them down to earth. The personal victories, sacrifices and compromises that made them so memorable and the lessons they learned and taught so enduring. There isn't any set order to reading the chapters and I would encourage you to read them in any sequence that you like. 'Greatest philosophers' is used subjectively because they have personally impacted my life. They are the figures that plucked me from the depths of uncertainty. That inspire me to dig deeper to understand myself and the world. To take one small step forward every day.

This book is also about exploring modern interpretations of philosophy for personal and business use. The 'Interviews' section features stories from modern philosophers and business owners who use the topic practically day to day.

If you find some classical wisdom to take away from this book, then that's awesome. If not, that's okay too. To reference a famous quote, the only thing I know is that I know nothing. And I'm not even sure of that. I find life gets a lot easier when you think like that. I'm not sure whether you'll enjoy this book or not, but I'd still encourage you to write a review.

Chapter 1

The Stoic Emperor and Resilient Leadership

171 AD. On a corner of the Danube River, the Roman town of Carnuntum perches like a great eagle on the edge of the world. Out on the frontiers of the empire, wildness and savagery run amok. The order and civility of Rome are far away. Outside of the city, Carnuntum is the most important location in the empire because it's where the emperor has made camp.

Inside his tent, Marcus Aurelius stirs. He gazes up into darkness, small cracks of morning light penetrating the tent, disturbing his slumber. The emperor turns onto his side, mind flooding with all the responsibilities and obstacles that have been set before him. His war against the Marcomanni tribe and all the other barbarians that sought to strike against Rome. The Antonine Plague spreading death across the empire, exacting a heavy toll on his people. The Senate and their constant demands. The men who'll challenge him, who will smile to his face and mutter about weakness behind his back. The frailness of his body and all the aches and pains that come with it.

As if his own flesh wishes to remind him of the last part, a rattling cough erupts in his throat. Marcus convulses and a part of him yearns to stay in bed. To throw the covers over his face and sink back into the peace of sleep. But duty calls to him. All the mentors who've shaped his life call to him across the years. His adoptive father Antoninus Pius, who taught him the values of respect, patience and self-restraint. His tutor Apollonius of Chalcedon, who instilled in him the meaning of virtuous character. His teacher Junius Rusticus, who showed him the way to be disciplined. Lucilla, his mother, who practised generosity and lived simply.

Marcus contemplates their character and reminds himself: *When you wake up in the morning, tell yourself: The people I deal with today will be meddling, ungrateful, arrogant, dishonest, jealous and surly. They are like this because they can't tell good from evil.*[1] He tells himself that even wrongdoers have the same nature as everyone else. A nature linked by the cosmopolis of human understanding. So, to feel anger or hatred towards any man or woman is a futile endeavour. To feel hurt or offended by their actions is unnecessary because it is outside of your control. Instead of turning your back on someone, you were born to work together, like the natural functions of the body, feet walking towards the same destination, hands building the same home, eyes seeing the same vision. Anything less is an obstruction.

Completing his morning meditation, Marcus rises from bed to start his day.

* * *

This mental technique was one of many philosophical tactics Marcus Aurelius applied to his daily life. Known as the last of the Five Good Emperors of Rome, Marcus practised Stoicism. The philosophy helped to guide him through a chaotic world, influencing his decisions as a leader, politician and human being. We know a lot about his life and Stoic perspective because he recorded his thoughts in the *Meditations*, a private journal Marcus never intended to be published.[2]

In his journal, Marcus explores concepts of duty, compassion, ethics and honour, reminding himself to improve, to change, to remember the Stoic teachings that steered him. Two thousand years later and the influence of the *Meditations* is still being felt, with people all over the world reading it and seeing their own struggles reflected back at them. And to understand Marcus's life, it's essential to understand Stoicism and what it meant to him.

What is Stoicism?

Growing up in England, the attitude of 'keep a stiff upper lip' was a part of my childhood. Put another way, it's describing someone who's stoic. The implication is an emotionless robot that doesn't talk about what's going on inside. I used to think that's what stoicism meant. Turns out that's unhealthy 'little s' stoicism. 'Big S' Stoicism is the complete opposite and it started with a guy called Zeno of Citium around 300 BC. What follows is a simplified version of Stoicism to emphasise its practical nature. Several great books go into the technicalities and deeper nuances of the philosophy. They include *How to Be a Stoic* by Massimo Pigliucci, *How to Think Like a Roman Emperor* by Donald Robertson, *365 Ways to be More Stoic* by Tim LeBon and *Being Better: Stoicism for a World Worth Living In* by Kai Whiting and Leonidas Konstantakos.

Zeno was a wealthy merchant. On a journey to Athens he got shipwrecked. Overnight, his entire life changed and he needed to find a way to move forward. So, he stumbled through Athens and wandered into a bookstore. As the story goes, he was rifling through texts when he came across a book by Xenophon, a student of Socrates. Reading the content of the book blew Zeno's mind and he asked the bookseller where he could learn from men like Socrates.

As luck would have it, a philosopher called Crates was wandering by the bookshop and the seller pointed him out. From that day forward, Zeno studied under Crates, who was a Cynic philosopher. Cynicism became an inspiration for Zeno's philosophy and when he'd developed his perspective, he went to a place in the Athenian marketplace called the *Stoa Poikile* (painted porch). The Stoa became a place where people debated ideas in public and where Stoicism got its name. Zeno built his philosophy around the understanding that practising virtue is the highest good and the path to a well-lived life. External concepts like wealth and pleasure are beyond our control and we can only focus on what we can control. This is our reaction to outside events and happiness isn't found in external things. It comes from practising virtue alone.

Put another way, the Stoics believed we must live in accordance with nature (which doesn't mean walking around without any clothes on in the woods by the way). This can be taken to mean human nature, the community and the environment. It's practising the four Stoic principles of justice, courage, temperance and wisdom. Stoicism isn't about being passive or individualistic. It's about being an active part of your community and engaging with the world. It's instilling a sense of social responsibility, helping others and living what you believe.

Zeno's students Cleanthes and Chrysippus helped to mould Stoicism into a clearer set of values and were the giants of the Early Stoa (3rd century BC). Into the 1st and 2nd centuries BC, the Middle Stoa developed under the guidance of people like Panaetius of Rhodes and his student Posidonius. They were responsible for bringing it from Greece to Rome and Stoicism further evolved to fit Roman society. Greek Stoicism tended to focus on individual experience and ascetic self-denial. Roman Stoicism had a more human feeling to it because it championed society and used reason to regulate emotion, not to deny it completely.[3] There also seemed to be a more relaxed attitude to external factors like being physically wealthy, which some of the most famous Roman Stoics were. For example, the politician Seneca and personal advisor to Emperor Nero had a vast fortune of 300 million sestertii. When reconciling the relationship between being materially rich and being a Stoic, there's the concept of the preferred indifferent. In other words, wealth shouldn't be recklessly sought after or at the expense of self-harm. But it can be better to be wealthy than not, especially if it's a byproduct of living a virtuous life.

By the time Marcus studied Stoicism it was well established among Roman high society. One of his greatest examples of learning how to apply it practically was by studying the teachings of the slave Epictetus. Here's an indication of the universal accessibility of Stoicism. Then and now it's a philosophy that can be embraced by people of all walks of life. By Marcus adopting Stoicism into his day-to-day life, some have idealised him as a philosopher king, a concept that Plato presented in his work *The Republic.* A philosopher king was someone who combined political skill with philosophical truth for the greater good of all. Another perspective is that Marcus wasn't a philosopher at all. When writing *Meditations,* he was repeating maxims and work back to himself that he'd previously studied. He didn't contribute any wholly original philosophical ideas and his journal can be appreciated without knowing anything about Stoicism. At one point, he even admits to himself that he shouldn't go expecting Plato's *Republic* and that he certainly didn't view himself as a philosopher king. Nevertheless, the life of Marcus Aurelius is a fascinating story of how a boy wise beyond his years was hand-chosen to become the most powerful man in the Western world.

Groomed for greatness

Born on the 26th April 121 AD, Marcus Annius Verus came from a privileged family that taught him the merits of a simple, good life. They lived in a town called Ucubi in the Roman province of Hispania Baetica before they moved to Rome. Marcus's father died when he was 3 and although he remembered little of him, Marcus recalled his compassionate attitude and took it with him later in life.

Raised by his mother and paternal grandfather, Marcus's family had a connection to the court of Emperor Hadrian. His grandfather was a trusted friend of the emperor and brother-in-law to Hadrian's wife. From his later writings, we know that both family members had a tremendous impact on how Marcus lived his life. From his grandfather, he learned the importance of sociability, constantly mingling with other patrician families as a boy, learning the flow of conversation, even though he would come to dislike the rhetoric and sophistry needed for politics.

From his mother, Marcus internalised frugality and unpretentiousness. She'd inherited a vast fortune and owned a brick and tile factory, though she lived a life that wasn't ostentatious like so many of the Roman elite. As she gave away her time and resources to honourable pursuits, so did her son. Marcus was known for gifting away the inheritances he received to kin. Another time, during his reign as emperor, Marcus discovered the royal treasury was empty. So, he auctioned off imperial treasures to the public to fund the First Marcomannic War in 166 AD.[4] Marcus's childhood was filled with other mentors like his painting master Diognetus, a man that may have been the future emperor's gateway into philosophy. He taught the boy to look into the details of the everyday, the things that could go unnoticed like the wrinkles on the face of an old man but were important for understanding the rhythm of the world.

One person took a shine to the young Marcus and would change the course of his life: Emperor Hadrian himself. Hadrian saw a boy wise beyond his years, nicknaming him Verissimus, which means most truthful one. Perhaps he saw a youth who wasn't afraid to question the nature of the world. Who stood apart from the other patrician boys in his court who were unable to think for themselves. Hadrian gave Marcus many honours, raising him to the rank of a Roman knight at the age of 6. At age 8, the emperor placed Marcus in the College of the Salii, a ceremonial order dedicated to celebrating Mars, the Roman god of war.

Despite Hadrian's praise, Marcus had little to say about him, other than as a reminder of how *not* to live his life. In *Meditations*, Marcus mentioned Hadrian's desire to be remembered as a great man, but the pursuit of fame is always fleeting and that he was as dead and gone as every other emperor before him. His name also isn't mentioned in Book 1 of *Meditations,* where Marcus lists all the people who influenced his life for the better.

There came a point where Hadrian knew he had to name a successor because he was childless. At first, he chose someone else to be his official heir. Yet that heir died a year later and the emperor had to go back to the drawing board. Although he wished for the 16-year-old Marcus to be his choice, Hadrian felt the boy was still too young. So, he devised a plan where

Marcus would be groomed for the throne instead. He wouldn't be *given* the title of emperor. He would have to *earn* it.

So, Hadrian adopted the husband of Marcus's aunt, Titus Aurelius Antoninus. In turn, Antoninus adopted Marcus as his son and Hadrian became the boy's adoptive grandfather. To mark this occasion, Marcus's name changed from Verus to Aurelius as part of his new father's household. Nothing was ever straightforward in the world of Ancient Rome. Hadrian's original heir had a son called Lucius. And so Antoninus adopted the boy too, making him Marcus's new brother.

What did Marcus make of being adopted into Hadrian's line? Did he see the role of the emperor as a chance to remake Rome in his own image as predecessors like Nero had? Would he go on to pursue pleasure and excess as Tiberius had? By all accounts, Marcus was distraught at the announcement. He had a hard time adjusting to the idea that he would have to leave his mother's villa and move into a world of insincerity, backstabbing politics and power-hungry senators.

As he lay asleep that night, Marcus had a dream. In it, his shoulders were made of ivory. He realised that he could bear the weight and duty that was expected of him. His Stoic training would help him to do this. Marcus was ready to embrace the path before him and there would be many teachers along the way to pick him up whenever he fell.

The heir apparent

After Hadrian's death in 138 AD, Antoninus became emperor without any struggle. He immediately set the tone for his reign by appeasing the Senate and sparing the men that Hadrian had condemned to death for various slights. An honourable and dutiful man, the emperor earned the name Pius and it was from this behaviour that Marcus took his lead. Still, the young heir was restless and anxious. He struggled to control his temper as anyone in a position of high power and responsibility would do. This image is at odds with the cold and emotionless stoic who doesn't feel their emotions. Author and CBT therapist Donald Robertson highlights that this is one of the key differences between the character trait and the philosophy. 'people … often think that it's about supressing feelings like anxiety, which they view as bad, harmful or shameful. That's not only bad psychology, it's also totally in conflict with Stoic philosophy, which teaches us to accept our involuntary emotional reactions, our flashes of anxiety, as indifferent: neither good nor bad.'[5]

Marcus's trajectory towards accepting his emotions and applying Stoicism didn't happen overnight. It was day-by-day progress and the sum of his lessons from teachers like Apollonius and Fronto. Both tutors had differing perspectives and hopes for their wayward student. Apollonius taught Marcus about the metaphysics and practicalities of Stoicism and how to use it to cultivate resilience for the self and for making hard decisions. Fronto didn't care for Stoic doctrine. He was more interested in instructing Marcus in the ways of rhetoric and public speaking because he saw these as being crucial for an emperor to rule wisely. He was well aware of Marcus's distaste for politics but speaking well was a necessary part of his station. He urged his young charge to accept that even if he attained all the wisdom of the Stoics, he would still have to don the imperial purple and carry out his duties.

Marcus's conflict between philosophy and rhetoric is felt throughout his writings, such as when he reminded himself: 'beware of becoming Caesarified, dyed in purple. It does happen. Keep yourself simple, good, guileless, dignified, unpretentious, devoted to justice, pious, kind, affectionate to others and resolute in carrying out your proper tasks.'[6]

Philosophy won the day for Marcus in the end and although Fronto was eclipsed by his other mentors, the young Caesar maintained a close relationship with his rhetoric teacher. The two exchanged letters over the years, with Marcus being able to relate to Fronto's chronic illness. He too suffered from a range of maladies and there is a deep intimacy and camaraderie between the men as Marcus laments his own illness, even saying that he wished to take on Fronto's sickness himself with all the pain and discomfort that came with it.[7]

Marcus's most influential philosophy tutor was Junius Rusticus. He helped Marcus fully embrace Stoicism and turn it from a set of theoretical ideas into a way of life. Having served as a general and soldier, Rusticus knew what it meant to contribute to a cause greater than himself. That to live in accordance with nature meant to be actively engaged in all aspects of life. Through his own journey, Rusticus met Arrian, a student of the renowned Epictetus and he may have possibly met the famous teacher in person. In any case, a copy of Epictetus's lectures was in his personal library and he passed the copy down to Marcus. According to author Ryan Holiday, 'Junius seemed to be willing to deliver truths to his pupil'. Marcus relates that he was 'often upset with Rusticus,' but the teacher and student always reconciled. It's a credit to both that 'Marcus was able to say he never became so angry with Junius's criticism or methods that he did something he later regretted'.[8]

During these years of training, a marriage was arranged between Marcus and his cousin Faustina the Younger. By all accounts, their relationship was strong and loving, though it wasn't without hardship. Marcus and Faustina had thirteen children, losing many to natural causes. Only six survived to adulthood, five daughters and a son. Marcus's relationship with his son Commodus is an enduring part of his legacy that we'll investigate later.

By 156 AD, Antoninus had ruled Rome prosperously for nearly twenty years. At age 70, his health started to fail him and he found it hard to keep himself standing for long periods. Nevertheless, he carried on serving Rome faithfully and Marcus took on more responsibility to help his ailing father figure. In 161, Antoninus finally succumbed. He called Marcus to his bedside, passing on the emperorship to his son. He spoke the word 'equanimity' which can be summed up as the way his rule and life are remembered.[9] Equanimity of spirit. Calm and composure. A steady hand steering a ship through turbulent waters. An example to be picked up and honoured by his heir.

Forged by war

When Marcus acceded to emperor, he didn't do it alone. His brother, Lucius Verus, also had a claim to the throne. Rather than risk political in-fighting, Marcus made the bold decision to name his brother co-emperor. Never had this been done before in Roman history. While the emperors were equal in rank, Lucius effectively took orders from Marcus and deferred to his judgement. The brothers were different in personality and temperament. Lucius enjoyed a life of luxury, throwing lavish parties and spending his time hunting. Distraction and vice seemed to be his philosophy, while Marcus doubled down on his Stoic viewpoint.

Still, the early reign of Marcus and Lucius was well received by the Roman public. Policies were put in place to support poor children, while free speech was permitted. An example of this was in the comic writer Marullus, who openly jested and criticised the emperors without any retaliation.[10]

Marcus was always open to learning and being proven wrong. He wrote, 'If someone can prove me wrong and show me my mistake in any thought or action, I shall gladly change. I seek the truth, which never harmed anyone:

the harm is to persist in one's own self-deception and ignorance.'[11] Marcus would need this open-mindedness and willingness to adapt. For there was war on the horizon and he would spend most of his reign far from Rome, fighting in distant lands.

Not long after the brothers' co-crowning, the Parthian king Vologases IV launched a bloody campaign into Armenia. As a client state of Rome, Armenia was under the protection of the empire, but the Roman soldiers were slaughtered and the governor of the region was forced to take his own life. To address the growing Parthian threat, Marcus sent Lucius to Syria to coordinate war efforts. After accompanying his brother to Capua, Marcus turned back to Rome to contend with state affairs – a disastrous decision.

Out of Marcus's sight, Lucius dallied and partied without restraint on his journey to Syria. Marcus had already sent the iron-willed general Avidius Cassius to discipline the troops stationed at the front. When Lucius arrived, he took command and sank further into hedonism, drinking, whoring and avoiding action, leaving men like Cassius to do the heavy lifting for him. Looking at it in a different light, Lucius may have suffered from conditions like alcoholism and depression. His pleasure-seeking was the only way he knew how to function and his addiction helped him cope in a world of violence and pressure.

After six years of fighting, Rome emerged victorious in the Parthian War. Lucius came home and carried on with his merrymaking, further testing his brother's Stoicism. Soon, the First Marcomannic War broke out and both emperors found themselves travelling to the northern frontiers of the empire. By this point, Marcus likely didn't trust Lucius to be able to handle himself alone and stepping in was unavoidable.

Early skirmishes went in Rome's favour and in 169 AD, Lucius longed to be closer to home. The brothers camped at Aquileia in northern Italy, where Lucius became ill. Three days later he died and there's a lot of speculation as to how it happened. Poison is one theory. More likely, the co-emperor died of the Antonine Plague that was ravaging the Western world.

Despite all the difficulties Lucius had caused Marcus, he likely mourned the loss of his brother dearly. The *Meditations* proves time and again that its author was an emotional person who felt loss deeply. And even though the emperor was a frail man, he soldiered on back to the front line. His philosophy demanded he continue to fight for Rome and her people.

Travelling around Gaul and the Danube, Marcus waged war against tribes like the Marcomanni and the Sarmatians. In the early stages of the war, the Romans suffered a terrible defeat at the Battle of Carnuntum, with a reported loss of 20,000 troops in one day. The emperor didn't shy away from the action, nor did he allow setbacks and his ill health to prevent him from performing his duty. His Stoic training would have been critical during these periods, and he embraced the concept of the inner citadel. This is a fortress or a place of refuge we can build inside ourselves when dealing with adversity. The inner citadel isn't a place where we cut ourselves off from emotion. It's recognising that an obstacle is in front of us, registering it and taking a step back. Once we've created a space for rational thinking, we can step out of the inner citadel and potentially turn an obstacle into a solution.[12]

Marcus cultivated his inner citadel every second he was on the battlefield. A famous example of how he turned a disadvantage into an advantage was during a battle against the Sarmatians, a tribe of fierce horsemen and women who wore scale armour and fought with bone-tipped lances. Marcus and his son-in-law Claudius Pompeianus lured the Sarmatians out onto the frozen Danube. The legionnaires planted their shields into the ice and supported each other to blunt the impact of the lances. With the Sarmatians stunned by their failed charge, the Roman soldiers rushed at them and found a way to make the horses fall over and dismount the riders. Roman spears thrust from behind the shield wall, sowing discord among the Sarmatians and destroying their own strategy. Fighting in hand-to-hand combat, the legionnaires would then switch tactics by wrestling the enemy to the ground and flipping them over onto the ice.

Marcus's resolve and leadership made him beloved by his troops. There are a few instances of his legions attributing his presence to divine miracles. The most famous was the Rain Miracle of 174 AD, when a group of legionnaires were outmanned, surrounded and without water. The emperor prayed to Jupiter and a sudden thunderstorm exploded in the heavens. Lightning struck down their foes and the rain quenched the thirst of the Romans, giving them the strength to fight on and win the day.[13]

Under Marcus's leadership, Rome finally overcame the tribes. But in 175 AD, a new threat loomed. A threat from within. Avidius Cassius, the general who had served the emperor faithfully through all his campaigns had steadily grown in power throughout the eastern provinces of the empire. Rumours of the emperor being dead were in the air and Cassius's jealousy of being passed over as successor by Claudius Pompeianus festered like a bad wound. Driven by a lust for power, Cassius allowed his men to crown him emperor which ignited a civil war.

On the other side of the empire, Marcus heard the news. It was delivered to him by an exhausted rider who'd travelled over 1,500 miles to deliver the message of betrayal. With Cassius becoming a serious threat to his authority, Marcus could have retaliated brutally. It was how Cassius liked to handle situations. Instead, the emperor vowed to *forgive* his former friend. Before his soldiers and advisors, Marcus proclaimed he was willing to grant Cassius and his followers clemency, that he was willing to bear what he must to end the civil war peacefully.

That Marcus showed no anger towards the betrayal is remarkable. It was the culmination of all the years studying with Rusticus, Fronto and Apollonius, of seeing Antoninus make decisions that impacted the fate of countless people from moment to moment, all those fleeting moments of fiery youth, of working every hour of every day to become a calm and fair-minded sovereign.

The Senate wasn't calm. They were terrified of what Cassius and his armies would do to Rome and declared him as public enemy number one. They sent their own forces along with the emperor's legionnaires to engage the usurper in Syria. Three months after the rebellion, Cassius was killed in his own camp. A centurion and a junior officer cut off the would-be emperor's head and delivered it personally to Marcus. He refused to look at it and instructed the head to be buried. While his legionnaires and the Senate rejoiced in Cassius's death, Marcus felt no joy. He kept his word to pardon the men who had served with his former ally and said that Cassius's family would live under his protection as they had done no wrong.

Not long after the rebellion, Marcus's wife Faustina died. For years, there had been rumours that she'd associated with Cassius and had wanted him to take power from her husband. Marcus had never cared for rumours and hearsay. He honoured his wife of thirty years, grieving and deifying her. Perhaps a part of him sensed that he would see her again soon. His health had continued to decline, yet he could still secure Rome's future with his heir and only son Commodus.

Going to the rising sun

March 180 AD. Marcus lay in bed, his body gripped by the diseases that had plagued him his whole life. Death was closing in, though he wouldn't be leaving Rome without a protector. For three years, his son had been ruling as co-emperor and he'd done all he could to make sure Commodus was prepared. All he could do now was wait for the end and accept it graciously. By his bedside, a young officer watched over him and the emperor uttered his final words, 'Go to the rising sun; I am already setting.'[14]

With that, the last Good Emperor of Rome died, a man who'd practised what he preached and would be remembered as perhaps the greatest emperor that Rome had ever known. His son would have a different legacy. Commodus lived an opposite life to his father, one that strayed far from the Stoic path. He overturned Marcus's decisions to spare the descendants of Cassius. He killed enemies indiscriminately. He played gladiator in the arena and demanded the people worship him like a god. He even had plans to rename Rome after himself when it burned down in 191 AD. His cruelty and capriciousness earned him an early death, as he was assassinated at the age of 31.

That Marcus would allow his unstable son to succeed him as emperor is one of the biggest criticisms of his legacy. It's an interesting question to explore and there have been several theories. One perspective is that Commodus wasn't naturally an evil person. He was simply weak willed and gullible, allowing himself to be coerced and flattered by sycophants. Donald Robertson mentions Marcus tried to surround his son with worthy advisors like Pompeianus. It was 'a safety measure but that was negated when Commodus simply fled from the (northern) front leaving Pompeianus and others behind and surrounding himself with individuals at Rome who further corrupted him'.[15]

We should also remember Marcus was as human as the rest of us. A parent can try their very best to steer a child in the right direction and we can imagine him making the attempt. Within his sphere of control, he tried to shape Commodus into a noble and wise ruler, but there would always be events beyond his control. To think otherwise would be foolish. Throughout his life, Marcus applied many practical Stoic exercises, some of which I've mentioned. Below is a list that you can apply to your own routine as you walk the path of Stoicism.

The view from above

Maybe you're feeling anxious or stressed. Close your eyes and picture that you're standing outside of yourself. There may be people in the room with you. Consider that they could be going through similar experiences of having a stressful day.

Next, imagine you're looking down at your city or town. There are people walking below you who are going through the same thing. They're struggling at work. They're facing adversity. They've been fired. They've lost a relationship. They're grieving.

Imagine yourself floating higher and higher. You're looking down at the whole world. Everyone on the planet is linked by the same strand of humanity. You're able to see that what you're experiencing is normal. That weighed against the grand scheme of things, it's not as bad as it seems. That you have the power to control how you react to the situation.

Slowly come back down to earth. Back to yourself. Open your eyes and think about how you're feeling now.

The premeditation of adversity

Consider you're going to meet people in life that you won't agree with or get on with. You're always going to be faced with situations that are uncertain and you don't know the outcome. Visualise what could *potentially* happen if a setback occurred. Visualise it as happening to you *right now* and think about how you'd respond and react.

It could be dealing with a difficult work colleague, contending with illness, a major financial decision. Rehearse the scenario a few times in your head to inoculate yourself against stress. If that scenario were to happen, you're more likely to be prepared to deal with the emotions of fear, anger or anxiety. The outcome doesn't matter. What matters is you did the work to expose yourself to stress in small doses.

Contemplating The Sage

In Stoicism, there's the idea of The Sage. A figure that's mastered the philosophy. That never gets angry or sad and has achieved *eudaimonia* (a flourishing life). And that's just it. The Sage is an *idea* and an *ideal.* Not a reality. It's an impossible goal and that's okay for a Stoic. It's something to reach for and aim at.

When doing this exercise, you can think about someone who inspires you. It could be someone living, fictional or historical. A figure that displays character traits you admire and want to model. When you must make an important decision, you could imagine someone like Marcus Aurelius guiding you. Imagine how he would handle the decision and follow through based on your best judgement.

The Stoic reserve clause

This is accepting that whenever you carry out an action the result isn't within your control. The reserve clause is saying to yourself, *Fate permitting, I'm going to help this person*. Or *if nothing stops me, I'll finish writing this report.* By attaching a caveat to the action, you can stay composed and not worry about the expectations of being successful. If you don't succeed, there's no need to beat yourself up about it because you had good and sincere intent.

Fate permitting, this has been a useful introduction to Stoicism for you and you can experiment with it in your life.

Chapter 2

The Philosophical Orator and the Slippery Slope of Pride

The fear of public speaking is one of the most common phobias in the world. Called glossophobia, it affects up to 75 per cent of people.[1] Whether it's the idea of being judged or messing up our words, this fear is natural. In the ancient world, the power of a speech could literally make the difference between life and death. The same could be said for certain instances in the modern world, whether it's a lawyer defending their client in court, or a CEO speaking to their staff and seeking to inspire them to grow a business. Varying degrees of life and death are based on the perception of the speaker.

But whatever the situation is, a well-delivered speech can move and change listeners for better or worse. That's stayed the same for millennia and even the greatest orators in history have found themselves struggling, adapting and learning to make their message land. To convince people of their point of view, create change and build a reputation. Marcus Tullius Cicero is counted among the most eloquent public speakers of all time. His ability to argue, persuade and inspire helped him climb from obscurity to the pinnacle of Roman society. In this chapter we'll chart his life and how he combined philosophy with rhetoric. Before we dive into that, it's worth asking the question about what rhetoric is and how it developed.

The art of rhetoric

What comes to mind when you think about rhetoric? A politician that pontificates on stage? A guru that claims to have all the answers? A form of manipulation? These are some modern interpretations of rhetoric that are based on truth. Like any tool, rhetoric can be used for good or bad. To twist a message, promote an unethical cause and coerce people into violence.

The original purpose of rhetoric was for a more noble and humane cause. In the 5th century BC, early forms of democracy were developing in the Western world. In Syracuse in Sicily, exiles were returning to claim property under a new regime but many were unable to reclaim their belongings because they didn't have any documented evidence. So, they were given the opportunity to pursue their case in front of a jury. To do so, they would hire specialists who could talk eloquently and argue in their favour.

The connection between eloquence and public forums continued into the Greek world, where Athens became the height of culture. Athenian citizens needed to defend themselves openly in court, which required them to know how to speak well, leading to the emergence of rhetoric teachers called Sophists. Early sophists like Protagoras of Abdera taught his students to question different sides of an argument, to focus on the act of persuasion, which could help a man defend himself verbally against the accusations of his peers and grow his political reputation.[2]

Over time, the Sophist movement became associated with the teaching of clever turns of phrases and metaphors – the use of language, patterns of speech and structure to influence people into believing a certain perspective. In other words, it was all flash and no substance. This was a chief argument of Plato, who claimed the sophists were only interested in money, wealth and fame. They wanted to fill their schools with wealthy students and get rich. Plato argued that sophists didn't have the knowledge to teach things like justice. They were only concerned with manipulating public opinion as a means to justice. In Plato's mind, his teacher Socrates restored philosophy to speaking in public by acting in the interest of values and morality.[3]

Later, Plato's student Aristotle would further develop rhetoric into a codified system. In his opinion, rhetoric was a tool that could be misused. But it was extremely helpful for a person with good intentions to learn about so they could use it to influence others for the better.

Aristotelian rhetoric also emphasises the point of proof. He believed that people are most likely to be convinced when something has been proven and a good orator won't need to distract people with big emotional appeals. With that said, Aristotle developed three principles of persuasion as follows:

- **Logos**: This is the rational part of an argument. It's appealing to the logic of an audience. This can include factual information and data, which can be misused with logical fallacies like the straw man concept. Ultimately, the speaker is trying to get the audience to buy into their argument.

- **Ethos:** This is when the speaker presents their character or the character of the person they are talking about. It's used for showing credibility. This may include the orator talking about their expertise, arranging a speech in an organised way and signalling you have good intentions with their presentation.
- **Pathos:** The orator appeals to the emotions of the audience. They may tell stories to elicit emotions like sadness or happiness or make people laugh.[4]

When the influence of the Greeks waned and Rome became the centre of culture and power in the West, rhetoric became entwined with the ideal politician within the Roman Republic. Cicero further added to the canon with his corpus of works. This spanned early manifestos like *De Inventione* (*On Discovery*) which he wrote when he was 20, to mature treatises like *De Oratore* (*On The Ideal Orator*), a master class on oratory as he saw it. A constant self-promoter and politician to his core, Cicero is largely responsible for creating his own myth as we'll see in the portrait of his life and presentation style.

From humble beginnings ...

Born in January 106 BC, Cicero's family came from the town of Arpinum, a town not far from Rome. The boy's name means chickpea in Latin, owing to an ancestor who had a dent in his nose that looked like the vegetable. Years later, when Cicero entered the world of Roman politics, his friends advised him to change his name to something less likely to bring him ridicule. In answer, Cicero vowed he would 'strive to make the name Cicero more illustrious than such names as Scaurus or Catulus'.[5] He would make it a name to be remembered and the envy of all.

Although Cicero's mother and father had connections to the Senate, they weren't members of the Roman nobility. This meant Cicero was considered a *novus homo* (new man) in the Roman political realm. He had no ancestors to speak of who'd attained high rank in the Senate and was thought of as country bumpkin by the patricians that he hoped to rub shoulders with. We can imagine Cicero dreaming big even in his childhood and committing to a political career that wouldn't be halted by anyone.

When his family moved to Rome, the aim was to increase the prospects of Cicero and his brother. Cicero got stuck in as soon as he was given the opportunity. He watched great speakers like Lucius Licinius Crassus and Marcus Antonius deliver in the public forum. He studied with legal specialists such as Quintus Mucius Scaevola, learning the ins and outs of court processes, of how to defend clients and state arguments. He also entered military service for a while and then a world that was torn apart by political strife and war. Two warring factions in the Senate jostled for control. The aristocratic Optimates led by Sulla and the Populares led by Marius, both using the people to advance their own political interests.

In 80 BC, Cicero found himself on the wrong side of Sulla in one of his first court cases. He defended a man called Roscius, who'd been accused by Sulla on trumped-up charges for killing his father. Cicero stepped in to help and leaned into the ethos part of Aristotelian rhetoric. He positioned Roscius as a humble farmer with good character who couldn't fathom a murder so brutal. On the other hand, those who'd accused him were motivated by greed and corruption.

> In this regard, I pass over what could have been an extremely powerful argument for me in maintaining Roscius' innocence – the fact that crimes of this sort are not generally born amid rustic manners, a frugal mode of living, a life rough and uncultured … this city breeds prodigality, and from prodigality greed necessarily develops, and from greed audacity bursts forth.[6]

Cicero's strategic use of rhetoric won the case for him and Roscius was acquitted. Although it won Cicero some acclaim, he wanted to escape the possibility of Sulla's harsh retaliation and took a sojourn to Greece, where he learned about philosophy and threw himself into studying all the major schools of thought. He soaked up Stoicism from Diodotus and Posidonius, educating himself on the idea of living in accordance with nature. He drank from the well of Epicureanism with Phaedrus, learning what it meant to live unseen on his intellectual journey. He paid close attention to the academic sceptic, Philo of Larissa, all of which helped him further develop his skills as a rhetorician.

Of all the schools, Cicero gravitated the most towards Academic Scepticism. He appreciated the fact that the school allowed for arguing on multiple sides to undermine the certainty of his future rivals in the Senate and make him a better speaker. By taking up this philosophy, Cicero could rationalise and explain all the contradictions that he would make in his political career and in his speeches. He could remain agnostic to all other philosophies and be driven to make a decision based on his own rational judgement.[7]

Eventually, news reached Cicero that Sulla had died and Rome had become a more stable place for ambitious new men to win their fortune. Returning to the city as a more seasoned orator, the nearly 30-year-old Cicero was ready to climb the rungs of the *cursus honorum,* the senatorial ladder, until he reached the top as Consul of Rome.

... to the greatest heights

Cicero consulted an oracle, who told him that he should rely on his own nature and not the opinion of the masses. Taking a cautious approach into politics, he started as a quaestor in Sicily. There he built up favours by being the lawyer for several young Roman nobles. He hoped this would win him praise in Rome, yet his name continued to fly beneath the radar. Doubling down, Cicero continued to strive for recognition and he finally got his chance when the Sicilians asked him to prosecute Gaius Verres.

The corrupt governor of the island, Verres was defended by the greatest lawyer of the day, Hortensius. Cicero won the case, catapulting him into the spotlight that he'd always desired. Soon, he was networking with the cream of Roman society. He joined the inner circles of the general Pompey and the richest man in Rome, Marcus Crassus, men who would go on to shape the future of the republic alongside Julius Caesar in the First Triumvirate.

As Cicero's star burned brighter, so did his political climb. Aedile, Praetor and at last, Consul in 63 BC. The new man without a noble pedigree had shattered all expectations by becoming the youngest citizen to ever achieve the highest office without coming from a patrician family.

During his year as consul, Cicero achieved what he would perceive as his finest moment. He uncovered a plot to overthrow the Senate by a bankrupt senator called Cataline. Through diligence and oratory, Cicero picked Cataline apart and denounced him before the Senate and the people. He deployed another ethos-based argument that can be summed up as a character assassination of his rival:

> What an extraordinary terrifying war it will be if Catiline will be leading this praetorian co-host of whores! Now, citizens, draw up your garrisons

> and armies against these outstanding troops of Catiline! First, post your consuls and generals against the wounded and worn-out gladiators; next, lead out the flower and strength of all of Italy against that castaway, debilitated band of shipwrecked men.[8]

Triumphant in stopping the Cataline Conspiracy, Cicero was named *Pater Patriae* (Father of the Fatherland). The victory emboldened Cicero but it would also become a double-edged sword. His journey to the top of the mountain had been meteoric and so would his downfall.

Fall from grace

In the years following the Catiline revolt, Cicero's political career began to unravel. The First Triumvirate of Pompey, Crassus and Caesar was growing in power and the former consul refused to support them because his views were at odds with theirs. Despite the triumvirs courting him as an ally, Cicero would not be swayed. And so, the Triumvirate were willing to let Cicero's enemies attack him without restraint. This was the perfect opportunity for Cicero's nemesis, Publius Clodius.

As tribune of the people, Clodius passed a law that outlawed any Roman who had put another Roman to death without trial. Cicero fell into this category by sentencing the Cataline rebels to death without a proper hearing. This forced Cicero into exile in 58 BC and his property was confiscated and destroyed in Rome. What followed was one of the lowest points of Cicero's life and he spent the next year and a half in Greece sinking into depression.

Being recalled to Rome by Pompey, the Triumvirate made the message clear to the former consul: do not interfere with our plans and do as we say. Forced to comply, Cicero spent the 50s defending his enemies. To find some sense of control and solace, he turned to writing and in this period he produced *On the Ideal Orator*, *On the Republic* and *On the Laws.*

In 51 BC, Cicero served as proconsul in the province of Cilicia, where he discovered some of his old political magic that helped restore order. But any hope of reclaiming some of his former influence was dashed on his return to Rome and the breakdown of the First Triumvirate. Crassus had died on campaign, while Pompey and Caesar were on a collision course to civil war.

During this period of uncertainty, Cicero sided with Pompey, championing the old Republican ideas that had helped him to rise to the consulship years before. When Caesar won his war against Pompey and brought Rome under his dictatorship, Cicero had the opportunity to speak out, to fight against the threat of the Republic being overturned completely as he'd done with Cataline. But he stayed silent. He chose to compromise and save his skin, while Stoics like Cato the Younger actively resisted Caesar. Philosophy had called to Cicero to do *something*. But he chose to be a fair-weather philosopher instead. Cato committed suicide in 46 BC, martyring himself for the ideals of the Republic. And Cicero eulogised him. But even then, he censored himself for fear of angering Caesar. This period of Cicero's life was personally difficult. His daughter Tullia had died and it left him grief-stricken, untethered. His only refuge was writing. He wrote *The Consolation*, a moving ode to his daughter where he recalled philosophy to soothe his grief. He went on to write extensively about philosophy and became a bridge for future readers to learn more about perspectives like Stoicism. According to Ryan Holiday,

> the one upside to Cicero's capitulation and his fair-weather commitment to philosophy is that by living he was able to continue writing, and to serve as a kind of bridge between Greek and Latin philosophical thought, especially in the area of ethics. And when it came to ethics, he knew of no better source in all of Greek and Latin literature than the Stoics.[9]

On the 15th March 44 BC, Caesar was assassinated and while Cicero had no direct hand in the plot, he was close to the men like Brutus, who'd driven his knife into Caesar's body. Brutus and his conspirators had kept Cicero out of the plot, perhaps believing he was too finicky and changeable to do what needed to be done.

Out of Caesar's demise came the Second Triumvirate, heralded by his heir Octavian, Mark Antony and Lepidus. Cicero attempted to muster one final stand. He rallied what remained of his oratorial spirit and spoke scathingly of Antony in speeches that became known as *Philippics*.

For the clever-tongued, eloquent Cicero, this would be his farewell address. The Second Triumvirate, Antony most of all, weren't forgiving. Cicero was sentenced to death without a trial and hunted down. Antony's assassins cut his head and hands off and brought them back to Rome. The body parts were presented on the *rostra,* the speakers' platform, the place where Cicero had always felt the most comfortable, pontificating and haranguing to the people.

The Ciceronian guide to oratory

Despite how he lived his life, Cicero's identity as one of the greatest speakers of all time is undisputed. There's a lot we can learn from him about public speaking and using rhetoric in an ethical way. Cicero's ideal speaker was a philosophical orator, that is someone who has a broad understanding of many subjects – art, politics, philosophy, history, law etc. – and can pull from these topics at will to craft a message. For him, practising and memorising a speech was better than reading theoretical handbooks, even though he wrote his own handbooks and often contradicted himself. His approach to oratory was based on five essential parts:

Invention

The first part involves finding the subject matter of your talk. This could mean researching specific topics or collecting a set of facts that are needed to state your case. You'll also want to consider the Aristotelian sources of proof which are logos, ethos and pathos. You can consider asking yourself questions like:

- What are the facts that I want to talk about?
- What are the most important parts of the cause I'm speaking about?
- What is my credibility or the credibility of the person I'm talking about?
- What is my experience and how many years have I been doing my job?
- What kind of emotions do I want to make the audience feel?
- What's the story behind my cause and are the parts that will make the audience feel the emotions I want them to feel?

Arrangement

Once you have the subject matter of your speech, it's time to organise it in the right order. This could be as simple as the beginning, middle and end. It could be more complex and arranged into how you want to make the audience feel. Cicero tended to organise his speeches in this structure:

- **Prologue/Introduction**: The opening of the speech should put the audience in the state of mind that you want them to be in. Strive to capture their attention as quickly as possible.

- **Narration**: This is sharing the story of your subject matter. It's presenting facts, anecdotes and interesting details. The three essential ingredients of narration are brevity, clarity and persuasiveness.
- **Confirmation**: This involves bringing in proof of what you're talking about. You might have testimonials, stats etc.
- **Refutation**: You might want to acknowledge an alternative opinion and state why you disagree with it.
- **Epilogue/Conclusion**: At the end of the speech, reiterate your main points and focus on stirring the audience's emotions for a final time.

Style

Now that you've figured out what you're going to say and the order of it, the next step is to plan out *how* to say it. This comes down to language and using the right words to convey your message. Brilliant subject matter can be obscured by a poor choice of words. Cicero believed there was no one type of style that would work. It came down to the speaker understanding their strengths and weaknesses. 'Between all of us here, then, there are great differences, and each of us has clear and specific traits. And amid this variety, the better is generally distinguished from the worse more by ability than by the type to which each belongs, and everything that is perfect in its own type is praised.'[10]

In terms of style types, he outlined three types:

- **Plain**: The plain style of speech uses simple language and positions the speaker on the same level as the audience. Language might be colloquial, words are short and the stories easy to picture and understand.
- **Middle**: The middle style uses a mixture of relaxed language and grand imagery to illustrate the point. This might also be used when balancing multiple perspectives and positioning the speaker as a mediator, or someone who can translate complex ideas.
- **Grand**: This was Cicero's favourite style. It positioned the speaker above the audience, used an aspirational tone, vivid stories and stately language.

In Cicero's opinion, the best speakers were masters of all three styles and understood which one to use based on their audience.

Memory

Memorising the speech came next and ancient orators like Cicero identified two important kinds of memory. Firstly, natural memory, is planted in the mind and comes with our thoughts. Secondly, artificial memory is what we learn from practice and discipline. It's developing connections in the brain that string the subject matter of a speech together, either through remembering certain lines, images or stories. According to Cicero,

> only those with a powerful memory know what they are going to say, how far they will pursue it, how they will say it, which points they have already answered and which still remain. Such people also remember much of the material they have used in the past and in other cases, and much that they have heard others use.[11]

Delivery

The final part of rhetoric, delivery, linked back to style. It was tone of voice, pauses, breaths, and body language. Here are some of Cicero's recommended delivery tactics:

- Modulate your voice to go higher or lower depending on the story you're telling.
- Study the delivery styles of speakers you admire and model their behaviour.
- Write down your speech and read the lines out loud. Experiment with different types of delivery.
- Identify how to deliver a complex idea in the simplest way possible. Find synonyms for the same word and focus on how they sound in your mouth when you speak them aloud.

Chapter 3

The Roman Socrates and Compassionate Living

Beneath the heat of Apollo dragging his mighty chariot across the sky, the Forum thrummed with the lifeblood of empire. Along the Via Sacra, plebs bustled towards the Coliseum, eager for their fill of violence and entertainment as laid out by the emperor, rubbing shoulders with young nobles and their entourages who desired to curry favour with the great Caesar.

Beggars rolled dice with each other beneath the sweeping colonnades, bartering their fates with Fortuna, while merchants haggled in the shadow of the Temple of Saturn, hoping to be blessed with wealth and prosperity.

Musonius Rufus pondered his view of wealth, while he listened to the sophist Marcellus deliver a speech on the love of money being equal to a love of the gods to the crowd that had gathered inside the basilica. On his way to see one of his favourite students, Musonius had stopped to listen, finding the man's subject matter instructive in the corrupting power of physical riches and for cultivating a better character. Marcellus spoke well enough for a charlatan, though there was no conviction in his arguments. His words were hollow, parroted rhetoric from speeches he'd likely learned by listening to magistrates and tribunes delivering public verdicts while begging in the streets.

Musonius reflected that if Thrasea was with him he would say men of Marcellus's ilk had become all too common under the reign of Nero. Men who lacked honour and lived in discordance with nature, harming the cosmopolis of humanity. Thinking of his headstrong student made Musonius smile. If there was ever a man who could continue to live up to the virtues of justice, courage, wisdom and temperance in his absence, he could think of no one better suited to the role. Musonius studied the crowd, and their reactions to Marcellus's words. He saw a mixed response of discontented murmurs and nodding heads. A young woman of fair complexion at the front of the throng seemed particularly disgruntled. Her lips were upturned, eyes narrowed.

Marcellus concluded his oratory, claiming those who believed in true wealth could make themselves richer by donating to messengers of the gods like himself.

'A rousing speech,' Musonius spoke, loud enough to be heard by many in the crowd. 'You have convinced me of your wisdom, good Marcellus. For only one truly blessed by the gods can know the real value of money.' Taking his coin pouch from his belt, Musonius held it up. 'I have a thousand sesterces to my name. Were I to give this to you, surely I would also be blessed with the wisdom of the divine. What say you?'

Marcellus gazed at the purse, a covetous gleam in his eyes. 'I would say you are indeed a wise man.'

'And I would call you a fool and anyone else who believes this man's lies,' came another voice. The young woman spoke up, hard brown eyes boring into Marcellus and Musonius. 'He is unworthy of such a gift.'

The woman's outcry emboldened several others, who also shouted to Musonius that Marcellus was a bad and vicious snake and not to be trusted. Marcellus's lips thinned, addressing the crowd as one entity. 'Do not heed the cries of this harpy. She is prone to raving. Look instead to the example of this man who speaks reason and truth.'

Musonius answered, 'I am reminded of Lycurgus, who drove extravagance out of Sparta and substituted frugality, who preferred a life of deprivation as means of producing courage to a life of excess and who did away with luxury as a corrupting influence and considered the will to bear hardships the salvation of the state. Trained in such noble and austere habits the ancient Lacedaemonians were the best of the Greeks and were so esteemed. Their very poverty they caused to be more envied than the king's wealth. For my part then, I would choose sickness rather than luxury, for sickness harms only the body, but luxury destroys both body and soul, causing weakness and impotence in the body and lack of self-control and cowardice in the soul.'

Musonius made eye contact with every person in the audience, finally settling on the young woman. 'You call this man a liar,' he smiled. 'Money is exactly what he deserves.'

He dropped the coin purse in front of Marcellus, his eyes still on the woman. She glared at him and left the basilica through the crowd. Musonius, ever intrigued by human nature, wandered after her into a marketplace with various stalls. 'Good lady, hold a moment.'

The woman turned to him, frustration etched into her face. 'What do you seek from me?'

'An answer to a question. What offence did Marcellus cause you?'

'That lout steals from my father. Takes advantage of his kindness when he sells his wares beneath Apollo's gaze. He is a jackal. Preying upon anyone who will listen to his lies and you are his latest victim.'

'That money was on loan from Nature. It was given and now it has been reclaimed,' Musonius replied, voice calm. 'Your father may feel something of the same when he commits acts of virtue. What is your name, good lady?'

'Cornelia,' the woman folded her arms, brow furrowed. 'You sound like those philosophers I hear screaming about divine wrath in the Forum. You all have such strange ways of looking at the world.'

Musonius smiled, taken in by Cornelia's bluntness. He found it refreshing. 'Perhaps. The words of sophists like Marcellus can be elegant. But they are lacking in the spirit of what true philosophy is. It is far more appropriate to put theory into practice.'

'And would a woman be able to learn this kind of philosophy?' Cornelia asked, glibness on her tongue.

'Women, like men, have a natural inclination towards virtue and the capacity for acquiring it. It is the nature of women no less than men to be pleased by good and just acts and to reject the opposite of these. If this is true, by what reasoning would it ever be appropriate for men to search out and consider how they may lead good lives, which is exactly the study of philosophy, but inappropriate to women?'[1]

Musonius finished his appraisal and bowed his head in acknowledgement. 'Thank you for answering my question, Cornelia. May the gods watch over you.'

Carrying on down the Via Sacra, Musonius moved away from the crowds, towards a network of *domus* – houses – where Rome's wealthiest citizens and the emperor's most loyal subjects lived. Musonius traipsed through the streets until he came to a modest *domus* with minimal finery on the outside. At the entrance hall, he was greeted by slaves who announced him to his student Gaius Rubellius Plautus, who had been deep in a book.

Crossing the atrium, the young man's face was full of warmth. 'Teacher. You've come at the right time. My mood already soars in your presence.'

Studying his student, Musonius noted the worry lines and dark shading under Plautus's eyes. Eyes filled with the quiet reserve of an old soul whose body had aged prematurely with the stress, fear and uncertainty that wracked him.

'It is good to see you again, my friend.' Musonius squeezed the younger man's shoulder. 'I came as soon as I could.'

'Your company is welcomed,' Plautus admitted, directing his slaves to pour two cups of water. 'I cannot thank you enough for your wise counsel in the matters of my cousin. Nero's wishes to have me far from Rome will be honoured. I confess to struggling with the tenants of our school lately. When I go to sleep, I fear for the safety of Antistia and the children. I fear I will wake up in the afterlife with them.'

'Remember what you feel are impressions. You have the choice to assent to them. What is up to us and what is not. Whenever you stumble, that is the first step to make again. Have courage in this exile and know that it is not an evil. That it will not deprive you of air, water, shelter and the company of good men and women to associate with,' Musonius counselled, empathising with Plautus's position while also aiming to provide a realistic perspective.

The emperor's whims changed with the wind. The chances of him trying to assassinate his cousin were high but that didn't matter. All that mattered was virtue. Exercising the four virtues of courage, wisdom, temperance and justice.

Plautus nodded, determination flickering in his eyes. 'I am grateful to count you among such company. I have sent my family to our villa beyond Rome's walls with an armed guard and the litter of those who will accompany us. I wished to stay here until you arrived and ride out of the city with you. Tonight, we will all share one final meal together and depart for Syria.'

'Then let us be away,' Musonius replied, finishing his water.

'As you say, teacher,' Plautus smiled, having his travel supplies packed and their horses readied. As they travelled back down the Via Sacra, a roar came out of the Coliseum, the voices of thousands of people calling for more blood, violence and sport. Musonius felt grateful to the universe for giving him this opportunity to practise his philosophy elsewhere.

The walls of Rome fell away to open countryside, to a world of infinite possibilities. Musonius breathed in the fresh air and engaged Plautus in a dialogue about the philosophers of old, who'd carried their messages with them wherever they went in the pursuit of wisdom. To be a lover of wisdom, that was a good enough legacy for anyone to leave behind.

Musonius the Uncompromising

That was a short story. But Musonius Rufus was a living, breathing, flesh-and-blood philosopher who's been called the Roman Socrates for his wisdom and simple approach to life. A proud Stoic, Rufus was the teacher of other giants of the school like the slave Epictetus and the hot-blooded Thrasea who led the Stoic Opposition against Emperor Nero. While not as well known as other philosophers, Rufus has much to teach us about compassion, parenthood, family dynamics and gender roles. Unique among his peers, Rufus advocated for women being able to learn philosophy. His teachings, written down and recorded, by two of his students, contain many progressive ideas that still have relevance today.

Born in 30 AD, Rufus came from an equestrian family, a rank that held a certain amount of privilege in Roman society. Yet Rufus didn't seek political office or to achieve great fame like a Cicero. He didn't bury himself in riches and physical wealth like his contemporary Seneca. As my short story hints, Rufus stood apart from gold and fame. He saw philosophy as a way of life, a panacea against glory-hunting and praise inflating the ego. He rejected the power and influence that came with his position as a respected public figure, which contrasted with the actions of some of his students.

One instance is with his pupil Dio of Prusa. Rufus needed to convince a group of soldiers about the advantages of peace over war. But the soldiers wouldn't listen to him and he had to back down to make sure he didn't lose his life. By contrast, Dio gave a grand speech to an army that threatened to turn against Rome.[2] He won them over to his cause based on his rhetoric. Rufus strived for an ideal that shouldn't be mistaken for passivity. He was unwilling to compromise on his beliefs, even when he failed – an attitude that made him a source of suspicion from the Roman elite. Still, he survived exile and the reigns of several emperors.

His first brush with exile came through his association with the Stoic Opposition and Nero's paranoia. The emperor had targeted his cousin Gaius Rubellius Plautus and Rufus chose to accompany his student into exile in Syria in 60 AD. He advised Plautus to 'choose to die well while it's possible, lest shortly it may become necessary for you to die, but it will no longer be possible to die well'.[3] Two years later, Nero's assassins came for Plautus and even though the threat of death had hung over him, the young man hadn't let it disrupt his daily routine. Rufus's teachings remained with him until the end.

In 65 AD, Rufus was briefly recalled, only to be banished again in the wake of the Pisonian Conspiracy. For years, growing dissatisfaction with Nero's sadistic rule had festered among the Roman nobility. The conspiracy involved several high-ranking senators and Nero's punishment of those who'd plotted against him was swift and brutal. Fellow Stoics like Seneca were forced to commit suicide, while Rufus was exiled to the island of Gyara.

A harsh, desolate place, Rufus could've bemoaned his lot. He could've given in to despair. No. Gyara was the ideal training ground for Stoicism. Rufus committed himself to suffering towards virtue. To use the hardship to cultivate resilience and aid fellow exiles on the island.

During this period of his life, several fantastic tales have circulated. One source claimed that he single-handedly discovered an underground spring that slaked the thirst of several political prisoners. Another story expounds how he dug a canal to benefit all of Greece. Yes, these stories should be taken with a grain of salt, but it shows just how highly Rufus was regarded throughout history. He believed exile wasn't evil, that struggle provided an opportunity to become a better person.

In 68 AD, Rufus came back to Rome under the emperor Galba. It wasn't long before he found himself at the heart of conflict once again. 69 AD, the Year of the Four Emperors, had been a time of great instability in Rome. Galba was replaced by Otho. He was replaced by Vitellius and in those final days of his rule, Rufus became an ambassador to sue for peace between the emperor and his rival Vespasian. Rufus's advice fell on deaf ears and it was said he threw himself into the path of troops that almost trampled him to death.

In the wake of Vespasian rising to power, Rufus didn't hide away from political engagement. He stepped right back into the fray to prosecute a traitorous Stoic called Publius Egnatius Celer. The man had sold out his Stoic brethren to Nero and after a momentous struggle, Rufus was successful in winning the case.

Now, Rufus's reputation was so great that Vespasian had to recognise his strength. This grudging respect spared Rufus another exile when other philosophers were banished from Rome in 71 AD. But the emperor eventually went back on his word and again Rufus found himself sent far from his home.

Rufus had every right to be angry. To rail and fight against his unjust fate. As a Stoic, he recognised it was beyond his control, that it was no different from his time in Gyara and that he could do good wherever he travelled. In Syria, Rufus taught kings and foreign rulers about the merits of philosophy, finding purpose in teaching the values of justice, wisdom, temperance and courage.

Years passed until Rufus was recalled in 79 AD by Vespasian's son, Titus. The cycle of violent and cruel emperors continued with Titus soon being replaced by Domitian. What remained the same was Musonius's dedication to putting philosophy into practice, of pursuing the highest good until his death in 101 AD. We don't know how Musonius died or if he was exiled for a fourth time. But his name lived on through students like Epictetus, whose fragments are a living record of the influence his teacher had on him.

Six timeless life lessons from Musonius Rufus

1 Practice is better than theory

'Theory which teaches how one should act is related to application and comes first; it is not possible to do anything really well unless its practical execution be in harmony with theory. In effectiveness, however, practice takes precedence over theory as being more influential in leading men to action.'[4]

Rufus was a firm believer in practice over theory. In a lecture that dealt with those subjects, he told the story of two physicians. One could speak beautifully about the art of medicine but had no experience in taking care of the sick. The other physician wasn't a great speaker, but he had the experience to help a sick person. Rufus then asked his interlocutor who would be chosen to attend to the ill. The response was the doctor with experience would be chosen.

This lesson can be applied to being compassionate in the modern day. You can talk about being compassionate, but if you don't actively show it in daily life, can you really be considered compassionate?

2 Treat everyone equally

One of Rufus's most provocative ideals for his time was that women should be allowed to study philosophy too. In his mind, both men and women have the same capacity to want to do good and the tools to make it happen. He also addressed the notion of whether daughters should be able to receive the same education as sons. The example he gave is men and women changing activities for a day. What would happen if a woman did gymnastic exercises and a man took up spinning? The only difference Rufus could see between why both genders stuck to these tasks was because of physical strength. But in some cases, he argued that it would be beneficial for women to take on more demanding tasks. From this attitude, we can take the idea that everyone is equal and that we must try to empathise with all genders and creeds in the pursuit of virtue.

3 *Philosophy is part of a good marriage*

In two lectures 'What Is the Chief End of Marriage?' and 'Is Marriage a Handicap for the Pursuit of Philosophy?' Rufus stated that philosophy wasn't a hindrance to a strong marriage. Although he went into the typical values of his age about how marriage was needed for procreation and family, he went far beyond this traditional view.

For Rufus, philosophy was necessary for building a relationship not based on transactional things like wealth and beauty. It helps to build a partnership on shared values, a desire to love each other and live a good life together. He even told a funny story about Socrates' relationship with his wife. How could one of the greatest philosophers the world had ever known believe that philosophy was a handicap if he himself had a spouse? Socrates' relationship with his wife is famously said to have been turbulent, which added further weight and comedy to Rufus's point. The philosopher concludes that a strong, equitable marriage is the highest form of virtue.

4 *Suffer towards virtue*

Suffering has negative connotations though Rufus viewed it in Stoic terms. 'Acrobats face without concern their difficult tasks and risk their very lives in performing them, turning somersaults over upturned swords or walking ropes set at a great height or flying through the air like birds, when one misstep means death, all of which they do for a miserably small recompense.'[5]

In this analogy, Rufus states that an acrobat is ready to endure hardship for true happiness. This perspective can be interpreted in many ways. It's accepting a little bit of pain in the moment to set up a better future for yourself. It's a willingness to take some knocks and learn how to be a better person. It's being able to adapt and overcome in a way that's appropriate to the situation.

5 *Great leaders are always learning*

Another core element of Rufus's teachings was that leaders should take up philosophy or dedicate themselves to lifelong learning. In an exchange with a Syrian king, the philosopher spoke of leaders having self-control, discipline and a natural inclination towards protecting their people. When the king asked what he could do to repay Rufus for his advice, he said, 'The only favour I ask of you is to remain faithful to this teaching since you find it commendable. For in this way and no other will you best please me and benefit yourself.'[6]

6 Always live in accordance with nature

Once, an older man asked Rufus what the best cure for old age was. He replied that the best thing for people of all ages is to live in accordance with nature – the Stoic concept of living in harmony with people and the universe.

To illustrate his point, Rufus compared human nature to animal nature. For example, we wouldn't see a dog as having reached its full potential if all it did was indulge in pleasure and didn't do the things that are thought to be good by a dog. In his words, 'nothing would be said to be living according to nature but what by its actions manifests the excellence peculiar to its own nature.'[7] Rufus finished his lecture by saying that the nature of all human beings is to live for virtue and the doing of good acts.

Chapter 4

The Old Master and Going With the Flow

One of the most interesting things about philosophy is how it's shaped by cultures. In the West, the schools of thought that came out of Greece and Rome have had a profound impact on our understanding of what philosophy is. This has led to a tendency for us to want to use philosophy like a rulebook. To have a manual for life that can be put into a neat structure. *If I follow these principles, then it'll make me happier. If I stand by this value that I can quantify, then surely all my problems will be solved.* I'm not saying these thoughts are a bad thing. Or that philosophy can't bring structure to a life.

Day-to-day of living just isn't straightforward. It flows from one moment to the next, like a river that's either turbulent and rocky or calm and manageable. This is where I see the benefit of Eastern philosophies. There's a *flow* that doesn't need to have structure. There's a focus on nature, on letting go and accepting what's in front of us instead of raging and thrashing against external forces. We can bend and be flexible instead of being rigid and shut off.

An Eastern philosophy that helps me go with the flow is Taoism, along with the teachings of its alleged founder Lao Tzu. Rather than being a set of rules for how to live one's life, Taoism is more of a spiritual sandbox for you to play in and explore at your own pace.

What is Taoism?

Taoism or Daoism is one of the three major Chinese philosophies alongside Buddhism and Confucianism. In a Western lens, it's become associated with martial arts, feng shui and t'ai chi and while these practices can be beneficial, it's important to ground Taoism in its origins and core teachings.

At the centre of the philosophy is the Tao. A word with multiple meanings. A word that isn't associated with a deity, spirit or god. It can be translated as 'way', referencing a path or movement to be followed. Tao is also the source of everything. The universe and time. An energy that's both attainable and unattainable.[1] If you're thinking that sounds like a paradox, you're right. Tao is the origin of movement and it's the way of moving towards something. Put another way, it's being in sync with the changing nature of the universe, moving graciously and spontaneously through the world and being open to change.

When practitioners embrace the Tao, they're following ideas like:

- **Harmony with the natural world**: The acceptance that all humans and animals are linked together and deserve to live side by side. An appreciation and respect for natural elements like fire and water and how they shape our environments. Spiritual fulfilment is found in the rhythms and energy of the world.
- **Respect for the body and mind**: The mind and body are one and the longevity of both is reliant on each other. Taoists promote good health by cultivating their inner alchemy as a form of mental and physical healing. As the body ages, practitioners seek to age in a healthier way. As the mind ages, practitioners seek to keep it open.[2]
- **The acceptance of opposites**: Taoists see that there is light and darkness to everything. That duality is found in all and there can't be one thing without the other. This is best represented by the yin-yang symbol of a circle being divided into two fish-shaped halves. One side is white with a black dot. The other side is black with a white dot.[3]

Key Taoist concepts

- **Inner alchemy**: The practice of gathering certain energies in the body to improve physical and mental wellbeing.[4]
- **Ch'i/qi**: This is the energy that's found in everything, including the human body. Alternatively, it can be viewed as life-force energy or the scientific building blocks of the universe. Ch'i is linked to tai ch'i and martial arts and the exercises that are done to cultivate inner alchemy.
- **Wu-wei**: The most basic way to understand wu-wei is learning how to go with the flow. This is sometimes mistakenly referred to as non-action. It doesn't mean not doing anything. It means not *forcing* things to happen. In accordance with the Tao, action is made without exaggeration or hyperbole. Think of how water flows naturally or the idea of 'being in the zone.'[5]

- **The Ten Thousand Things:** A combination of the five Taoist elements: fire, water, earth, metal and wood. A way of referring to all natural phenomena like mountains, animals, woods, the sky, humans etc. Everything in existence.[6]

The life of the old master

According to popular belief, Taoism is traced back to 500 BC by a man called Lao Tzu. This historical figure is shrouded in mystery and debate and we should be careful when calling him the 'founder' of Taoism. It wasn't created to be formally organised in the way of religion, even though it would be developed into a philosophy and religion by various lineages and schools in the centuries to follow.

Lao Tzu is also an honorific meaning 'old master' and it's generally accepted that he was either a fictional character or the amalgamation of several historical figures. Still, it's worth looking into the legends about his life. According to one tale, Lao Tzu was known as Li Dan and served in the royal court of the Zhou dynasty (1046–256 BC). As an official court scholar, he specialised in divination and astrology and protected sacred books.

In another story, Lao Tzu acted as a teacher to the younger Confucius. When the two met, Confucius was eager to learn more about the Tao. The old master chastised the younger man for his pride, ambition and impatience. In awe of Lao Tzu, Confucius hailed him as a mighty dragon that understood the inner workings of the world.[7]

Then there's Lao Tzu's legendary departure to the West. Disillusioned with the warring factions of China and unable to get his message of embracing the Tao to the ruling class, Lao Tzu decided to abandon human society. While walking through the Western Pass of China, the gatekeeper Yin Hsi recognised Lao Tzu. The gatekeeper begged him to write down his teachings and so Lao Tzu wrote everything he had to say before departing. No one knew where he went after that.[8]

Years later, Lao Tzu would be turned into a god and Taoism would be officially organised into a religion called the Way of the Celestial Masters, in 142 BC by Chang Tao-ling. The differences between religious and philosophical Taoism are arbitrary, loosely consisting of different 'ways' that are a matter of personal taste. Author Elizabeth Reninger acknowledges 'there are two distinct terms associated with this difference. Taoist philosophical texts (particularly from the Classical period) are referred to collectively as *Tao-chia.* The organised religious institutions of Taoism are referred to as *Tao-chiao*',[9] But the two are now so deeply connected that both need to be considered to truly understand Taoism.

Another legend is Lao Tzu writing the influential *Tao Te Ching*, which contains all the wisdom Taoism teaches. Most likely, it was written by several authors, adding their own interpretations. The book consists of aphoristic life lessons that seem mysterious and understated. There is paradox, double meanings, playfulness and curiosity in every line. Take this quote 'If you try to change it, you will ruin it. Try to hold it, and you will lose it.' Or 'All streams flow to the sea because it is lower than you are. Humility gives it power. If you want to govern the people, you must place yourself below them. If you want to lead the people you must learn how to follow them.' Or what about this perplexing passage? 'Close your mouth, block off your senses, blunt your sharpness, untie your knots, soften your glare, settle your dust. This is the primal identity.'[10]

It feels like the author(s) are having some fun at our expense. We can strain as much as we want to try and unpick the word puzzles but to do so would be to miss the point entirely. Lao Tzu and the other Taoist sages deliberately used jokes and metaphors to hint that trying to find wisdom in words isn't so much an intellectual pursuit but a feeling that doesn't need to be explained. It's the same intangibility that's inspired people from all walks of life, from the original practitioners of Taoism thousands of years ago, to films like *Star Wars* using the Tao as inspiration for The Force.[11] There's an undeniable freedom to be found in discovering your own path and here are some of the Ways of Taoism that you can try out for yourself:

1. **The Way of Ceremony**: This path is focused on honouring the Taoist deities and immortals through rituals. It involves prayers, music, singing hymns and ideas associated with traditional religious worship.
2. **The Way of Divination**: This path centres on divining the patterns and rhythms of the world. It's incorporating practices like feng shui and using appropriate divination tools.
3. **The Way of Martial Arts**: This path celebrates physical and mental health and longevity. It's doing activities like t'ai chi and kung-fu. It's trying healing practices like acupuncture, herbal medicine and Taoist callisthenics.

4. **The Way of Imagination:** This covers creativity and artistic expression. Painting, writing, using the imagination to keep the mind healthy and developing good mental health routines. This also has similar crossovers with the Way of Meditation.
5. **The Way of Wandering:** This was the original form of Taoism that Lao Tzu advocated. It's strolling freely through different landscapes, acting spontaneously and finding places where you can cultivate inner peace.

Practical Taoist exercises

The Three Treasures

The Three Treasures are the most basic virtues of Taoism: compassion, simplicity and patience. These are good reminders of how to conduct yourself in various situations. It's being compassionate to people who need a kind word or people who look like they don't deserve it. It's understanding the importance of moderation, being thrifty and acting with restraint. It's having the patience to wait for the good things, to fail and get back up again and keep going.

Holding to the One

This exercise is meant to bring you in line with the essence of the Tao. The first step is to start from a place of wanting to unlearn and putting yourself in the right state to do so. This could be through meditation, a certain ritual or martial arts. In step two, you make the conscious effort to let go of any structure and embrace unlearning in the void. For step three, the boundary between yourself and the world is dissolved and self-awareness is heightened.[12]

Turning the Light Around

A kind of meditation technique. The light that's being referred to is your awareness. It's turning your attention away from the external world and shining the light of awareness back on yourself.

- Find a quiet place and close your eyes. Don't think about the world outside of you. Focus only on your breathing.
- Become aware of your heartbeat and the slowness of each breath you're taking. Any movements of your body.
- Become comfortable in the awareness for a few minutes.[13]

Creating a Taoist Altar

A useful exercise for practitioners following the Way of Ceremony. While there are lots of variations, a Taoist altar will always have certain objects present:

1. A picture of the deity or immortal that you want to honour or that inspires you.
2. The Sacred Lamp. Placed at the centre of the altar, the lamp represents the light of Tao and the eternal spark of charge. It's usually lit continuously to reflect the eternal Tao.
3. Two candles placed either side of the Sacred Lamp. They represent yin and yang and the duality of life. They also represent the sun and moon.
4. Three cups arranged in front of the Sacred Lamp. Each is filled with a different substance. The cup on the left contains water to signify yang (male energy). The second cup on the right features tea to signify yin (female energy). The final cup contains uncooked rice to demonstrate the union between yin and yang.
5. Five plates of fruit placed in front of the cups. They symbolise all five Taoist elements of fire, water, metal, wood and earth.
6. An incense burner with three sticks signifies the lower abdomen area of the human body. This is linked to inner alchemy and the cultivation of the three treasures of compassion, patience and simplicity. It's placed in front of the fruit plates.[14]

Chapter 5

The Architect of the City of Ladies and Defying Expectations

A young woman sits in her study. For hours, she's been poring through texts in search of knowledge. Seeking a break from the heavy material, she turns to something light-hearted. She chooses a book by the poet Matheolus, a writer of great wit and style. She's never read it before. All she knows is that it comes highly recommended as a book that praises women. Before she can turn the first page, she's called away by her mother for supper.

In the morning, the woman returns to the poet's book with a clear head. She's even more excited to read it. And as she reads the pages, that excitement turns to disappointment and shock. The words of the poet aren't of praise for women. They are damning, painful words. A book that scorns womankind as wicked and immoral. The downfall of good men.

From that reading, an idea forms in the young woman's mind. A realisation that Mathelous isn't the only man to write so poorly about women. All manner of philosophers, orators and writers have painted women with the same dark brush. This young woman, Christine de Pizan, no matter how much she turned the question over in her mind, could she find an answer that satisfied her. She thought about it so hard that she fell into a deep trance and called out to God to give her the answer. Christine beseeched Him to help her understand: 'Oh, Lord. If you created men in your own image, then surely women have been created in your own image too? How could you have made any mistakes? Didn't you make us with all the qualities you wished a woman to have? But here we stand. Judged and condemned. I don't understand these contradictions. How can we be guilty of the crimes men accuse us of so often?'[1]

Before despair consumes her, Christine sees a bright light before her eyes. When it fades, three women stand before her: Lady Reason, Rectitude and Justice. The ladies inform Christine they have been sent by God to help her undertake a momentous task. A calling that cannot be ignored. Reason, Rectitude and Justice tell her that they will help her build a magnificent city full of illustrious women who extol the greatest virtues of humanity. Women who're courageous, loving, compassionate, faithful, wise and just. Great queens like Artemesia who claimed victory after victory. Queen Ceres who gave the world agriculture. The noble Elissa, who became known as Queen Dido and the founder of the city of Carthage. Talented creatives like Sappho, Minerva, Isis and Arachne. Prophetesses of great renown. Far-seeing Erythrea who predicted the fall of Troy, the rise of Rome and the coming of Christ. The city grew with every name Reason, Rectitude and Justice called out and Christine forges stone by stone. Wall by wall. Home by home.

And while piecing together the city, she asks questions. Why do men think women shouldn't be educated? Why do they believe us to be incapable of sound judgement? Why do they claim women have brought only evil into the world? The trio answer all her questions patiently and practically.

At last, the City of Ladies is complete. Christine admires her handiwork and addresses all women to find refuge within the walls, that women of the past, present and future can find shelter and be shielded from slander. 'My ladies, see how these men assail you on all sides and accuse you of every vice imaginable. Prove them all wrong by showing how principled you are and refute the criticisms they make of you by behaving morally. Act in such a way that you can say, like the Psalmist, "The evil done by the wicked will fall on their own heads."'[2]

Raised to be an outlier

When Christine de Pizan wrote *The Book of The City of Ladies* in 1405, there had never been a text like it. A book that celebrated the nature of being a woman and striking back against the tide of misogyny that men had been writing for hundreds of years. A poet, copyist and philosopher, De Pizan broke the mould on how traditional medieval women were meant to think and act. So prolific is her body of work, that there are over 200 manuscripts that survive, pointing towards a writer with a powerful understanding of classical knowledge during an era where the role of a woman was strictly defined. Often called a proto-feminist, Christine's life will be examined to see if that label is accurate.

Born in 1364 in Venice, Pizan's journey into the literary world started with her father Thomas de Pizan. An astrologer and scholar, his formative years had been shaped by books and creativity too. He'd been a student at the Italian University of Bologna and been in the same environment as the famous poet Petrarch.

When Christine's father accepted the position of court astrologer to King Charles V, he moved his family to Paris. Here, Christine would have access to the greatest intellectual culture in Europe. King Charles was the kind of ruler who celebrated the arts and saw it as the gateway to the highest form of learning. He'd created the *Sapienta* (knowledge) project, where he invested in new books being put into the Louvre and commissioned various writers and artists to create those works. It would've certainly attracted Thomas and he saw no problem with his daughter having the best education his connections could afford.

Through her father, Christine learned rhetoric, philosophy and other pursuits that would be typically reserved for men. Interestingly, Christine's mother was against her education and wanted her to learn more practical pursuits like sewing.

By the time she was 15, Christine had married a royal secretary called Etienne du Castel. The union, arranged by her father, ticked his boxes as du Castel was also university-educated. By all accounts, the marriage was a happy one. In Christine's own words he 'was so faithful to me, and so good ... that I could not praise highly enough the good things that I received from him'.[3] Over ten years, Christine and Etienne had three children, two of whom survived. Their daughter went on to become a nun, while their son became a distinguished writer in his own right.

These happy times weren't to last. In 1389, Christine's husband died in an outbreak of plague and even before this tragic event, fortune had stopped smiling on her. In the decade 1380–1390, Christine was personally impacted by the death of King Charles V, who'd been a patron and protector to her family. Her father also died, leaving Christine as the head of the family in her mid-twenties. Further difficulties came from Christine struggling against lawsuits to settle her husband's estates. Yet it's important to remember that her situation wasn't so bad that she was forced to give up the trappings of the noble life she'd been born into. Christine and her brothers were able to inherit their father's estates in Italy and France.[4] Still, with two children and a family to feed, Christine couldn't afford to become a lady of leisure.

She had to maintain the powerful connections that had been cultivated by her father and husband in a political climate that was only going to become more turbulent.

Politics and the pen

Christine's writing career started around 1393, writing poetry in popular formats – ballads, fixed forms and collaboration pieces – that explored themes of love and artistry. Her skill with verse brought her to the attention of some of France's most powerful patrons of the arts. Nobles like the Duke of Burgundy and Charles the V's brother Philip and the Queen of France Isabeau of Bavaria.

By becoming a part of this world, Christine grew in confidence, and she shifted into writing political texts. Although she was Italian by birth, Christine had an intense, patriotic love for France and she used her books as a vehicle to try to influence the decision-makers that would decide the fate of the country. We see this in texts like *The Book of the Deeds and Good Conduct of the Wise King Charles V* and *The Book of the Body Politic* written against the backdrop of a destabilising French government.

During the reign of Charles V, France benefited from an age of artistic enlightenment and relative peace. When he died in 1380, tension over who would rule next broke out between the Duke of Burgundy, the late king's son Charles VI and his bother Louis of Orleans.

Unfit to rule due to mental illness and youth, Charles IV's position was usurped by his uncle, while Louis believed the crown should go to him. This ignited the Armagnac–Burgundian conflict that tore France apart for decades and bled into the Hundred Years' War that devasted Europe.[5]

Seeing these events unfold before her, Christine couldn't sit back and do nothing. While she wrote texts like *The Book of Deeds of Arms and Chivalry*, she was a sworn pacificist. She implored readers to end the war peacefully and reached out directly to Queen Isabeau through moving pieces like *Lamentations of Frances' Ills* and *Epistle to the Queen of France.* In one passage, she called for Isabeau to step into action to save her country: 'Oh, crowned Queen of France, why are you still sleeping? Who prevents you from restraining now this side of your kin and putting an end to this deadly enterprise? Do you not see this heritage of your noble children at stake?'[6]

By engaging in the political dialogue, Christine was playing a dangerous game. She was in a position where she had patrons on both sides of the conflict and would need to be careful about how she addressed events. It was crucial that for her own safety and that of her family's that she be seen to remain neutral. It's a testament to her writing skills that she was able to do so in everything she wrote without ever suffering deadly backlash for her stances. She would carry on writing within the political sphere even after she fled Paris, which we'll come back to shortly, because no exploration of Christine's legacy would be complete without her role as a copyist and how she brought her books to life despite all the political turmoil.

Bookmaking in medieval Paris was a collaborative experience, involving the laborious process of making and sourcing parchments, long hours of writing uncomfortably with a quill and knife to scrape away mistakes, illuminating the pages with rich imagery and the cost of gathering all these necessary materials together. Christine had access to a vast network of artisans who could help her in creating her manuscripts. What stands out about her work is that Christine actively participated in writing out her works by hand instead of dictating to scribes to write them for her. Several traces of her writing and editing have been detected and remain wonderfully persevered.[7]

That Christine published, edited and wrote her own work also lends to her identity as an entrepreneur embedded into the commercial bookmaking trade of Paris. This let her have great control over her public image, which informs much of how we perceive her today.

A partnership that helped in this was with her illuminator and book artist known only as the City of Ladies Master. He was responsible for the images in many of her greatest works, including the book from which he gets his name. In all of Christine's work, he painted her consistently. She's shown to wear a trailing blue gown and white wimple.[8] Through her creative autonomy, networking and output, Christine perfected her philosophy on womanhood. She was able to make her voice heard by her upper-class readership.

A proto-feminist?

Christine's stance on women's rights is characterised by her being critical of men demonising women and the misogynistic attitudes of the day. The best example of this is in *The Book of the City of Ladies*, where she makes a case for the celebration of women and creating a safe space for them.

Framed as an allegorical vision with herself as the protagonist, Christine is visited by the three wise ladies of Reason, Rectitude and Justice to help her build a metaphysical city. Every famous woman that these figures mention becomes another metaphorical building block for the city and gives Christine the freedom to express her views that 'all women, whether of high, middle or low social rank should be especially alert and on your guard against those who seek to attack your honour and your virtue'.[9]

Throughout the text, Christine demonstrates how well read she is through retelling the stories of ancient queens, warriors and women of her time. Cleverly, she uses rhetoric to play devil's advocate with the ladies while the city is being built. She positions herself as a mouthpiece for all the misogynistic arguments that have been thrown at women, asking the trio to prove their arguments in the form of a dialogue.

For example, she says to Reason, 'I'm delighted to hear from your lips that so much good has been brought into the world thanks to the intelligence of women. Yet there are still those men who go around claiming that women know nothing of worth. It's also a common way to mock someone for saying something foolish by telling them that they're thinking like a woman.'[10] In this passage, she agrees with Reason's assertion. Other times, she's a contrarian:

> I can't help myself from mentioning a custom which is quite common amongst men and even some women, which is that when wives are pregnant and give birth to a daughter, their husbands are very often unhappy and disgruntled that they didn't bear them a son … why is it, my lady, that they are so displeased? Is it because girls are more trouble than boys or less loving and caring towards their parents than male children are?[11]

We must also remember that Christine was a devout Catholic writing about the Christian perception of women in the fourteenth and fifteenth centuries through the male lens. The crux of her argument in *City of Ladies* is that it's human nature to sin and men are just as likely to do it as some women are. But both can make informed moral decisions.

Elsewhere, Christine continued to rally against religious hypocrisies in her famous letters concerning the epic poem *The Romance of the Rose.* Written between 1230 and 1275, the poem tells a tale of seduction between a male protagonist and a young girl represented as a rosebud. The girl is passive and objectified, while the man proceeds to woo and take her virginity in a scene that Christine describes as 'a barely disguised description of sexual intercourse, if not rape'.[12] Further anti-female sentiments are delivered by a persona called the Jealous Husband who spews out a torrent of hatred, which ends with him beating his wife. Here's a snippet of his speech: 'All of you women are, will be, and have been whores, in fact or desire, for whoever could eliminate the deed, no man can constrain desire … for no amount of beating or upbraiding can change your hearts.'[13]

Christine took up an impassioned debate about *The Rose* with some of her male contemporaries who defended the poem, stating that she didn't believe in the female weakness that the poem portrayed. She even gave a tongue-in-cheek response about referring to her own 'feminine weakness' to undercut a letter from one of those defenders called Gontier Col. The tone of a letter to her seemed to be that he was amazed a woman could understand and be so engaged with works that covered so many different intellectuals and authors.[14]

In these works, the question must be asked: Was Christine a feminist? It's tempting to see her daring rebellion against societal norms through our modern lens. But we must take care to ground her within the Middle Ages. Firstly, it would be anachronistic to call Christine a feminist because the term wasn't coined until the mid-nineteenth century. Secondly, she wasn't advocating for female equality in her writings because such a concept didn't exist. Nor did she argue anywhere that women were equal to men within the confines of the period.

Where this difference becomes clear is in Christine's follow-up to *City of Ladies* called *The Treasure of the City of Ladies.* She wrote the book as a survival guide for upper-class women who lived day to day in the world as it was. Christine wrote about the etiquette that high-ranking ladies should stick to and how they should act during times of war and politics, supporting their husbands and being mediators. She believed they should obey their husbands without resistance[15] and learn to look the other way when they cheated.

Christine also counselled that the woman's role should extend as a caregiver towards her children and in-laws too:

> She will love and honour the relatives of her husband and show it in the following ways. She will honour them and make them feel very

> welcome when they come to visit, and when other people are present she will honour her husband's family more than her own.[16]

And while Christine wrote about women from poorer backgrounds, they weren't her main audience. In context, she'd secured many wealthy patrons and the idea of books being available to anyone beyond the elite of society would have been peculiar indeed.

But Christine was trying to show her support for women in her own way. *The Treasure of the City of Ladies* is filled with coping mechanisms that her readership would've used in their daily lives. The book also features instructions for working-class women, despite it not being aimed at them, reflecting the medieval penchant for inclusivity when dealing with a book of conduct. So, while Christine was a champion of her sex, there are stark differences between her approach and modern feminism, as her biographer Charlotte Cooper-Davis points out: 'Although her concern with improving the lot of women is one that Christine shares with modern feminists, because her views do not approximate to equality between the sexes, her works should only be considered pro-feminine (in other words pro-women) or proto-feminist at best.'[17]

After Christine had finished writing *The Treasure of the City of Ladies*, she was 40 years old and could look back on a prolific writing career. But she wouldn't be able to do so from Paris. The political chaos had become too much for the city and when civil war broke out in 1418, she escaped to a convent, possibly the one where her daughter lived as a nun.

Up until her death around 1429–1431, little is known of Christine's final years. But we do know about one final work: *The Hymn to Joan of Arc*. What's striking about this short work is that it's the only record of Joan of Arc's accolades beyond the trial records written in her lifetime. In Joan, Christine saw a real-life example of her City of Ladies. Here was a female contemporary fighting in the name of France and standing up for the good fight. Christine may not have lived to see how it ended for Joan of Arc, but she lives on through every generation of women who reinterpret her and add to the City of Ladies through their own accomplishments and dreams. And this city, both metaphorical and physical in the minds of those who add to its foundations, deserves to be protected and championed by men, women and identities of all kinds. Because to do so is human.

Chapter 6

The Prince of Politics and Making Your Own Luck

Democrats, Republicans, Conservatives, Liberals. Every name and label comes with a certain association in the political world. They divide, shape, focus and unite us across ideas and ideologies. Here's another word associated with politics: Machiavellian. What do you see when you think of a Machiavellian politician? A person without scruples and morals? Someone who'll do whatever it takes to get ahead? That word, so bound up with immorality and ambition, has become an enduring part of the legacy of Niccolo Machiavelli.

A philosopher who courted as much controversy in his own time as today, Machiavelli's work has both fascinated and repulsed for his ends justify the means approach to life. Called a 'teacher of evil'[1] and a figure associated with the devil incarnate as 'Old Nick',[2] it would seem Machiavelli's reputation speaks for itself in the court of public opinion. But to find out if it's warranted, we must examine the life and ideas of the man who said, 'Everyone sees what you seem to be, few really know what you are, and those few do not dare oppose themselves to the opinion of the many.'[3]

Born of fortune's wheel

Arguably the most important theme of Machiavelli's work is his relationship with fortune and the desire to master it. To defend against unwanted blows, to adapt to changing times and to be in the most advantageous position as the wheel of fortune continued to turn. In some sense, he was born into fortunate circumstances.

The Machiavelli line traced its origins back to the village of Giogoli, south of Florence. They came from the same stock as the lords of Montespertoli and increased their wealth through the centuries. Several distinguished members of the family had served in public office, giving them high status, which Machiavelli's father Bernardo benefited from. With a background in law and access to a private library of some of the greatest classical texts of the era, Bernardo created an educated household with his wife Bartolomea.

Machiavelli's mother came from an intellectual background too. Her childhood years were steeped in humanist texts and the fruits of a family that had been tied to the poet Petrarch in the previous century. Before her marriage to Bernardo, she'd already had a husband and born him a daughter. But in 1457, Bartolomea was widowed and her subsequent union with Bernardo produced four children: Primavera, Margherita, Totto and Niccolo.[4]

While we can imagine Niccolo growing up in a happy household filled with reading, laughter and song, his childhood wasn't as stable as this picture would suggest. By his own admission, he was 'born into poverty … and at an early age learned to scrimp rather than to thrive'.[5]

Machiavelli's dismal assessment of his formative years probably stemmed from the lot of his father. Florence, like so many other city-states across Italy during the Renaissance, was a cultural hub of the world. A thriving republic, Florence attracted the most brilliant thinkers, architects and writers of the era.

A large part of this influence came from the powerful Medici family, bankers whose pockets were bottomless and whose wealth could put Croesus to shame. The Medicis used their riches to control the politics of Florence and the head of the family, Cosimo de Medici, encouraged the arts, building monuments and raising the city to new heights of cultural enlightenment. This approach was carried on by his son Piero and grandson Lorenzo *il Magnifico.* And so, the Medicis ruled behind the scenes for decades, presenting a republic to the people, while governing like monarchs.[6]

Bernardo was not a fan of the Medicis, but he wouldn't dare to openly criticise them in public. While a member of an anti-Medici group, the elder Machiavelli appreciated how Lorenzo championed humanist writers and made classical education a pillar of Florentine society. But this appreciation for the classics wasn't enough for him to achieve any station of note.

For all his life, Bernardo had lived with the possibility that he was a bastard, which meant he faced legal restrictions. Under Florentine law, bastards couldn't practice law or join certain guilds. His reputation became further tainted by the decades-long tension with the Medicis. The *ottimati* (elite) of Florence had become tired of the Medicis using the city as their private enterprise and worked to oust the family from power however they could. Bernardo's second cousin, Girolamo, had been one of the most vocal against Cosimo de Medici and eventually he was captured and tortured for conspiracy. Girolamo confessed everything, naming rebels in Bartolomea's side of the family too. It's doubtful Bernardo ever had anything to do with the conspiracy, yet suspicion would inevitably be cast his way and make him a victim of circumstance.

Debt further added to Bernardo's troubles, which he'd inherited from his father and uncles. So, he relied on his country farms for produce, selling what was grown from the land and renting out his properties. Whenever he was short-changed by a tenant or customer, Bernardo fought for every last penny and he and his wife took great pains to keep up appearances for their children at home.[7]

Despite these hard times, Niccolo received a first-rate education in Latin, rhetoric and classical literature. His father knew with this kind of knowledge, his son would be able to enter public office. But while Machiavelli was studying for a far-off career in politics, things were about to change in Florence.

As had happened with his grandfather Cosimo, Lorenzo de Medici faced opposition from his fellow citizens that he could no longer ignore. He turned to the Signoria, the dominant governing body of Florence, reshaping it to his specifications and placing men inside of it upon whom he could rely. This stoked further resentment among the *ottimati*, as many noble families felt there was an uneven distribution of favours and wealth with the new reforms that Lorenzo had brought in. *Il Magnifico*'s challenges continued to build through the newly elected Pope Sixtus IV strengthening his grip on the Papal States, the declining fortunes of the Medici bank and the pope's decision to ally with his rivals.

The last straw came in a confrontation between Lorenzo and the pope over naming a new archbishop of Florence. Lorenzo wanted his brother to fill the role, but the pope voted in his own nephew. When the nephew died a year later, Sixtus brought in a man called Francesco Salviati, a man often accused of gambling and sinful behaviour. Lorenzo refused to let this insult rest and forced the Signoria to back his ambitions and compel the pope to appoint his brother-in-law as the archbishop. This back-and-forth pissing contest finally ended with Salviati taking the position.

The consequences of Lorenzo's stubbornness would be felt through Florence. A committee came together to finally strike against the Medicis once and for all with the assassination of *Il Magnifico* and his brother Giuliano. But the conspirators overplayed their hands and Lorenzo gathered his men to wipe them out, Salviati and members of the rival Pazzi family among them.[8]

Machiavelli was still a boy when Lorenzo cleaned house and though he wouldn't have understood the true ramifications, he would've sensed that things were changing for his family. For the next few years, his education would be stopped and started with different teachers, with one of his most prominent being Paolo Sassi. With Sassi, Machiavelli sat beneath the learning trees of Cicero, Virgil, Terence and Livy, absorbing the nature of the law, the mechanics of speech making and the flourishes of letter writing.

Sassi pushed his students to seek moral and political lessons recorded by the ancients, a lesson that Machiavelli would've laughed bitterly at. For all the talk of virtue and good conduct that Sassi spoke of, he sexually abused his students, a practice that although illegal, was still considered by some to be a necessary part of a young man's education. Recent documents have shown that Sassi was a prolific paedophile without any regret. His abuse of children was unveiled a decade after Machiavelli left his care. We can't know how badly Niccolo was mistreated, only that it would've been deeply traumatic and served as a building block for his philosophy that dealt with the harsh realities of the world.[9]

Fortune had indeed spun her wheel constantly in his childhood, the needle twirling from civil war, family troubles, psychological scarring and situations changing at the drop of a hat. It'd also equipped Machiavelli with a determination to survive against all odds.

Blown by the changeable winds of politics

Sometime between 1485 and 1487, Machiavelli started his university education at the Studio Florentino, where his burgeoning literary talent got him into a group surrounding the Medicis. In the circle, Lorenzo's son Piero and his two brothers were the centre of the universe and Machiavelli wasted no time in trying to gain their favour. Specifically, he seemed to have focused on the youngest brother Giuliano, writing him poetry with amorous undertones. This appeared to have a positive effect and Machiavelli seemed poised to inch himself into the good graces of the most powerful family in Florence. Yet this decision was poorly timed.

Following the death of Lorenzo the Magnificent in 1492, Piero took his place as the de facto ruler of Florence. But he lacked the political shrewdness of his father, causing him to lurch from one disaster to the next. Piero created a group of sycophants who obeyed him alone and alienated both the *ottimati* and *popolani* (upper-class artisans and merchants).

The most humiliating blow to Piero's credibility was dealt by King Charles VII of France. The king planned to claim the kingdom of Naples for himself and asked Florence for aid. In a delicate position, Piero couldn't withstand Charles's bullying and gave him everything he asked for. The Florentines were appalled. Not only had Piero overstepped his boundaries, he'd given away many of Florence's most valuable possessions.

Another coup against the Medicis soon followed. This time it was led by Fra Girolamo Savonarola, a friar with supposedly divine foresight who decried Piero as a tyrant. Before the Signoria, the Medicis found themselves in dire straits. Vastly outnumbered, Piero and his men were forced to retreat from Florence. The Medici reign was officially over and they were declared outcasts, their properties confiscated and loyal advisors executed.

In this power vacuum, Savonarola rose to prominence, while the constitution was restructured. The Signoria agreed to set up a Great Council, which oversaw the election of major political offices. This would be made up of a thousand legitimately born Florentine citizens. The Great Council was further complemented by the Council of Eighty. The smaller group would be chosen from the Great Council to pick ambassadors and military commanders.[10]

And what of Machiavelli? Where did he stand in all this political upheaval? Up shit's creek without a paddle. While it could never be claimed he was a close associate of the Medicis, Machiavelli's desire to court Giuliano's approval hardly helped his standing. Family woes didn't help his situation either. He'd inherited more responsibilities from his father and needed to defend his family's interests in a dispute with the Pazzi who wished to claim a Church benefice that had been with the Machiavellis for years. Niccolo realised it was a losing battle and if he didn't do something soon, he would be swept away in the torrent of Savonarola's reforms.

To escape his rocky prospects, or perhaps to spite them, Machiavelli turned to jokes and wit. His sense of humour, characterised by dark bawdiness and a sharp sense of irony, manifested in many of his later carnival songs and plays, most notably the *Mandragola* and *Clizia.* An early work where this became apparent was by translating *Andria*, a comedy by Terence. Not only did he translate the original text, but he also updated it with his own observations and modern slang, even taking a subtle dig at Savonarola for his prophetic visions.[11]

Around the time he was translating *Andria*, Machiavelli met a man who would change his life forever – a man named Marcello Adriani. A powerhouse orator adept at navigating the storm of Savonarola's Florence, Adriani took Machiavelli under his wing and helped him look past recent disappointments, to look deep into the past and conjure the wisdom of the ancients with his lessons and speeches. Bolstered by Adriani's mentorship, Machiavelli became drawn to the poet-philosopher Lucretius, who contended that forces like Fortune and God were disinterested in human affairs and freedom came in taking fate into your own hands.

While Machiavelli immersed himself in this new doctrine, Savonarola's influence in Florence began to wane. His prophecies and predictions had failed to come true and increasingly hypocritical behaviour turned the city against him and in these cracks of dissension, ambitious young men like Machiavelli found openings into the Florentine government.

In 1498, Machiavelli seized upon the opportunity to be named Second Chancellor, a job that involved dealing with subject towns and domestic issues. Even though he lost the election, to be recommended for such a position without any political experience and a scant reputation was still an accomplishment. Adding to this growing swell of momentum was the fact that his mentor Adriani had been elected to First Chancellor. Something had to give soon.

Then, Savonarola pushed his luck again. The once proud and influential friar had led the bonfire of the vanities, burning books, art, statues and objects that he considered to be sinful and immoral. Even though he'd been excommunicated on orders from Pope Alexander IV, Savonarola defiantly led another bonfire and continued to preach openly. Antagonism between the pope and Savonarola became so severe that the Signoria, to protect the autonomy of Florence, agreed to shut the friar up once and for all. With multiple factions vying for his blood, Savonarola couldn't escape the inevitable. He, along with two of his most loyal supporters, were arrested, tortured and hanged in the Piazza della Signoria on the 23rd May 1498.

The winds of change quickly swept through Florence. Anyone even remotely associated with the friar was executed, exiled or removed from office. One such casualty was the Second Chancellor Alessandro Braccesi. With his removal, a more capable replacement was found based on his relative obscurity and untapped potential. At the age of 29, Machiavelli finally shrugged off all the missteps of his youth, becoming Second Chancellor. At last, he'd been able to bend Fortune to his will.

The road of rocky diplomacy

Machiavelli's early diplomatic missions would prove to be instructive for him in several ways. His first major outing involved him negotiating with the mercenary commander Jacopo d'Appiano, who was trying to take advantage of his relationship with Florence to hold out for more money before he and his men committed to reconquering Pisa on behalf of the Florentines. He also expected the Signoria to authorise him to raise forty extra men-at-arms. The commander, known for his stubbornness and tight-fistedness, would've tested the skills of even the most seasoned diplomat. The inexperienced Machiavelli had his work cut out for him.

For two days, Machiavelli negotiated with d'Appiano, stating the case of his superiors. The Second Chancellor informed the mercenary that Florence had been grateful for his past service. But they couldn't agree to his demands as there was a clear contract in place. Also, Florence didn't have the cash d'Appiano was asking for anyway. In terms of the forty soldiers, d'Appiano was free to take up his query with the Duke of Milan, who'd agreed to pay for his expenses when the contract had been first signed. But as the political situation was so unstable with the Pizan campaign, he would have to wait for a reply. Machiavelli demonstrated his shrewdness by getting the mercenary commander to agree with Florence's position.[12] Other times, Machiavelli would have a harder time acquitting himself to the standards of the Signoria. His next important mission involved dealing with Caterina Sforza of Forli, a woman who expected Florence to protect her city in the shifting power dynamics of King Louis XII of France and the pope's son Cesare Borgia in the Romagna. A savvy and politically gifted player, Caterina was as happy to go to Milan for help as she was with Florence. She knew both cities were in desperate need of troops for their campaigns. The Signoria sent Machiavelli to negotiate with her about a deal.

After a lot of toing and froing, Machiavelli believed it was in the best interests of Florence for the Signoria to agree to her terms. Only the decision-making process was slow, and Machiavelli felt trapped between the inaction of his colleagues and the pushiness of Caterina. In the end, he had no choice but to accept that the deal couldn't be saved, due to his relative inexperience and the rapidly changing political situation of King Louis pressing his attack. All the Signoria cared about were results. Machiavelli returned to Florence empty-handed with no alliance and the prospect of leaving Forli undefended against Cesare Borgia. Plus, his failure damaged his reputation with colleagues and left the long-term future of Florence's safety in question.[13]

Machiavelli didn't let these experiences deter him. He continued to serve the Signoria through handling negotiations with France and the rising threat of Cesare, who expected Florence to become his ally in his ongoing campaigns. These undoubtedly stressful years were made brighter for Machiavelli by settling down to marry the well-born Marietta Corsini and starting a family.

Despite carrying on affairs with prostitutes, gambling and getting blackout drunk with friends, there's evidence that Machiavelli cared deeply for his wife. Their letters to each other convey a great depth of love and Marietta gave as good as she got in the relationship. Whenever she was displeased with her husband, she let him know and took charge of the household while he was away.[14] But as much as Machiavelli cared for his wife and as much as he would carouse with other men and women, politics would always be his favourite mistress. Affairs of state soon called him away again and he got wrapped up in more alliance talks with Cesare in Imola. Eventually he found himself unable to carry out his duties and asked his superiors to be withdrawn as the chief Florentine diplomat with the impatient duke.

In Cesare, Machiavelli saw a capable general and statesman, an exemplar of all the virtues that he would write about years later in *The Prince.* Yet for all his military talent and ambition, Borgia was outmanoeuvred by his rivals. Machiavelli wrote, 'Borgia became a prince by his father's influence and despite his best efforts, could not maintain his state after his father's influence failed … Borgia then made a mistake by not preventing the election of a Pope hostile to him.'[15] After the death of his father in 1503, Cesare's position gradually weakened until he was killed in Spain in 1507. He'd been fighting a rebellious count called Louise de Beaumont and in the ensuing chaos of his siege failing, Borgia rode off after a group of fleeing knights. Too late, Borgia realised he was outnumbered and was cut down by de Beaumont's men, who'd had no idea whom they'd just killed. An ignoble end for a man of such high ambition and power.[16] And like his subject, Machiavelli too fell from his lofty position, suffering a reversal of fate.

Outcast to historian

In 1512, after years of slowly rekindling relationships and waiting for the right opportunity to strike, the Medicis returned to power in Florence. First Chancellor Piero Soderini, both a friend and mentor to Machiavelli, was forced to step down and flee the city for fear of his life. The political landscape of Florence was uprooted, the Republic dissolved, and Machiavelli found himself alone and vulnerable.

His association with Soderini made him a target and he was thus willing to sacrifice any goodwill he had towards the man to save himself. Desperately, he wrote to the Medicis in a letter known as *Ai Palleschi*. He verbally destroyed Soderini and everything he represented.[17] Machiavelli's flip-flopping made no difference. Soon, he was accused of being part of a conspiracy against the Medicis which he likely had no part in.

Imprisoned, Machiavelli went through a painful torture called *strappado.* First, his hands were tied behind his back and he was lifted by a rope so he was never more than a few inches off the ground. This was done to him six times and for three weeks he rotted in jail, the outside world rapidly changing around him. When Giovanni Medici took the mantle of Pope Leo X, the Medicis could afford to be merciful and issued a pardon to many who'd been caught up in the conspiracy.

Among those released, Machiavelli may have hoped that he could return to political favour, though he would be bitterly disappointed. He tried to mend fences with Soderini, who'd found favour with the pope as a cardinal, using his friend Francesco Vettori as a messenger. This was not to be as the former Second Chancellor was still considered a liability.

Now a political outcast and exile, Machiavelli left Florence for his farm in the hamlet of Sant'Andrea in Percussina. Here, Machiavelli could find some solace among Marietta and his children, even if his heart still yearned for the rush of intrigues and diplomatic missions. He consoled himself by writing to Vettori, which helped him keep up to date with what was going on in Florence. It was in this period of his life that Machiavelli sat down to write his most famous political treatises like *The Prince* and *The Discourses on Livy.* The former work, written to gain favour with the Medicis, was never read by his intended audience. Twice, Machiavelli was rebuffed, causing him to pour scorn onto the family that he'd orbited, loved and hated for all his adult life. *The Discourses* was a longer work that dealt with similar themes as *The Prince*. It focused on the rise of the Roman Empire and the positive outcomes of factional struggles between the Senate and the plebs being the only way to achieve true liberty.

Outside of his political musings, Machiavelli found enjoyment at the Orti Oricellari, a secluded garden where he could talk and debate philosophy, art and the most important issues of the day with like-minded men. In this garden, he could shrug off the weight of the past and dedicate himself to new pursuits, to reinvent himself as a dramatist by writing comedic plays like the *Mandragola,* which was widely praised in his time. Still, Machiavelli felt an itch that needed to be scratched, that would only be completely satisfied by doing what he'd done best in his years as the Second Chancellor.

In 1520, he was finally recalled from the wilderness by the Medicis to oversee a situation that Machiavelli's compatriots thought was better suited to 'an accountant or a pen-pusher'[18] rather than a man of his acumen. Nevertheless, Machiavelli happily agreed and even though some of his closest friends believed he should come to terms with his political star having long since waned, he damned all opinions and was determined to prove his worth once and for all.

To do this, Machiavelli would write the history of his glorious Florence to be able to record everything the city had achieved. After much persuasion, he was granted his wish and commissioned to write an official history of Florence by the Studio Fiorentino. The term official is used loosely here. As Dr Alexander Lee states in his biography of Machiavelli, such works were written 'not only to memorialise the city's past, but also to shape its identity in the present … more often than not, they had provided a justification of its system of government … as such the writing of "official" history could not be entrusted to just anyone. It required … the "right" political outlook'.[19]

Indeed, Machiavelli's *Florentine Histories* were greatly embellished, presenting a version of Florence heightened by imaginary battles, drama and invented speeches. While retreading the same ground as the *Discourses*, Machiavelli homed in on the role the Medicis had in the battle between tyranny and liberty over the city. In some sense, it appeared that Machiavelli was openly criticising the Medicis by referring to how they had taken away Florence's liberty in the past. But he'd intended it as advice as to how the future of Florence could be shaped for the better, that his dream of a new republic *could* be forged, so long as the Medicis listened to him. Yet the more things change, the more they stay the same and the power of the Medicis wouldn't last.

In 1527, Rome was sacked by the Duke of Bourbon and his forces during the War of the League of Cognac. In the wake of this crushing defeat, Medici rule disintegrated and they were abandoned on all sides. Machiavelli had been away on another diplomatic mission at the time and when he returned to Florence, it must have felt like he was stepping back in time. For a new republic was born and Machiavelli dared to dream that he could once again be restored to his role as Second Chancellor. But it wasn't to be: he'd spent too long in the Medici camp, been on the wrong side of history too many times. For all his ambition and intelligence, the author of *The Prince* had been too short-sighted to see which way the wind was blowing and once more he was cast out by those in political power.

This bitter realisation, coupled with chronic stomach issues, caused the 58-year-old Machiavelli's health to decline. In June 1527, he took to bed, plagued by visions of Heaven-bound people, of the philosophers Seneca, Tacitus, Plato and Plutarch who told him they were destined for Hell. 'So many interesting people to talk to. Perhaps I'll be happier in Hell,' Machiavelli chortled darkly. Perhaps a part of him believed that. Perhaps another part was so terrified of his end that humour was the last defence mechanism left to him before he breathed his last breath.[20]

Machiavellian philosophy

Now that we've looked at the experiences and situations that shaped Machiavelli's life, we're in a better position to examine his philosophy and ideas. Much of our understanding of Machiavellianism comes from *The Prince*, first published in 1532. One interpretation of the book is that it's a manual for tyrants, that a prince must do whatever it takes to secure his power and look beyond concepts of good and evil. This is an oversimplification and there's much more to the themes of *The Prince*.

Firstly, Machiavelli is concerned with realism over idealism: 'How one lives is so far distant from how one ought to live, that he who neglects what is done for what ought to be done, sooner effects his ruin than his preservation.'[21] As nice as it would be for a ruler to behave kindly towards their subjects and allies all the time, that isn't how the real world works for Machiavelli. They must be willing to act immorally for the protection of the state. That doesn't mean they should be cruel for cruelty's sake. In fact, it was one of the fastest ways for a prince to be undone. Machiavelli used the example of Cesare Borgia as a figure who was pragmatic with his cruelty, using it to subdue the Romagna. As a result, Borgia was able to restore order and so cruelty was used in the ultimate service of compassion. This is the part of Machiavelli's philosophy that has become synonymous with the ends justify the means. What he was referring to specifically was a prince behaving wickedly to serve the state and protect it. This was linked to a prince's *virtu*, the qualities that he needed to possess to be effective in his role.

One of Machiavelli's favourite words, *virtu* wasn't the same as virtue. His word contained no moral or religious connotations. It meant strength, ingenuity, courage and a willingness to act with necessity. By embracing *virtu*, a prince could protect himself from the blows of *fortuna*, the force of unpredictability that changes lives on a whim. The dichotomy of these two forces can be seen in Machiavelli's perspective on whether it's better to be loved or feared as a ruler: 'The answer is, of course, that it would be best to be both loved and feared. But since the two rarely come together, anyone compelled to choose will find greater security in being feared than in being loved.'[22] To Machiavelli, love is based on fortune. It isn't reliable or sustainable. Fear is in the wheelhouse of *virtu* because it's constant, even in a changing world.

Another interpretation of *The Prince* is that it was a guide for how leaders shouldn't behave and that Machiavelli's later works were a rallying cry for Republicanism. The philosopher Jean-Jacques Rousseau admired Machiavelli for this perspective, writing in his *Social Contract* that 'whilst pretending to teach lessons to kings, he taught great lessons to people'.[23]

Whether a proud Republican or a teacher of the unscrupulous, Machiavelli has also been considered the father of modernity. His philosophy is built on a contrast between the ancients and moderns. In his eyes, the ancients were strong and the moderns were weak, but those ideas could be brought forward to create a new kind of politics. Modernity wasn't so much a time or a place, but a way of looking at the self for Machiavelli. His Italy wasn't a united nation. It was a land of feuding regimes where religious figures and mercenaries caused chaos for their own gain. His prince was the modern man sent to solve this political problem.

Machiavelli's influence is still felt today, from political systems down to the actions of individuals, sometimes in the most unexpected of places. An example is the rapper Tupac who changed his name to Makaveli after reading his work while in prison. It wasn't that he idealised the philosopher, so much as the way of thinking to achieve goals whatever it takes.[24] As have so many others who've internalised Machiavelli's teachings, for better or worse.

So, who was Machiavelli really? A statesman who loved his country above all else. A philosopher who courted controversy wherever he went. A man of many contractions. We can only decide for ourselves, to dare to be bold, to fly in the face of tradition, or take it up as our mantle and make informed decisions to see the world as it is to make the changes that are needed for the right reasons. To make those decisions, looking to the past is instructive. Just as Machiavelli did himself.

> At the door, I take off my clothes of the day, covered with mud and mire, and I put on my regal and courtly garments; and decently reclothed, I enter the ancient courts of ancient men … there I am not ashamed to speak with them and ask them the reasons for their actions and they in their humanity reply to me.[25]

Chapter 7

The Everyman Philosopher and Not Knowing Anything

Of all human fears, death may be the one that unites us all. Perhaps because of its finality. Perhaps because it brings with it a sense of unimaginable suffering and pain. Or it's the fear of the unknown of what's on the other side. Is there a world beyond, determined by how we choose to live? Or is there nothing at all? What is certain is that when we encounter death, we are all impacted in different ways. And for some of us, it's life changing.

Let's take the case of a 36-year-old man alive in sixteenth-century France called Michel de Montaigne. For many years, he'd obsessed over death, of an end he couldn't see. Rather well off, Montaigne had recently taken full responsibility for his family's chateau and estate in the Dordogne and spent as much time as he could escaping from his morbid thoughts by travelling around the family's vineyards or riding to Bordeaux to fulfil his role as a magistrate.

One day, while riding through the forest with his entourage of servants and acquaintances, on one of these escapades, Montaigne began to daydream. The daydream became so intense that he didn't pay attention to where he was going or what was happening around him. Suddenly, Montaigne felt a huge weight slam into him like the crack of an arquebus. His mind snapped in wild directions. Had he been attacked? Had he been shot? Those thoughts were all he remembered as he hit the ground roughly and lost consciousness.

Actually, Montaigne hadn't been shot at all. One of his servants had decided the retinue was moving too slow for his liking. So, he guided his horse into a full gallop and crashed into Montaigne, knocking him to the ground and knocking him out. As his servants tried to revive him, Montaigne hacked up blood and thrashed about all the way back to the chateau as he drifted between life and death. And in that space, he felt an inner sense of calm that contrasted with his outward flailing. As he'd later write, 'it seemed to me that my life was hanging only by the tip of my lips; I closed my eyes in order … to help push it out and took pleasure in growing languid and letting myself go.'[1]

For Montaigne, the riding accident became a sojourn into death, to put himself before it, not as a brave warrior who'd marched into battle, but as a regular bloke who slipped into it by mistake, and somewhere along the way, that slope down became relaxed and enjoyable. But Montaigne didn't die that day. He woke up in bed and spent the next several nights feeling aches and pains that would continue for the next few years. What remained beyond the physical discomfort was clarity. A profound understanding that death didn't have to be feared. That it didn't have to be worried about at all because 'nature will tell you what to do on the spot, fully and adequately. She will do this job perfectly for you; don't bother your head about it'.[2]

This led to Montaigne doing something that had never been done before. To write about himself in such a way that he became the subject of his literary world, to retrace all the internal sensations that he'd felt on that day from moment to moment. He created the essay genre, which came from the French word *assay*, meaning to try. He tried to understand himself and the world around him by writing 107 essays over a period of twenty-two years. Often there was no rhyme or reason to his thoughts, as he wrote in a stream of consciousness that split off into rivers and bends that circled back as much as they diverged.

What this did was turn Montaigne into an everyman philosopher who can have a conversation with any reader of any generation.

An uncommon upbringing

Born on the 28th February 1533 into a merchant family, Montaigne's introduction to life would be very different from most children of the era. His father Pierre, a fan of the Renaissance ideas that had come over from Italy, had served in the French army and been exposed to those ideas while fighting overseas. Later, he became mayor of Bordeaux, dedicating much of his energy to improving the family estate as the local *seigneur* (lord).

In his son, Pierre found an opportunity for daring experiments. When his little Micheau (an affectionate nickname from father to son) was perhaps one or two years old, Pierre sent him to live with a peasant family and have a peasant wet nurse. The reason for this was probably because Pierre wanted his son to know what it was like to grow up around the people who would one day look to their lord for help. A possible downside to this was that Montaigne missed out on those crucial bonding experiences with his father and mother Antoinette, though it didn't seem to bother him later in life.

When he returned to the chateau, Pierre decided on an even more radical experiment. It was agreed that Micheau would be brought up as a native Latin speaker. At the time, to have command of the Latin language marked you as a person of high refinement and education. It opened the door to a respectable legal job and many other avenues. The only problem? Pierre barely knew any Latin and his wife's and servants' were non-existent. The head of the Montaigne household came up with a two-step solution. First, he hired a Latin teacher called Dr Horst who was fluent in the ancient language and knew only a little French. Second, Pierre banned everyone in the chateau from speaking to his son in any language that wasn't Latin. He and Antoinette brushed up on their skills too and so the experiment went on.

By all accounts, it was a great success. Montaigne spoke Latin beautifully and naturally, being complimented by Dr Horst and other early teachers. However, a consistent part of Montaigne's character would become his inconsistency. His desire to explore new things, to examine them and put them down again before moving on to the next phenomenon that caught his eye. As he grew older, his lack of Latin practice reduced him to the same level as other young noblemen who'd been expected to learn the language. He also learned to speak French decently enough but would never be accused of being the most eloquent man in the room when he spoke it.

Yet his unconventional upbringing helped shape Montaigne into his own person. Someone who couldn't just be satisfied with one answer. Someone who needed to question and investigate the world from multiple angles, having spent time in the company of peasants and unlocked a gateway to the ancients by internalising an ancient language. And this thirst for learning and questioning carried over into books as he stepped into the College de Guyenne in Bordeaux, where he'd spend the next decade of his life.

The young Montaigne's reading habits had a distinctive philosophical flavour. Expected to study writers like Horace in depth, Montaigne may have been bored to death if not for his reading of books that weren't typical classroom reading. Excitement and wonder came to him through reading Ovid's *Metamorphoses*, Virgil's *Aeneid* and Terence's comedies.[3]

After devouring these books, his appetite changed. He moved on to biographers like Plutarch, who'd become Montaigne's favourite writer. The way Plutarch packed things, sensations and conversations, into his work appealed to Montaigne's desire to see how people really lived instead of an imagined life. And when he read into adulthood, Montaigne didn't make a cult out of books or philosophers as his father did. While he certainly respected the authors he read and housed their books in his personal library, Montaigne wasn't a Christine de Pizan. He didn't spend long periods constructing an artificial city out of ancient voices. Nor was he a Niccolo Machiavelli, changing his clothes to reverently communicate with the dead. Montaigne chided, prodded and called out the philosophers he read. He had conversations with them, dialogues that would come out in his essays. Plus, he called himself a lazy reader who read only for pleasure and forgot most of what he read anyway. By his own admission, 'I leaf through now one book, now another, without order and without plan, by disconnected fragments ... actually I use them scarcely any more than those who do not know them at all.'[4] (This contradictory statement is classic Montaigne.)

Lazy as he claimed to be, it didn't stop him from gaining a magisterial position in the town of Perigueux, where he was fast-tracked into the Bordeaux *parlement.* Montaigne started his career in law by assessing cases that were too complex to be taken care of right away by the main judges. It wasn't up to him to pass judgement, but to write down accurate accounts of what each party said. What he found in his work was extremely troubling, as the Bordeaux courts were mired in needless bureaucracy and many people chose not to seek justice at all, for fear of never having their voices heard or worse.

Montaigne felt that the people who passed the judgements were as fallible as anyone else and he saw his point proven in many guises. Especially when sent on errands to other *parlements* and to communicate with the royal court. On one visit, Montaigne met King Henri II, with whom he wasn't impressed – with France besieged by warring religious factions such as Protestants, Calvinists and Jesuits, strong leadership was vital. But it never came from the royal family and the country fell into pogroms and massacres for many years.

The ever-flexible Montaigne managed to stay in the good graces of every religious faction he crossed paths with, even being a trusted diplomat for the likes of Catherine de Medici and her sons, and heirs to the French throne, Charles IX and Henri III.[5] But the most important relationship of

Montaigne's life would come early into his career when he encountered fellow magistrate Etienne de la Boétie.

A once-in-a-generation friendship

A rakish twenty-something-year-old, Montaigne met La Boétie at a dinner party. Both had already heard of one another. Montaigne's reputation for bawdiness had reached La Boétie's ears, while the former knew of the latter through a provocative manuscript called *On Voluntary Servitude.* A couple of years older than Montaigne, La Boétie had a cooler, wiser head on his shoulders and we know what he thought of his friend through a poem he wrote about the young Montaigne. He saw a man in danger of wasting his potential, who squandered his time on pretty women and idle pursuits.

The two of them engaged in the quintessential philosophical friendship of two men living under each other's gaze, learning, growing, sharing ideas together and expressing deep love, which has been interpreted as erotic in some circles. But as Sarah Bakewell states about Renaissance male friendships in Montaigne's biography 'while any hint of real homosexuality was regarded with horror, men routinely wrote to each other like lovestruck teenagers. They were usually in love less with each other than with the elevated ideal of friendship absorbed from Greek and Latin literature.'[6]

Tragically, their relationship lasted only a few short years. La Boétie caught the plague in 1563 and Montaigne diligently stayed by his bedside, recording his friend's final hours. At times, Montaigne portrayed La Boétie as dying a perfect Stoic death, seeing his end rationally and bravely. That's only one interpretation. Montaigne couldn't write a wholly idealised version of his friend's death no matter how hard he tried. His wry sense of humour shone through, for example depicting La Boétie's farewell speeches: 'The whole room was full of wails and tears, which nevertheless did not interrupt the train of his speeches, which were a little long.'[7]

In the days after La Boétie's death, Montaigne sank into grief and depression. And while he'd never fully be able to shake off the melancholia of his best friend's death, he made La Boétie live on through himself and his work. Montaigne made sure of this through bringing the man's *On Voluntary Servitude* to a wider audience, although he had to be careful about how the work was presented. The text struck a revolutionary tone with some audiences because of its themes of refusing to submit to tyranny. While he'd intended to make it a part of his *Essays*, Montaigne didn't want to taint his friend's name. So, he included a dedication that spoke of La Boétie's conviction.

Even though his friend was gone, Montaigne knew he still had a duty to carry on and in his own opinion, he'd reached an age that was ideal for marriage. At 32, he married Françoise de la Chassaigne. Their marriage seemed to be typical of the period. Montaigne and Françoise spent time away from each other in the family property, as the realms of men and women were expected to be different. Montaigne probably would've avoided marriage all together if he could, saying 'of my own choice, I would have avoided marrying Wisdom herself, if she had wanted me. But say what you will, the custom and practice of ordinary life bears us along.'[8] That didn't necessarily mean their relationship was loveless. Montaigne spoke of his wife with great affection in an early publication he dedicated to her. They went on to have several daughters together, only most of them died young. Montaigne tried to remain stoically detached from these blows, as infant mortality was an expected misfortune of his time. Death seemed to be closing in on him from every direction. The demise of his daughters must have been made even more painful by the loss of his father and the sudden death of his younger brother in a freak sporting accident.

With all this tragedy bearing down upon him, we can see why Montaigne found it difficult to keep morbid thoughts at bay. It all converged into the riding accident that changed his perspective forever.

Explorative retirement

After Montaigne's brush with death, he lost the burning desire to write his *Essays.* He started up a few years later in 1572; his first one didn't involve his accident or what he experienced. What truly marked his rebirth was a retirement from public life. Montaigne sold his magistracy at the Bordeaux *parlement*, choosing to focus on his estate and a life of contemplation. He even marked the occasion a year after committing to it, painting a Latin inscription in the wall of his library. It read, 'at the age of thirty-eight, on the last day of February, anniversary of his birth, Michel de Montaigne, long weary of the servitude of the court and of public employments … retired … where in calm and freedom from all cares he will spend what little remains of his life now more than half run out.'[9] In retirement, he found the opportunity to write and meditate on all the human foibles he observed in his tower and library, or the room behind the shop. This was Montaigne's sacred space, where he could withdraw from the world. Not to cut himself off from family and friends but as a method of cultivating his inner world and healing from the grief and pain of his losses and put them down into his *Essays.* And as he explored his inner workings, Montaigne presented himself with shameless openness. He loved having debates, loved turning his estate into a waystation for neighbours, friends and colleagues. A walking paradox as ever, Montaigne wore his openness as both shield and *savoir faire.* By being so genial, he believed he was safer from thieves and bandits than if he were to keep the gates of his estate closed or lock himself down emotionally and spiritually. Often, this belief saved him from trouble.

Once, he was attacked in a forest by twenty masked men. They took him hostage and considered holding him for ransom. Overhearing their conversation, Montaigne suspected they would put a high price on his name and if no one could match that sum then he would surely die. Damning the consequences, Montaigne spoke up and said they'd already had everything they could take from him. It didn't matter how high the ransom was it would make no difference.

The leader of the group went up to Montaigne and removed his mask so the two of them could speak face-to-face. The decision had been made and they would let him go. The bandits even returned some of Montaigne's possessions and his money. Montaigne believed what had saved him was his frankness and his ability to stand up for himself when the time had called for it.[10]

For the rest of the 1570s, Montaigne played around with his first batch of *Essays,* publishing them in 1580 with a Bordeaux publisher. These original chapters held duelling points of view, imbued with their writer's curious, witty tone of voice that charmed the French nobility. King Henri III ranked among those who were drawn to Montaigne's thought experiments, to whom the author gave a personal copy in Paris. With his work well received, Montaigne was free to expand his *Essays* over the next decade, turning rivulets of inquiry into vast torrents of human complexity and turning him into a literary star.

The runaway success of his work surprised Montaigne. Enough that it made him want to shake up his routine and embark on a sojourn of international networking where he could continue to learn about himself. There was also the matter of painful kidney stones that he had inherited from his father which made his life difficult. Abroad, perhaps he could find a cure. So, in the summer of 1580, Montaigne left his estate in the hands of his wife and set off across France, Germany, Italy and Switzerland.

Just as he did on the page, Montaigne followed no fixed path on his travels. Accompanied by a band of servants and acquaintances that he tried to break away from at every possible turn, he took in all the sights, sounds, tastes and smells of the lands where he arrived. He always ate local food. He marvelled at leashed ostriches in Augsburg. He traversed the waterways of Venice in a gondola. He studied an exorcism in Rome. He recorded the ups and downs of his urinary tract, sometimes voiding kidney stones that were as big as pinecones and came in 'exactly the shape of a prick'.[11] We know all this detail because Montaigne kept a journal that he dictated to his secretary and added to as well.

An illuminating part of Montaigne's travels occurred in Rome. A place of conflicting ideals for him, the Holy City was both cosmopolitan and narrow-minded. A copy of his *Essays* was confiscated from him and rigorously examined. Four months later, Montaigne received the book back with suggested amendments, though nothing more serious happened to him beyond that. Evidently, Montaigne wasn't too concerned as he applied for Roman citizenship, which was approved.

In 1581, he left Rome for Loreto, seeking more relief from the stones in the spas of La Villa. Here, an unexpected message came to him. Unknowingly, he'd been voted in as the new mayor of Bordeaux by the governing body and that he needed to return to the city as soon as possible; it was the last thing Montaigne wanted to think about. In the typical fashion of weighing multiple perspectives, the new mayor of Bordeaux took his time with responding to the summons. He didn't outright refuse, nor did he hurry. He meandered back home, detouring through Lucca, Sienna and Milan. Finally, on the 30th November, Montaigne presented himself in Bordeaux, ready to take up a position that he'd never wanted. Or did he want it? Much has been said of Montaigne retreating from the world of politics altogether. But some scholars like Philippe Desan have said that he had never given up on his political ambitions. The popular image of him being a lone philosopher living and writing in solitude was a construct of the nineteenth century from the likes of Nietzsche and Emerson. According to Desan, Montaigne desired to be made ambassador to Rome. When that fell through, he was given the mayorship of Bordeaux as a consolation prize.[12]

Whatever his motivations, Montaigne expected that being mayor wouldn't be a walk in the park. It required him to pick city officials and *actually* judge cases this time around, a full-circle moment for a man who'd started his career writing down opinions. When not deciding local laws, Montaigne hobnobbed with royal envoys, cleaning up the damage that had been left by his predecessor Arnaud de Gontault, who'd alienated Henri III and other nobles. Luckily, his sceptical approach to life helped him get along with everyone, while maintaining his equanimity. His four-year stint as mayor wasn't without criticism, however. Some accused him of being disengaged and lazy, when in fact he was living by the ancient philosophies of Stoicism, Epicureanism and Scepticism he so loved by remaining selectively detached. While his contemporaries claimed to be engaged for the sake of personal advancement, Montaigne never stopped being honest. He would give as much as duty demanded of him and would never act falsely or mince his words for self-interest.

A test of Montaigne's commitment to duty as mayor came between June and December 1585. Bordeaux, hit by a destructive heat wave and plague epidemic, lost roughly a third of its population and people left the city as quickly as they could. Montaigne, safe in his estate, coming to the end of his mayorship, was scheduled to do a handover ceremony in Bordeaux. He travelled to Libourne, which was near enough to the city but far enough away from danger for him to write for advice to his colleagues. Should he or should he not enter Bordeaux? The answer to his letters has been lost to history, though it seemed in the end that Montaigne chose to return to his estate rather than risk entering the city. By the time he did, his time as mayor had already passed.[13]

Interestingly, no one in his own time accused Montaigne of cowardice or lacking in courage. That critique came 270 years later when a host of writers condemned him for his failure of duty. It was enough for them to question the entire framework of *The Essays*. How could a book that supposedly told one how to live be taken seriously when its author had failed in such a key moment?

The flesh-and-blood Montaigne carried on writing his *Essays* and being called ever higher up the political ladder. Becoming increasingly wrapped up in defusing religious strife in France, he acted as a sounding board for Henri de Navarre and Henri III over the divide between Catholics and Protestants. In his stint as mayor, he'd helped to keep the peace between both.

In these later years, Montaigne also made one of the most important connections of his life. He met a young woman called Marie de Gournay, a woman who'd become his spiritual daughter and editor of his *Essays,* making him live on much as he'd done with La Boétie. Gournay had read a volume of his work in her teens, walking the path that so many future readers would travel by seeing themselves reflected in Montaigne's ramblings. And like most of the life-altering encounters in Montaigne's life, Death had a say once again. Only this time it was a mistake. For when Gournay inquired about meeting him, there were rumours that he'd died.[14]

But in 1588, on a trip to Paris with her mother, Gournay found out he was very much alive. At the time, Montaigne had been tasked with a secret mission by Henri de Navarre to speak with Henri III. A mission that apparently was unsuccessful. As if the whole experience for him wasn't dramatic enough, Montaigne reportedly received a message from Gournay out of the blue for him to call on her family, a bold move indeed. Montaigne thought it bold too and accepted the invitation.

After their meeting, Montaigne was sufficiently impressed by Gournay to explore an adoptive relationship (though it could've been more her idea, than his). He already had a healthy biological daughter named Leonor who didn't seem at all perturbed by this unexpected new addition to the family. She and Gournay got on well in later years, while Montaigne praised her for her diligence in editing his third volume of *Essays.* In one passage he wrote, 'she is the only person I still think about in this world. If youthful promise means anything, her soul will someday be capable of the finest things, among others of perfection the most sacred kind of friendship.'[15]

Whether those were Montaigne's or Gournay's words is still debated, though it's likely her exuberance and curiosity helped Montaigne in many ways. At this point in his life, he was juggling chronic illness and political pressure, with the latter reaching its head after siding with an exiled Henri III and being imprisoned in Paris's Bastille in July 1588. Luckily, he was released quickly by Henri's mother Catherine de Medici and he swiftly returned to his estate.

The stones that'd plagued Montaigne for years finally caught up with him in 1592. In September that year, an infection led to a throat inflammation called quinsy. His throat swelled, making it harder and harder to breathe. Pained as he was and though he couldn't speak, Montaigne communicated through writing notes. He probably knew that his end was coming and for three days he lay in bed, visited by a steady stream of family and servants. Having arranged his will, Montaigne reportedly had a mass conducted in his room. Then, on the 13th September, he passed away at 59.

If not for the attack of quinsy, Montaigne likely would've carried on writing his *Essays*. Who knows what kind of labyrinth of the self he would've continued to build? It turns out that future generations would do that for him, constantly reinterpreting his work for their own purposes.

What makes Montaigne the everyman philosopher?

It's my belief that you don't have to be interested in the subject of philosophy to appreciate Montaigne. His writing style and free-flowing observations create a living canvas to be coloured with your own interpretations. The reason is because of Montaigne's personal philosophy that blended several schools of thought. He appreciated the practical meditations of Stoicism, while enjoying the freedom of withdrawal that Epicureanism offered. The latter, also founded in Ancient Greece, advocated for moderation and a deliberate stepping back from the world to live simply.[16] Montaigne interpreted Epicureanism as side-stepping painful situations and diverting attention away from the issue, techniques that helped him cope with the loss of La Boétie and presumably others he cared for.[17]

The ancient wisdom tradition Montaigne loved most of all was Scepticism, which informed his habit of exploring multiple perspectives across his *Essays* and why he was potentially able to move between so many different circles without alienating himself and still maintaining his independence.

To clarify, Montaigne applied Pyrrhonian Scepticism, which acted as a form of therapy and a path to figuring out how to live, rather than just questioning for the sake of knowledge or a desire to be proven right. This original Sceptic, a man named Pyrrho, worked from the basis that he would always suspend judgment and that life doesn't have to be taken seriously. Montaigne took that approach to heart too in his expression *je souitens* (I hold back).[18] Sure, Montaigne enjoyed questioning for the fun of it. He also questioned so he could make an informed decision, expand his horizons and imagine situations from the point of view of someone else.

An entertaining example of Montaigne's Scepticism at work was his enjoyment of telling stories about animals and engaging in thought exercises with his cat. Famously he said, 'When I play with my cat, who knows if

I am not a pastime to her more than she is to me?'[19] Montaigne had no problem viewing himself through the eyes of his pet to further examine his appearance, mind and behaviour. It's the same as saying, 'the only thing I know is that I know nothing. And I'm not even sure of that.'

The delight that came with writing about anything that came to mind was a thing Montaigne was certain of. He had no qualms waxing lyrical about how he could no longer satisfy a woman like he used to or that he apparently had a small penis. He could jump to the defence of Seneca and Plutarch, only to poke fun at them a few sentences later. He wrote down the sensations of his illnesses like they were everyday conversations. 'If only I were like that dreamer in Cicero who dreamed he had a woman in his arms and had the faculty of ejaculating his gallstones in the bedclothes! My own gallstones monstrously unlecher me!'[20]

Of course, not every reader appreciated these details. In the years following Montaigne's death, he was called a subversive and *The Essays* were banned by the Catholic Church in 1676, where they stayed on the Index of Prohibited Books for roughly 200 years. Philosophers like Voltaire and Pascal saw him as a threat to reason and dignity. Rosseau saw a kindred spirit who wrote about noble savages and championed the environment. Romantics and Libertines either thought Montaigne wasn't being intense enough with his emotional reveries or obsessing over the relationship and supposedly hidden messages between him and La Boétie.

Following this tradition of personal interpretation, I see Montaigne's perspective as crucial for our modern age. His authenticity, his willingness to question, to take his time with decision-making, is useful for a world where information is currency. Whether it's fake news or people being locked into shiny object syndrome, it's become all too easy to fall into the snare of snap decisions. To not take the time to see a situation from more than one angle.

Montaigne is also partially responsible for the glut of information and personal opinions shared in blogs, think pieces and articles in every corner of the internet. His *Essays* paved the way for blogging and if he were alive today, there's a good chance that he'd throw himself into every online debate he could be a part of with his natural wit and healthy scepticism. And that's the most important takeaway for me. To question to understand yourself as much as the people you're talking to. To question to build the life that you want. To question the question and realise that you'll never have all the answers no matter how hard you try.

Chapter 8

The Foremother of Feminism and the Vindication to Live

'My own sex, I hope, will excuse me, if I treat them like rational creatures, instead of flattering their *fascinating* graces, and viewing them as if they were in a state of perpetual childhood, unable to stand alone.'[1] Such a rallying cry for the power of women has a modern tone to it. It's straightforward. It's stating the obvious. In eighteenth-century England, this statement was radical and provocative. It was spoken by Mary Wollstonecraft, a woman who for decades was remembered more for her unhappy personal life than for being one of the foremothers of feminism and her contributions to philosophy.

A writer and disruptor, Wollstonecraft stood out in the conservative English society that'd raised her to expect only a narrow life path for her gender. This was best personified in her ground-breaking book *A Vindication of the Rights of Woman*, where she argued passionately for women to have the same rights to education as men. Here we'll chart her life and show how she struggled and fought to have her voice, and the voices of so many other women heard.

Escaping into education

Born in the overcrowded, stifling district of Spitalfields, London, Wollstonecraft had an unsettled life ahead of her, filled with noise and chaos. Edward, her father, worked as a silk weaver, while her mother, Elizabeth, came from a wine-merchant background. For all intents and purposes, the family were financially comfortable, but never financially *secure* due in large part to the actions and antics of Edward Wollstonecraft. A quick-tempered, quick-to-jump-into-new-ventures kind of man, he moved the family around several times in Mary's youth. First to Epping Forest, then to the market town of Barking, where he took up farming without knowing how to do it properly.

Then, the Wollstonecrafts moved up North to Beverly in Yorkshire and Edward's fortunes or temper didn't get any better. In alcoholic rages, he abused his wife, Mary and her siblings. And as Mary got older, she forced herself into the protector role, shielding her mother and siblings from Edward's anger. Often, she'd spend nights sleeping on the landing outside of her mother's room to make sure her father wouldn't hurt her. A saving grace for Mary in Yorkshire was her friendship with Jane Arden. The two girls attended lectures from Arden's father and read frequently. In this intellectual atmosphere, Mary found a refuge from the dysfunctions of her home life.

In 1775, when Mary was 16, the family moved back to London. Edward had decided to chase after another pipe dream. Cut off from Jane and restless, Mary looked to learn new things wherever she could. She found a teacher in a neighbour called Reverend Clare, who showed her the works of John Locke and Johnathan Swift. Through the Reverend, Mary met Fanny Blood, starting up another close friendship. Soon, her father had them moving again, this time to Walworth and Mary's restlessness continued to build. A temporary cure seemed to be in the stories told by a bank clerk that she and her family lodged with. The clerk regaled her with the lives of ancient philosophers like Plato, stories that fascinated Mary and that she would take to heart in later years.[2]

By the time she was 16, Mary didn't want to be stifled by her parents any longer. Against her mother's wishes, she took a job as a companion to an elderly widow in Bath, which proved to be a trying experience. Even more trying, perhaps, was being called back to London to look after her dying mother in 1780. A few years later, another painful blow struck, to do with her younger sister Eliza.

Recently married and a new mother, Eliza suffered from post-partum depression, made worse by her husband. Their relationship deteriorated so much that Eliza wanted to leave him, a difficult prospect under the laws of the day. Women needed to carry out their duties. Mary refused to sit back and let her sister be handcuffed by such restrictive laws. Nor would she let Eliza be continually abused by her husband, just as she'd watched their mother suffer in silence all those years growing up. So, in 1784, Mary did something daring and dangerous – she convinced Eliza to leave her husband and daughter. Fleeing Eliza's home, the sisters hid out in Hackney, a decision that would have tragic consequences. Eliza's daughter died, while she was labelled a social pariah. Never again would she be able to remarry and so spent the rest of her life destitute.[3]

Even in these dire straits, Mary wouldn't leave her sister to fend for herself. She had a clear vision of the world and set about making it a reality with her friend Fanny Blood. Having lived with the Bloods for two years, Mary and Fanny had become like sisters. They decided to found a girls' school together, first in Islington, then the bohemian community of Newington Green with their siblings. While an idealistic idea, the schools both failed under the realities of economic conditions and changing circumstances. Blood soon married and moved to Portugal, hoping that the warm weather would improve her health.

When her friend's condition got worse, Mary left England to look after her, only for Blood to die. The loss of her friend and schools had left Mary at a crossroads. Would she finally conform to the standards of her age that expected her to be married, motherly and obedient? Of course not. She decided to walk a path paved with literature and discourses that she'd write and shake the foundations of Western society.

The unfortunate situation of females left without a fortune

With the help of friends, Mary secured work as a governess for the wealthy Kingsborough family in Ireland. As had been the case years before with the widow she'd worked for in Bath, Mary's iron will and independence left her at odds with Lady Kingsborough. Yet her teachings rubbed off on one of the daughters, Margaret, who later wrote that Mary 'freed her mind of all superstitions'.[4] Her tenure as a governess lasted less than a year, as Mary decided that she was fed up with the limited lot that women of respectable backgrounds had. Vowing to become an author, she returned to London, eventually collaborating with the liberal publisher Joseph Johnson. Armed with her pen and convictions, Mary wrote reviews and translated texts like *Of the Importance of Religious Opinions* by the political economist Jacques Necker.

Her first defining work, *Thoughts on the Education of Daughters*, would come in 1787. In the book, Mary makes the case for women becoming strong mothers and daughters by doing away with artificial social graces in favour of living by a moral and virtuous character. For example, she wrote, 'the emotions of the mind often appear conspicuous in the countenance and manner. These emotions, when they arise from sensibility and virtue, are inexpressibly pleasing. But it is easier to copy the cast of countenance than to cultivate the virtues which animate and improve it.'[5] In another chapter, Mary lamented the kind of education system that led women of her background to be left with little in the way of prospects: 'Painfully sensible of unkindness, she is alive to everything, and many sarcasms reach her, which were perhaps directed another way. She is alone, shut out from equality and confidence, and the concealed anxiety impairs her constitution; for she must wear a cheerful face or be dismissed.'[6]

In writing *Thoughts*, Mary was following the tradition of conduct books for ladies, the kind like Christine de Pizan's *Treasure of the City of Ladies.* But she was also adding a new dimension to the genre by openly critiquing the traditional education for women, ideas that would become fully formed in *A Vindication of the Rights of Woman.*

The book, well received by critics, emboldened Mary to keep writing and mingle with some of the most eminent thinkers of the day. She joined the circle of one of the future Founding Fathers of America, Thomas Paine, as well as entering the orbit of the rockstar philosopher William Godwin. A man with a utopian and optimistic view of the world, Godwin's ideas were far more bombastic and radical than he was in person.[7] On their first meeting, Mary was unimpressed and spent the whole night arguing with him. This combativeness *didn't* set the tone for the rest of their relationship. Mary felt drawn to another man, the artist Henry Fuseli. In him, she saw sparks of wild genius and fire that captivated her. Neither seemed to mind that Fuseli was already married and they carried on with each other until Mary came to his home and proposed that she, Fuseli and his wife have a three-way arrangement. Horrified, Fuseli's wife would stand for no such thing and Fuseli quickly broke off the relationship.[8]

Humiliated and looking for a new project to dedicate her time and energy to, Mary travelled to France in 1792 to support the Revolution that reignited her life spark. Her support for the Revolution was made more prominent by her disagreement with Conservative MP Edmund Burke, who wrote *Reflections on the Revolution in France* in 1790. Burke had once been a member of the liberal Whig party, a group that supported the American revolutionaries. So, many of his contemporaries expected him to be in favour of the French Revolution. When Burke derided the movement and promoted traditional values and faith in the aristocracy, it sent shockwaves throughout Europe.

Burke's conservative views angered Mary so much that she penned her response, *Vindication of the Rights of Men,* only a month after his book had been released. Initially, the work was anonymous, while a second reprint credited Mary as the author. In her work, Mary argued that Burke would see an equal society built on the passivity of women and the maintenance of slavery. That people shouldn't be judged on how they were born, but on their character. That Republicanism starts with the personal happiness of an individual in the home, connected to wider family values in an agrarian society. In one famous passage, Mary dismantled Burke's depiction of Queen Marie Antoinette being surrounded by women who were 'furies of hell in the abused shape of the vilest of women'.[9] She countered this description with 'probably you mean women who gained a livelihood selling vegetables or fish, who never had any advantages of education'.[10]

Cleverly, she also reversed and redefined the definitions Burke had created for women with phrases like sublime and beautiful. To him, the sublime meant the strength of masculinity, while beautiful represented weakness and femininity. Mary wrote that he might have convinced women that 'littleness and weakness are the very essence of beauty ... not to cultivate the mortal virtues that might chance to excited respect and interfere with the pleasing sensations that were created to inspire. Thus confining truth, fortitude and humanity within the rigid pale of manly morals'.[11]

Respectably unrespectful

Mary's scathing attack made her an overnight sensation at home and abroad. And when she arrived in Paris, she quickly joined up with like-minded British thinkers like Helena Maria Williams and associated with the moderate Girondins group instead of the more aggressive Jacobins. During this time of her life, Mary wrote and published her now-iconic *A Vindication of the Rights of Woman* during 1791 and 1792. An extension of her previous works, the main argument of the essay was that better-educated women would be able to contribute to a better society, that men and women were equal in various aspects of life, but not gender equality as we know it in the modern day. Like the work of Christine de Pizan, we should root Mary's perspective in the context of her time.

For example, Mary blended her rational thinking with religious faith by stating that women and men should be equal in the eyes of God, implying that both had an obligation to respect the sanctity of marriage. This was a radical double-standard exposure of the day. In other parts of her discourse, she calls directly on men, not women, to be the agents of change: 'Let it not be concluded, that I wish to change the order of things; I have already granted, that from the constitution of their bodies, men seem to be designed by Providence to attain a greater degree of virtue.'[12] Elsewhere, 'I appeal to their [men's] understandings and as a fellow-creature, claim, in the name of my sex some interest in their hearts. I entreat them to assist to emancipate their companion.'[13]

Mary's defence of her sex wasn't just theoretical. She intended to put it to the test in the pandemonium sweeping across France with the Reign of Terror and mass executions. To do this, she remained staunchly opposed to the Jacobins, who were against equal rights for women and subscribed to Rosseau's perception of women being limited to their roles as mothers and subordinates to their husbands. She flew in the face of what was 'respectable' for a British woman of her class by starting a relationship with the American adventurer Gilbert Imlay, sleeping with him out of wedlock.

As a British citizen and known friend of the Girondins, Mary came under suspicion when many of the leaders of the group were being guillotined. Imlay helped her by lying to the American embassy in France that Mary was his wife, giving her immunity from arrest. Besotted with Imlay, it wasn't long before Mary was pregnant with a girl. Naming her daughter Fanny after her closest friend, Mary looked forward to a life where she and Imlay could raise the girl together. But it was not to be. Imlay had no interest in raising a family and created distance between them by travelling on long voyages and neglecting to return her letters.

During 1794 and 1795, Mary moved between London and Paris, celebrating the downfall of the Jacobins and writing *An Historical and Moral View of the French Revolution*, which recounted how ordinary French people experienced the events. She cobbled together letters and documents, presenting a complex picture of the brutality of the Jacobins and the Reign of Terror. Still, she believed the Revolution was a wonderful accomplishment and that she could offset the British idea the French Revolution had been motivated by madness.

For all the clarity she placed into her writing, Mary still chased after Imlay, finding him in London in April 1795. He rejected her, a crushing blow that made her attempt suicide by drinking laudanum. Recovering,

Mary agreed to go on a business trip for Imlay to Scandinavia, attempting to find a Norwegian captain who'd stolen silver from him – a ruse on Imlay's part to get rid of her.

Arriving in Scandinavia with her daughter and maid, Mary spent the next three months travelling across Denmark, Sweden and Norway. Of these experiences, she recorded them in a book called *Letters Written in Sweden, Norway, and Denmark*. A beautiful precursor to the travel writing genre, *Letters* is filled with vivid observations of nature and its healing properties, for example, 'the more I see the world, the more I am convinced that civilisation is a blessing not sufficiently estimated by those who have not traced its progress; for it not only refines our enjoyments, but produces a variety which enables us to retain the primate delicacy of our sensations.'[14] The journal also became a way for Mary to process Imlay's constant betrayals through the emotional sensations nature caused within her: 'The impetuous dashing of the rebounding torrent from the dark cavities which mocked the exploring eye produced an equal activity in my mind. My thoughts darted from earth to heaven, and I asked myself why I was chained to life and its misery.'[15]

Returning to England and accepting their relationship was truly over, Mary tried to kill herself for a second time. She jumped into the River Thames on a rainy night, only to be saved by a stranger. Of her suicide attempt, Mary believed it came from a rational place, not from an emotional outburst. Having struggled to find a happy medium between her intellectual pursuits and true love, Mary would finally achieve that balance in the coming weeks and months.

Bittersweet acceptance

In some ways, Mary's failed suicide had reset the clock for her. She was free to rediscover old friendships and feelings. Returning to the circle of Joseph Johnson, Mary crossed paths with William Godwin once again. All these years later, perhaps she and Godwin were different people. Or maybe they had experienced so much that they could finally afford to drop their guards and appreciate one another's views. At any rate, Godwin courted Mary in a slow burn, the step-by-step advance of two people not having all the answers but figuring it out as they went.

Eventually, Mary became pregnant and she and Godwin were faced with a dilemma: Should they marry to legitimise their daughter's name and make sure she was protected? Or should they hold true to the principles they'd had for years of not believing in marriage? In the end, they chose the first option and were ostracised and mocked for their compromises. To Mary, it didn't matter. She had finally found someone who treated her as an equal in all things[16] and could look forward to the birth of their daughter Mary. Yet this brief period of joy wasn't to last. In 1797, Wollstonecraft suffered a complex birth. Contracting post-partum infection, she spent several days in pain. And on the 10th of September, she died from septicaemia.

The world had lost one of its brightest minds and Godwin was heartbroken. He resolved to honour his wife's memory by publishing her life story in *Memoirs of the Author of the Rights of Woman*. And while Godwin had the best of intentions, the book wasn't received how he wished it to be. Many readers were shocked by Mary's affairs, suicide attempts and illegitimate children. So damaging was the reaction that Mary's reputation suffered for over a century,[17] until later generations exhumed her legacy as that of a proto-feminist icon.

Mary's immediate legacy carried on with her second daughter, Mary Wollstonecraft-Godwin. History knows her best as Mary Shelley, the author of *Frankenstein.* Raised to cherish the memory of her mother, Shelley's earliest reading experience was of visiting the graveyard where Mary was buried and learning to trace her name from the gravestone.[18]

Many others were influenced by the philosophical and political works that Mary Wollstonecraft brought into the world. The Romantic poets William Wordsworth and Samuel Taylor Coleridge aped the natural aesthetics found in her travel writing. Novelist Virginia Woolf felt her living presence. American crusaders for women's rights Margaret Fuller and Elizabeth Cady Stanton were inspired by her example. For better or worse, Mary chose to live life on her own terms and use her philosophy as a guiding light through the stormiest of waters.

Chapter 9

The Art Critic and the Architecture of the World

John Ruskin watched the morning sky. He watched it peer through the boughs of the trees, the contrast of dark lines against a light canvas. Lines to be mapped with absolute accuracy onto his drawing paper. Lines that formed the roundness of Nature in all things. Not perfect globes, but of various curved surfaces: leaves, stones, boughs, the clouds themselves.[1] Ruskin loved recording the proportions of Nature. One could even go so far as to say he worshipped and venerated the practice of drawing the waterways, woodlands and green spaces of the world. Preserving the transient beauty that God extolled. The purple and crimson glory of a sunrise. A glittering river wending onwards, inciting wonder. Falling petals in the rapturous space between dropping from a branch and wilting into the dew-encrusted grass.

Today, Ruskin could take no joy from his vocation. He was filled with too much anxiety and dread. Feelings that had been with him since the beginning of spring. In the past few months, he'd been seeing queer patterns: abnormal clouds, peculiar, grim sunsets, dawns that didn't come on time. He'd checked his cyanometer often enough, always matching the colour of the sky with the shades of light and dark cobalt blue, testing and documenting changes. Something disturbing was happening to the earth. Ruskin felt it in the air and though he couldn't say for sure *what* it was, there had to be something he could do about it. And so, he opened his journal:

> It is the first of July 1871 and I sit down to write by the dismallest light that ever yet I wrote by ... For the sky is covered with grey cloud; – not rain-cloud, but a dry black veil, which no ray of sunshine can pierce; partly diffused in mist, feeble mist ... And everywhere the leaves of the trees are shaking fitfully ... to show the passing to and fro of a strange, bitter, blighting wind.[2]

The disturbance that the English philosopher John Ruskin recorded in his drawings was signs of climate change. In 1884, he delivered a lecture called *The Storm-Cloud of the Nineteenth Century* with a ferocious, manic energy, spilling out the unnatural weather systems that he'd observed in the Lake District and above his home of Brantwood.

> In those old days, when weather was fine, it was luxuriously fine; when it was bad – it was often abominably bad, but it has its fit of temper and was done with it – it didn't sulk for three months without letting you see the sun … it looks partly as if it were made of poisonous smoke; very possibly it may be; there are at least two hundred furnace chimneys in a square of two miles on every side of me. But mere smoke would not blow to and fro in that wild way. It looks more to me as if it were made of dead men's souls.[3]

To back up his tirade, Ruskin showed painted diagrams of clouds in motion and pointed towards this growing storm of the wrath of God. It was typical of his browbeating, prickly style of delivery, demanding his Victorian audience think deeply about their environment. The kind of attitude that had won him both renown and infamy through his years as a writer, lecturer, art historian and critic. Members of his audience were sceptical, claiming Ruskin to be mad and delusional about the changes he suggested.

At the time of writing this book in the 2020s, a similar story continues to play out about the existence of climate change and the importance of sustainability. As one of the pioneers of sustainable thinking, Ruskin is an intriguing figure to study for his efforts to protect the environment, both natural and man-made. We must also contrast his passion for environmentalism with his troubled personal life to paint the true portrait of a man who inspired the likes of Gandhi, Proust, Tolstoy, Wilde, Lloyd Wright and people from so many different disciplines and life paths.

Wrapped in cottonwool

Born in 1819, Ruskin was the only child of John James Ruskin and Margaret Cox. The elder Ruskin and his wife were first cousins and their backgrounds cast a shadow over their son through his childhood and beyond. John James, a sherry and wine importer, inherited the business after his father committed suicide and acted as the head of the bank of mum and dad for Ruskin in his later years. Margaret's side of the family were pub landlords and there was the feeling that she'd been rescued from such a life and brought into the wealthier camp.

John James, the opposite of his father, a shrewd and prudent businessman, nevertheless took on all the debts that had been left behind and the anxiety of bankruptcy was never far away. An engagement that happened in 1809 finally turned into marriage in 1818 and it was more like a business transaction than a celebration.

While Ruskin was growing up, there was no passion or sentimentality between his parents. And thus his childhood became sculpted by duty to his parents, the strict Christian evangelism of his mother, the ambitions that his father set on his shoulders. Yet Ruskin wasn't without beauty in his early life. His father schooled him in Romanticism, insisting he learn the works of Byron and Scott, lessons that would stick with him, as in 1836 Ruskin called the former the 'greatest poet after Shakespeare' and seemed to have modelled his early writing style on Byron.[4]

Another lens for beauty came through the extensive travelling the young Ruskin did with his parents. They often travelled by private carriage and one magical trip in 1833 stuck out when the family trekked into Germany, then onto Como, Milan and Genoa. The Ruskins finally turned back home when Margaret found the heat to be too much. But The Alps had left a lasting impression on Ruskin: 'They were clear as crystal, sharp on the pure horizon sky, and already tinted with rose by the sinking sun. Infinitely beyond all that we had ever thought or dreamed.'[5]

Nature enraptured the boy. Wherever he looked, whether in the small garden of his London home, or the sweeping hinterlands of Wales and the Lake District, he found beauty, truth and meaning. Ruskin felt drawn to water, its movement, shape and connectedness to all. He investigated this 'universal element' from different vantage points, looking for it in clouds, snow, pools, lakes and rivers. He saw it in the flow of the poems he read, the torrential overflow in the treatises and books he'd write about art and architecture.[6]

No matter how entrenched Ruskin became in the natural world, the roots of religion ran deep within him. His parents hoped he would join the clergy and he studied at King's College in London, learning from the evangelical Thomas Dale. Later, he studied at the University of Oxford as a gentleman-commoner and even here he couldn't escape his parent's influence. His mother took rooms in the High Street and Ruskin would visit her every evening for tea, while his father joined them on weekends.

The hawkeyed view his mother kept on him extended to his love life as well. At 17, Ruskin met his first love, Adele Domecq. The daughter of his father's business partner, Adele visited the family home with her sisters. Ruskin found these fiery, Roman Catholic girls to be like creatures from another planet. He tried to win the 15-year-old Adele's affection by writing her a story where he played a dashing Neapolitan bandit and her a fair maiden. Adele wasn't impressed with the awkward floundering of the English boy who spouted dogma about the Spanish Inquisition at her. For his part, Ruskin felt his father would have been happy to arrange a marriage between them but his mother had other ideas.[7]

She couldn't fathom her only child marrying a Roman Catholic. Ruskin later discovered that Adele had become engaged to a French nobleman and around this time, he started coughing blood, leading to his parents whisking him out of university and back on the road to travel.

But even with this strict religious upbringing, Ruskin didn't go into the Church. Art and writing became his calling, his creative works infused with the pomp and haranguing of a preacher. So, how did this happen?

All great Art is Praise

Ruskin's appreciation for art had been a constant of his childhood and the artist that propelled him forward was J.M.W. Turner. Becoming aware of Turner at age 13, Ruskin became enthralled by the vivid landscapes rendered in watercolours. Turner's work was a gift to him, informing 'the entire direction of my life's energies'.[8] When Ruskin discovered that his hero's work had been savaged in the 1836 summer exhibition of the Royal Academy of Arts, he felt personally offended. Writing an impassioned essay in defence of Turner, Ruskin had his father send it to the artist. Though his words didn't impress Turner and the essay went unpublished. Ruskin didn't give up and paid no mind to the age-old never-meet-your heroes concept. In 1840, he came face to face with Turner at the house of a picture dealer, later writing, 'everybody had described him to me as coarse, boorish, unintellectual, vulgar. This I knew to be impossible. I found in him a somewhat eccentric, keen-mannered, matter-of-fact English-minded gentleman ... bad-tempered evidently, perhaps a little selfish, highly intellectual.'[9] Their relationship waxed and waned like the moon, sometimes bright and full, other times cold and distant. Most importantly, Ruskin's discovery of Turner was a catalyst for his philosophy of all art being an expression of the divine, a celebration of God synthesised through the creation of paintings and buildings and how they represented the characters of the land and people. It led him to become an art critic, writing the influential book *Modern Painters* from his defence of Turner, over seventeen years.

Ruskin argued the 'truth of art' had to be found in Nature, that natural elements should be captured as they truly were, instead of being idealised. Steeping his language in rhetoric from the Bible, Ruskin presented landscapes as communications from God and that artists should spend as much time as they could in the natural world, channelling that spirituality into the canvas. And when he saw artists cutting corners, he wasn't forgiving. Even with Turner. Ruskin felt that he didn't depict water realistically, that it wasn't wet enough. When analysing two Turner paintings called *Shipwreck* and *Calais Pier*, Ruskin consulted a friend who'd been a naval artist, who said the water should be 'several shades lighter, and greyer or cooler … in any ordinary breezy weather, when you see boats knocking about at Spithead, and if the sun is shining through the sails … the transparent wet parts give a very beautiful effect'.[10] The little details mattered to Ruskin and he demanded it from every artist he critiqued. This radical new approach to art criticism put him on the map, kicking off another travelling tour for Ruskin with his parents, where he found the time to make some bold claims about architecture as well. In Rouen, he saw churches that were the perfect harmony of religion, art and nature. In Italy, he found a call to arms that galvanised him to defend ancient buildings, especially the buildings of Venice.

First visiting the city at 16, Ruskin returned to Venice in 1845 to gather fresh material for his second volume of *Modern Painters*. He became consumed by her buildings: the tracery of window openings, the grand beauty of the Doge's Palace and St Mark's Basilica. It was his duty to protect this Paradise of Cities from the hell of restoration, a fate he saw happening to St Mark's Basilica. Restoration for Ruskin was 'the most total destruction which a building can suffer … as impossible as to raise the dead, to restore anything that has ever been great or beautiful in architecture'.[11] In the past, Ruskin had threatened to knock men from scaffolding in his attempts to preserve original architecture. With his beloved Venice, he channelled his righteous indignation into *The Stones of Venice*, a deep rumination on the buildings of the city, along with detailed sketches and commissions to remember and protect the man-made wonders that were so important to him.

A particular aspect that Ruskin was keen to emphasise was the majesty of Gothic architecture. He defined six ideal characteristics of the Gothic in both the buildings and the builders:

1. Savageness.
2. Changefulness.
3. Naturalism.
4. Grotesqueness.
5. Rigidity.
6. Redundance.

What these characteristics sum up is that the Gothic is never content to be perfect. It's wonderfully weird, misshapenly beautiful, stylishly strange. The Gothic architect is like a novelist who never relies on hackneyed tropes or repetition. They take risks and go against convention, living by the creed of 'pointed arches do not constitute Gothic, nor vaulted roofs, nor flying buttresses, nor grotesque sculptures, but all or some of these things [are there], and many other things with them, when they come together as to have life'.[12]

Looking at the bigger picture, in his *Seven Lamps of Architecture*, Ruskin claimed that good architecture is illuminated by sacrifice, truth, power, beauty, life, memory and obedience. Sacrifice means crafting works to the best of our ability, either for God or because sacrifice has value in of itself. Truth references Ruskin's truth of materials argument, highlighting an honest construction process. The lamp of power ties into the awe that should be experienced when one gazes at a building. The lamp of beauty speaks of natural ornamentation drawn from God's creation. The fifth lamp of life comes from the hands of the builder, while the sixth lamp of memory is about buildings being an extension of the culture in which they've been created. And the final lamp of obedience details how a building doesn't have to be original for originality's sake. All the original things of the world were determined long ago, and so a man will take up the style of his day and become the best he can be at it.[13]

The lyrical way Ruskin wrote about architecture, the tenderness in which he presented Venice, reads like that of a man in love. And it was indeed

Bust of Marcus Aurelius. (*Via public domain, Wikimedia Commons*)

ortrait of Lao Tzu from *Myths nd Legends of China* by Edward heodore Chalmers. (*Via public omain, Wikimedia Commons*)

Christine de Pizan. (*Via public domain, Wikimedia Commons*)

A miniature of the poet Sappho from Christine de Pizan's *The Book of the City of Ladies*. (*Via public domain, Wikimedia Commons*)

Portrait of Niccolo Machiavelli by Santi di Toto. (*Via public domain, Wikimedia Commons*)

Portrait of Niccolo Machiavelli by Cristofano di Papi dell'Altissimo.
(*Via public domain, Wikimedia Commons*)

Portrait of Michel de Montaigne. (*Via public domain, Wikimedia Commons*)

Montaigne bust. (*Via public domain, Wikimedia Commons*)

ESSAIS

DE

MICHEL SEIGNEVR

DE MONTAIGNE.

A PARIS,

Chez ABEL L'ANGELIER,

au premier pillier de la grand

Salle du Palais.

Auec Priuilege du Roy.

An early cover of Montaigne's essays. (*Via public domain, Wikimedia Commons*)

Portrait of Mary Wollstonecraft by John Opie. (*Via public domain, Wikimedia Commons*)

William Godwin, husband of Mary Wollstonecraft by James Northcote. (*Via public domain Wikimedia Commons*)

ary Shelley, daughter of Mary Wollstonecraft by Richard Rothwell. (*Via public domain, Wikimedia Commons*)

Photograph of a young John Ruskin by William Downey. (*Via public domain, Wikimedia Commons*)

hotograph of Albert Camus with Maria da Saudade Cortesao and the poet Murilo Mendes in Rio de neiro, 1949. (*Via public domain, Wikimedia Commons*)

Photograph of Richard Wright by Carl Van Vechten. (*Via public domain, Wikimedia Commons*)

Promotional still for the original Broadway production of Richard Wright's *Native Son*. (*Via public domai Wikimedia Commons*)

'hotograph of Sojourner Truth. (*Via public domain, Wikimedia Commons*)

Photograph of Roland Barthes, first published in the Argentinian magazine *Periscopio*. (*Via public domain Wikimedia Commons*)

a love affair he had with Venice, beginning with a flaming passion and then cooling as he saw the city become torn and ravaged by the Austrian occupation of the late 1840s. But he still wrote of her with the giddy rush of a schoolboy recalling his first love: 'St Mark's lion, lifted on a blue field covered with stars, until at last, as if in ecstasy, the crests of the arches break into a marble form; and toss themselves far into the blue sky in flashes and wreathes of sculpted spray.'[14]

Ruskin couldn't muster the same love and affection for the women in his life, a problematic part of his legacy that we'll now turn to with the relationship that continued to damage his reputation years after it ended.

Lost in fantasies

In 1841, Ruskin wrote a fantasy story, *The King of the Golden River*, for a precocious 12-year-old girl named Euphemia 'Effie' Gray. Despite there being a nine-year age gap between them, Ruskin saw a bright spark in the girl that only grew more intense for him as she matured. The Grays and the Ruskins were friends and when Effie came to stay at the Ruskin home in 1847, she was on the periphery of John's infatuation with the granddaughter of Sir Walter Scott, Charlotte Lockhart. Our Ruskin had been courting Charlotte in the hopes of marrying into the family of one of his literary heroes. But it didn't go anywhere and the ever-astute Effie saw that Ruskin wasn't truly in love with Miss Lockhart.

Among these changing circumstances, Margaret Ruskin saw the 19-year-old Effie as a good match for her son. As did her parents. And so, in 1848, Ruskin and Effie were married, yet it mirrored the same unsteady course that Ruskin's parents had charted. The date was moved several times to suit his mum and dad and the engagement was mismanaged from the start. When the newly married couple honeymooned in Venice, Ruskin was more concerned with cataloguing architecture than supporting his grieving wife, who'd lost her aunt to fever. Their personalities were a sharp contrast to each other – Ruskin, solitary and singularly focused on his work, Effie, sociable, bold and effervescent.

The distance between them was more than emotional. Perhaps the most enduring part of their relationship is the lack of sex between them, with Ruskin never consummating the marriage. By 1854, Effie got an annulment from Ruskin and was free to be with the gregarious painter John Everett

Millais. She won the case on the grounds of incurable impotency, a shadow that dogged Ruskin for the rest of his life; before we move on, it's worth lingering on the fixation that Ruskin had on young girls. Was he impotent or was he a paedophile?

Throughout his life, Ruskin showed a repeated attraction to teenage girls. Before Effie, there was Charlotte Lockhart, who was in her late teens. After Effie, there was Rose La Touche, a Protestant girl who he'd taught to draw and there was a significant age gap between them as well. Ruskin proposed to her when she was 18, but she kept him waiting for an answer, as she was hesitant about their religious differences. (Ruskin had begun to explore Catholicism.) Then, Rose got sick and died at 26. Her death shattered Ruskin. Like the buildings he fought so hard to preserve, his 'Rosie' would be persevered in his memory and writing as he remembered her best: 'a marvellous little thing when she was younger but – which has been one of the things that have troubled me – there came on some overexcitement of the brain, causing occasional loss of consciousness, and now she often seems only half herself, as if it partly dreaming.'[15]

Trying to reconcile the proclivities of a philosopher with their transformative ideas is a philosophical exercise in itself. One could say that Ruskin was in love with the idea of beauty, but that he was blind to how it matured. His attitude toward women has multiple shades of colour, like a kaleidoscope that changes based on the angle you look at it from. In his essay *Of Queen's Gardens*, Ruskin wrote that women should be free to explore the same educational opportunities as men: 'Let a girl's education be as serious as a boy's. You bring up your girls as if they were meant for sideboard ornaments, and then complain of their frivolity. Give them the same advantage you give to their brothers.'[16] He wrote the essay in response to the narrow conventions of Rose La Touche's upbringing, putting forth a bold system for women's education, even as he wrote of women being helpmates and that the genders are separate in the Victorian mindset. What we can conclude is that it's possible to separate a person from their ideas, as much as both must be acknowledged at the same time.

After his separation from Effie, Ruskin went back to his various educational pursuits, finding new causes to take up. His travel experiences inspired him to want to make culture accessible to all through a 'national store'. In 1871, he founded the Guild of St George, a group built on Ruskin's radical utopian ideas of going back to the land. In 1875, he opened the St George's

Museum in the Sheffield neighbourhood of Walkley. In it, Ruskin housed books, art, plaster casts and minerals, bringing the cultures of France and Italy to the working-class metalworkers of Sheffield, wanting to inspire them to create. (Today, all these treasures can be found in the Ruskin Collection in the Millennium Gallery.)[17]

Another arena Ruskin thrust himself into was social criticism and politics. Rallying against capitalism and socialism, he spoke out against unstable employment and the notion that workers could be treated like machines to be used for cash production. He was against anarchy and never turned away from his belief in hierarchies and the monarchy, but he did believe that the factories had failed workers. That the rabid machine of the Industrial Revolution was harmful to the environment and the people –an opinion he could shout about from his privileged position of belonging to no party and having the wealth to have his opinion taken seriously by the parties he shouted at.

Ruskin's key arguments for political reform centred on the idea that the rich wanted to be rich because it afforded them power over their fellow man. That it could only be overturned through education of the consumer and sidestepping an unequal system through the simpler pleasures of nature and an environmental model. In his writings, he coined the term 'illth' in that ill is the opposite of well, so illth is the reverse of wealth. The term refers to work that causes destruction and devastation. Ruskin's political concepts were too controversial for some and his editor stopped giving him space in *The Cornhill Magazine* where he published his thoughts. Ruskin collected his essays on political economy in *Unto this Last.*

As enthralling and provocative as Ruskin's political lectures were, his 1870s activities would be the last hurrah of a sharp mind dulled and destroyed by mental breakdowns.

Melancholy maturity

When Rose La Touche died, a part of Ruskin died with her. A crushing melancholy swept over him, afflicting him on and off through the years, leading to manic episodes and hallucinations, made worse by a cocktail of grief, pressure and a loss of standing. In 1878, he suffered public humiliation in an incident with the artist James Whistler. Ruskin had critiqued his work the year before, calling his *Nocturne in Black and Gold: The Falling Rocket* piece the work of a charlatan and not worth the 'two hundred guineas for flinging a pot of paint in the public's face'.[18] Whistler retaliated by taking Ruskin to court, an act that brought further stress to Ruskin's mental state. In his defence, Ruskin asked his friend artist Burne-Jones to speak on his behalf. It didn't do any good. Ruskin lost the case and his standing as the influential art critic who had burst onto the scene in his youth. Whistler didn't fare any better, filing for bankruptcy and losing his home because of legal costs.

Into the 1880s, Ruskin's downward spiral reached its crescendo. He wrote his autobiography *Praeterita*, a book filled with unreliable narration and idealised memories, tinged by his illness. But there are flashes of Ruskin's timeless visual philosophy, the care he took with recording flowers, woodland and water.[19] In these final years, he was looked after by his cousin Joan Agnew, a woman who seemed to have finally fulfilled the long-term companionship Ruskin had always yearned for. Through this familial relationship, he was able to appreciate what age brought to beauty. 'I think of her a great deal prettier now than I did then … I am certain that everybody felt the guileless and melodious sweetness of her face.'[20]

Ruskin died in 1900, at his Brantwood home in the Lake District. He left the world at key turning points across everything he touched. In art, the movement of 'art for art's sake' emerged, fanned in part by his case with Whistler. In architecture, the Arts and Crafts movement expanded from his work to protect buildings. In politics, his theories birthed green socialism and the creation of Ruskin Land in the Wyre Forest, where volunteers continue to work outdoors and live off the land to give back to nature. Through all his efforts, Ruskin's main purpose was to leave behind something to look at, so we can better understand our place in the world. I'd say he achieved his purpose.

Chapter 10

The Philosophical Writer and the Absurdity of Life

King Arthur is riding through a forest. Well, riding is a bit generous. It's more like he's miming the gesture while his faithful squire Patsy bangs coconuts together. Up ahead, Arthur hears a fight going on. Two knights are locked in combat. A black knight and a green knight. The Black Knight overpowers his opponent, stabbing him through the visor slit of his helmet. Then, he returns to the bridge he's been guarding. Impressed with the knight's performance, Arthur 'gallops' over. The king offers the Black Knight a place at his Round Table and the knight refuses. Disappointed, Arthur intends to ride on.

'None shall pass,' the Black Knight booms, his voice a dark rasp.

'What?' Arthur exclaims.

'None. Shall. Pass.'

'I have no quarrel with you, brave Sir Knight, but I must cross this bridge.'

'Then you will die.' The Black Knight is unmoved.

Resigned to the fight, Arthur draws his sword. King and knight clash, their swords ringing through the forest. The Black Knight charges, convinced he'll run his opponent through. Then he looks down and sees that his left arm is missing, blood spurting from the open wound.

The king tells him to stand aside.

''Tis but a scratch,' the Black Knight replies and fights on, completely assured that he will soon be the victor. When his other arm comes off, a change of tactics is in order. The king sinks to his knees in prayer. Perfect. A good kicking is the answer. A boot to his opponent's face and the Black Knight carries on with the battle.

'Just a flesh wound,' he bellows in the face of the king's incredulity.

At some point, the Black Knight becomes aware that he's now missing a leg. But he's still standing. 'I'll do you for that! Come here,' he rages. He barks that he's invincible, that he *always* triumphs, that he's … The Black Knight notices his arms and legs are gone. 'All right, we'll call it a draw.'

As Arthur 'rides' away, fury burns in the Black Knight. How dare this coward run from him. He'll bite the yellow bastard's bloody legs off.[1]

That whole situation sounds absurd, didn't it? In Monty Python's *Holy Grail*, the Black Knight character believed he could still defeat King Arthur even with all his limbs missing. As an example of absurd comedy, his extreme denial and obsession is funny. But the situation is also absurd because the audience must accept that the Black Knight genuinely believes he can win and is acting rationally on his own terms in an irrational situation. This is a starting point for Absurdism. I like to think that the father of this philosophy, Albert Camus, would get a good chuckle out of watching *Monty Python* sketches if he'd been alive to see them. A man who lived and breathed his philosophy, Camus' ideas about meaning, purpose, revolt, life and death made him one of the most influential philosophers of the twentieth century. And there's still so much we can learn from him today.

Football, freedom and French connections

Born in 1913 to an Algerian working-class family, Camus grew up without knowing his father, who'd died in the First World War, while his mother Catherine did housework so she could keep a roof over their heads. They lived in a poor district of Algiers, living in the shadow of a French-occupied Algeria as *pied-noirs* (lit. 'black feet', French or Europeans born in Algeria).[2] In a cramped apartment, Camus shared the space with his mother, elder brother Lucian, grandmother and a paralysed uncle.

The circumstances of how someone is born should never define who they become, and Camus never let his humble beginnings hold him back. Excelling in primary school, under the watch of his teacher Louis Germain, Camus won a scholarship that admitted him to a distinguished secondary school.

A love of sport, especially football, brought the young Camus solace in between his studies. Whether in goal or on the pitch, Camus took to football like a duck to water, revelling in the tribalism and community that his team brought to him. At age 16, he played for the Algiers Racing University as part of the team that won the North African Champions Cup and North African Cup in the 1930s. Outside of the game, he felt antsy and restless, cut off from a cause that was bigger than himself. He kicked cans down streets, resisted the nagging of his grandmother, who didn't like him kicking a ball and damaging his school shoes.[3] Years later, when Camus had reached the zenith of the literary world, he called football and theatre his only two real universities. When asked by a friend Charles Poncet which he preferred, Camus said, 'football, without hesitation.'[4]

Sadly, all hopes for a football career were dashed when Camus contracted tuberculosis at 17. This would have been a death sentence for most people, both physically and socially for Camus and his family. Not only was TB potentially contagious for his family, but the disease carried the cultural stigma of weak character and deviancy. On the order of the authorities, Camus was placed in quarantine at his uncle's butcher shop. Among the smell of slaughtered animals and feelings of isolation, Camus found an oasis of purpose inside the first-ever room he had to himself. His anarchist uncle provided him with French and Algerian classics to read and stimulate his mind. It must have been hell for Camus, cut off from all the pleasures of the external world, yet in time he would refer to his condition as a 'fortunate illness',[5] acknowledging it opened new possibilities that might have never happened, without downplaying the severity of its limitations.

At this time, Camus began a lifelong friendship with his teacher Jean Grenier. Having noticed Camus was absent from class, Grenier tracked the wayward youth down and Camus felt ashamed of his poverty and illness. Grenier broke through the stone-faced silence of the boy and pulled him up by his bootstraps, encouraging him to carry on with his education. With Grenier's influence, Camus finished secondary school and enrolled in the University of Algiers, where Grenier became his lecturer and diploma supervisor. During his convalescence, Camus had read the works of Plato and other philosophers, so it's no surprise that he chose to study philosophy.

A new world of thought was opened to him through the works of novelist-philosophers like Franz Kafka, André Gide and Thomas Mann and he set his own thoughts to paper in his thesis called *Christian Metaphysics*, where he explored the relationship between Ancient Greece and Christianity through the figure of Plotinus. Writing for Camus became a raison d'être, an endeavour needing 'a certain constancy of soul, and a human and literary knowledge of sacrifice … to someone who asked Newton how he had managed to construct his theory, he could reply: 'By thinking about it all the time.' There is no greatness without a little stubbornness.'[6]

Camus would experience what sacrifice meant many times throughout his life. An early experience came when he was 20 and he met the beautiful

Simone Hié. Camus' uncle didn't approve of their relationship, as Hié was addicted to morphine. That didn't stop Camus from wanting to help her fight the addiction and they were soon married. A year later, they'd divorced, as Camus had found out she'd been having an affair with her doctor.

Even in his early twenties, Camus wasn't above getting involved in politics, illness be damned. In 1935, he joined the French Communist Party (PCF), believing at the time that it was the best way to promote equality between Europeans and native Algerians. He saw communism 'as a springboard and asceticism that prepares the ground for more spiritual activities. In short, it's a way to shirk false idealism and mechanical optimism and establish a situation where man can rediscover his sense of eternity.'[7] Still, he remained uneasy about its political dogma, even as he moved over to the Algerian Communist Party (PCA) in 1936 for its more peaceful approach. With his association with both parties, Camus couldn't shake his growing disillusionment with politics in general, feeling that no matter what he heard in speeches there was nothing but lies and the absence of human dignity.

As tensions increased in Europe and shifted towards more radical ideologies, Camus was expelled from the PCA, which hardened his resolve to promote justice and freedom in his later works. His strong feelings led him to journalism and he worked for the leftist newspaper *Alger-Republicain*, writing about the mistreatment of Arabs and Berbers by French authorities and continuing to advocate for a better relationship between his home and France. But as Anakaren Cervantes writes in her essay on Camus' role as a journalist, although 'he could empathise with Algerian nationalists and their desire for self-determination and freedom from the French government … he could not bring himself to believe that all French colonials in Algeria were exploitative and parasitic. Moreover, he never fully embraced the idea of a fully independent Algeria.'[8]

In 1939, the Second World War broke out, the culmination of all the upheaval and political anathema Camus had witnessed. When he tried to enlist, he was declared unfit to serve because of his tuberculosis. The following year, *Alger républicain* was banned, meaning Camus found himself in need of a new job. So, he flew to Paris to become editor-in-chief of the newspaper *Paris-soir*. In the City of Light, Camus would be able to fight for what he believed in in more ways than one.

Absurd men, strangers and plagues

The Paris of 1940 was eerily quiet. A Paris holding its breath in dread of the oncoming German invasion. Camus arrived in this oppressive atmosphere in March, feeling out of place in a place that felt the same about itself. Living in a hotel in the district of Montmartre, Camus' sense of isolation was magnified by his surroundings.

A symbol of bohemian culture, Montmartre was a city within a city, a haven for artists and creatives that brought little relief to Camus as he travelled back and forth on the long metro journey to his job at the *Paris-soir.* His work at the paper felt uninspiring, casting a fog of *ennui* over Camus, which he wrote about in his journal: 'What does this sudden awakening mean, in this dark room, with the sounds of a city that has suddenly become strange? And everything is strange to me, everything, without a single person who belongs to me, with no place to heal this wound.'[9]

After finishing his night shift at the paper and returning to his dank hotel room, he picked up writing the novel that consumed him. A novel that sprung from the intense alienation that he couldn't shake off. Time and again he kept coming back to a key phrase: 'A Stranger, who can know what that word means.' By May, Camus had finished the first draft of the book, which had come so clearly to him it amazed him. Much easier than his first attempt at a novel called *A Happy Death.* He called his book *The Stranger*, writing about his sense of awe at its creation to his fiancée Francine Fraue:

> I still imagine that the reader of this manuscript will be at least as fatigued as I am.. ... and I don't know if the continuous tension felt within it will not discourage many souls. But that isn't the question. I wanted this tension and I worked to transmit it. I know it is there. I don't know if it is beautiful.[10]

The Stranger focuses on an indifferent young French Algerian called Meursault. The novel starts with his mother dying and Meursault feeling no grief or emotion. He wanders through his life, apathetic in the blazing Algerian sunshine. Eventually, Meursault decides to help a neighbour get revenge on his girlfriend and he lurches from one volatile situation to the next. It culminates in Meursault shooting an Arab man on the beach and him not really knowing why he did it. Imprisoned, Meursault still feels detached, with the judge focusing more on the young man's inability to cry at his mother's funeral, instead of the murder. Finally, Meursault is sentenced to be executed. As he confronts death, it awakens an understanding within him. He compares his circumstances to the death of his mother, finding comfort in the fact that he can accept 'it was as if that great rush of anger had washed me clean, emptied me of hope, and gazing up at the dark sky spangled with its signs and stars, for the first time, the first, I laid my heart open to the benign indifference of the universe.'[11] It's exactly that indifference that makes him feel like he has a place in the universe. Meursault feels happiness in that knowledge.

The Stranger formed the beginning of Camus' cycle of the absurd and process. Each cycle featured a novel, an essay and a play built around a timeless theme with the modern and the classical placed side by side. Camus followed up *The Stranger* with *The Myth of Sisyphus*, an essay on the nature of suicide, freedom and the meaning of life. The central core of the essay is on Sisyphus, a man condemned by the gods never to die and to forever push a boulder up a hill. Whenever Sisyphus got to the top of the hill, the boulder rolled back down again and he had to start all over again. Camus proposed the idea that we're all like Sisyphus pushing our own boulders and that the essence of the absurd lies in the awareness that we can choose to find meaning in the act. That it's possible to find happiness and joy. That absurdism teaches us to live passionately and freely rather than to die passively. 'One always finds one's burden again. But Sisyphus teaches the higher fidelity that negates the gods and raises rocks. He, too, concludes that all is well … the struggle itself towards the heights is enough to fill a man's heart. One must imagine Sisyphus happy.'[12]

The least acclaimed of this cycle, *Caligula*, focused on the mad Roman emperor. Like the Black Knight of *Monty Python*, Camus' Caligula finds an absurd logic in his actions. In the rejection of all love, friendship and honour, the emperor realises that his quest for freedom in murder and death has provided no freedom at all and he orchestrates his own assassination.

After finishing *The Stranger* in Paris, Camus left the city, just before the Germans arrived.

He followed the *Paris-soir*, relocating to Lyon and marrying Francine. When he was laid off from his job, he and his wife returned to Algeria, where Camus taught in primary schools. In 1942, he prepared to send out his novel for publication, though a bout of tuberculous derailed him. Seeking medical treatment, Camus got permission from the Algerian authorities to return to France.

Resting in the Alps, Camus found himself cut off from his wife and family and in the heart of pro-allied territory. This forced solitude may have been even greater than the isolation he felt when he first came to Paris. Yet, he persevered and started on his second cycle on the theme of revolt, writing *La Peste* (*The Plague*). Set in Oran, the city is going through a deadly epidemic and Dr Bernard Rieux does what he can to help its victims. Rieux understands that there's little more he can do to treat his patients, reflecting that small acts at a time of crisis are sometimes the only real course of action. Individuals are powerless to control their destinies against greater external forces. In one sense, *The Plague* can be read as a metaphor for France's rebellion against Nazism. In another sense, Camus was asking the reader directly what it means to rebel and be responsible for our own actions.

Returning to Paris, Camus entered the existential circle of Jean-Paul Sartre and Simone de Beauvoir, philosophers with rockstar reputations of their own. Camus had discovered Sartre in 1938, reviewing his work *Nausea* and finding it aligned with his own sensibilities. Likewise, Sartre had plenty of praise for *The Stranger* and *The Myth of Sisyphus.* A brief meeting in 1943, at the opening of Sartre's play *The Flies,* blossomed into fast friendship and competitiveness on similar and differing ideas. Both were novelists and philosophers, viewing shades of the absurd in the human condition. But where Sartre seemed to take a negative view of human reality and physicality, Camus revelled in its positivity and the sensuality of the physical. Sartre often wore his existentialist label proudly, while Camus always rejected belonging to that school.[13]

Camus' belief in revolt compelled him to take a stand in the war effort. In 1944, he joined the clandestine newspaper *Combat* as editor-in-chief, writing on behalf of the French Resistance. Camus tended to remain anonymous or use pseudonyms when producing issues, both to avoid capture and to remove himself as an intellectual. He was just another participant in the revolution, using language that promoted a sense of collectivism among *Combat*'s readers. He explicitly named areas of France associated with the working class, creating an inspiring liberal message. Even after the war ended, Camus continued to write for *Combat* and fought to keep it independent of capitalist intent.[14]

Revolts, reprisals and women aplenty

The war changed so many people and Camus was no different. He'd been privy to death and genocide on a mass scale, writing about it on the front lines of rebellion and he'd had more than his fill of it. He took a hard line against capital punishment and the brutal reprisals against Axis collaborators. For him, 'capital judgement upsets the only indisputable human solidarity – our solidarity against death.'[15]

In 1945, Camus put his thoughts into action by signing a petition for mercy in the case of a guilty verdict at the trial of Robert Brasillach, the former editor of a fascist magazine. But it made no difference, as Brasillach was executed by firing squad. Here Camus split from peers like Sartre and De Beauvoir, who believed that the death penalty was necessary for ushering in a better future. The friends would continue to drift even further apart until a hard break became unavoidable, which all stemmed from a difference of belief between Camus and Sartre.

By 1951, Camus' stance on communism had changed dramatically with his release of *The Rebel.* In the essay, Camus pointed out that revolt is a necessary part of history, vastly different from the result of a Communist revolution. Society was built on rebellion, with groups rising up against their oppressors to define the next generation. Man rebelled against life itself to impose limits on himself. For Camus, *that* is true rebellion – drawing lines to maintain moderation and stop tyrants.

This viewpoint didn't sit well with Sartre, who fully embraced the idea that justice and freedom could be gained through Communism. He felt *The Rebel* was a personal attack on him – he'd been at the centre of political pressures and conversations for years. Perhaps he felt he had a duty to move beyond personal affection at a time in history when people would be judged for their actions. He had to be resolute in what he believed. So, he had his colleague Francis Jeanson review *The Rebel* for his *Les Temps modernes* magazine. Jeanson savaged *The Rebel*, leading to Camus writing a letter to the editor that his work had been misrepresented. He never named Sartre, though the pain he felt over the incident was palpable, writing, 'I am beginning to become a little tired of seeing myself ... receive endless lessons in effectiveness from critics who have never done anything more than turn their armchair in history's direction.'[16] This prompted Sartre to fire back with a tirade that killed their friendship once and for all. Camus, left feeling disturbed by the whole ordeal, never published his reply to the letter. His personal life only became more difficult, due to his constant womanising.

Throughout all his work, Camus' love of women and passionate relationships is front and centre, from casting himself into the role of Don Juan in *The Myth of Sisyphus*, to his celebration of women's bodies in *Summer in Algiers*. He never tired of asking the question of why one had to love rarely in order to love much, penning letters to the women who'd captured his heart. One of his most publicised affairs was with the Spanish actress Maria Casares, an affair that caused his wife to have a mental breakdown. Depressed and feeling guilty, Camus tried withdrawing from public life, though he couldn't help but be drawn into the struggles of the Algerian War. The public wouldn't allow him to draw back. They expected an answer from him on his stance. Also, he was about to receive the most distinguished award of his writing career.

Prizes, portents and death

In 1957, Camus was told he'd won the Nobel Prize for literature, arguably the highest award that any writer could aspire to. At 43, Camus was the second youngest writer to win after Rudyard Kipling. Yet the news shocked him, as he'd expected his friend, rival and contemporary André Malraux to win.

As the story goes, there was a lot of politicking behind the scenes with the Nobel Prize committee refusing to honour Malraux because of his association with the right-wing government of French president Charles de Gaulle. Both authors opposed each other's political views, though Camus remained gracious and humble. He believed Malraux deserved to win more than he did and surely would have if not for his politics. On the surface, Malraux remained gracious too, even if deep down he was furious with the slight.[17]

In his acceptance speech, Camus expressed his surprise and spoke of why he used his art – to live and to serve in the pursuit of truth and liberty:

> None of us is great enough for such a task. But in all circumstances of life, in obscurity or temporary fame, cast in the irons of tyranny or for a time free to express himself, the writer can win the heart of a living community that will justify him, on the one condition that he will accept to the limits of his abilities … the service of truth and the service of liberty.[18]

During the speech, Camus was asked about his failure to support the rebels in the Algerian War and he continued to live by his philosophy of there being causes to die for, not kill for. 'People are now planting bombs on the tramways of Algiers. My mother might be on one of those tramways. If that is justice, then I prefer my mother.'[19]

Now at the height of his career, Camus could have laid down his pen. But he still felt his work was unfinished and began work on an autobiographical novel called *The First Man*. He also used the money from the Nobel Prize to fund a theatre production of Dostoevsky's *Demons.* The Camus of the late '50s wanted to explore moral learning, how people expressed their ethics in the real world. A shining example of this was the philosopher Simone Weil, who truly lived her philosophy of attention by suffering and sacrificing her health to help the working class. Camus had found a kindred spirit in her years before and made sure her works were posthumously published and that she would never be forgotten.[20]

In 1960, we can imagine Camus looking with hope towards a better future. Tragically, he would not get to see what this new decade would hold for the world. On the 4th January, he was riding in the front passenger seat of a Facel Vega with the nephew of his publisher, Michel Gallimard. Having spent the Christmas holidays in Provence, they were returning to Paris. Originally, Camus hadn't intended to go back to Paris in a car. His wife and their daughters, Catherine and Jean, had travelled by train. By this point in their relationship, Camus had decided it was more appropriate to think of Francine like a sister and had been writing ardent letters to a mistress at the time that 'this frightful separation will at least have made us feel more than even the constant need we have for each other'.[21]

Still, his love for his family carried him onwards to see them. But he never made it back, as 65 miles outside of Paris, in the town of Villeblevin, the car crashed into a tree, instantly killing Camus and injuring Gallimard, his wife and daughter. On Camus' person, the return half of a train ticket was found, along with 144 pages of his manuscript *The First Man.* An absurd end for the man who'd popularised absurdism. Later reports confirmed that Gallimard hadn't been speeding and the surface of the road hadn't been dangerous, giving rise to all kinds of conspiracy theories as to how the crash happened. Camus' premature death shocked the world. Many mourned him and wrote fitting tributes, like his one-time friend and rival Sartre, who said 'the accident that killed Camus was a scandal because it suddenly projects into the centre of our human world the absurdity of our most fundamental needs. At the age of 20, Camus, suddenly afflicted with a malady that upset his whole life, discovered the Absurd – the senseless negation of man. He became accustomed to it, he *thought out his* unbearable condition, he came through.'[22] Indeed.

Camus' experiences are as relevant as ever in the modern day. During the height of the COVID-19 pandemic, sales of *The Plague* went through the roof as people grappled with a physical and metaphysical pestilence that kept them locked inside their homes, forcing them to confront the isolation that Camus had felt when he was writing in his dingy hotel room in Paris. His thoughts of the absurd permeate pop culture franchises like the *Assassin's Creed* gaming series. There's a line in the *Myth of Sisyphus* where Camus writes, 'the absurd does not liberate; it binds. It does not authorise all actions. "Everything is permitted" does not mean that nothing is forbidden.'[23]

Nothing is true. Everything is permitted. That line is the credo of the Assassin Order, a motto that the protagonists of the long-running series must come to terms with as they run through historical periods, fighting an eternal war of ideals against the Templar Order. Chaos and order. Light and dark. Two sides of the same absurd coin. Camus' ideas endure because at his core he identified more as a writer than as a philosopher. He resisted being called a philosopher because he didn't paint his world with arguments. He painted his world with images. All images and ideas, at some point in their shaping, are absurd. Camus knew this instinctively and it's why he remains one of the greatest philosophical writers of all time.

Chapter 11

The Outsider and the Philosophy of Otherness

1925. Jackson, Mississippi. Smith Robertson Junior High. A young, black man has been chosen as the valedictorian for his school. He's written a speech to deliver for graduation and he's been called into the headteacher's office.

'Well, Richard Wright. Here's your speech.' The headteacher slides papers across the desk to him expectantly.

'What speech?' Richard asks.

'The speech you're going to deliver on the night of graduation.'

'But professor, I've already written a speech.'

The headteacher finds this funny. He informs Richard that there are going to be white and black people attending the graduation and it's better that he reads what's been given to him.

Richard protests. He insists that he'll read the speech *he's* written. The headteacher gets angry. He threatens Richard with the prospect of never graduating, even though he's passed all his exams. 'I'm the one who decides who passes around here,' the headteacher huffs.

'Then I don't graduate.' Richard starts to walk away.

The headteacher takes another tack. He baits Richard with the idea that he could help him get a teaching job. He tries throwing his weight around, cajoling and browbeating the 17-year-old who's refusing to do as he's told. He should know his place in the world. That he should accept what he's been given.

Richard answers, 'I want to learn, professor. But there are some things I don't want to know.'

That night, a boy named Griggs, a classmate, calls on Richard at his home. He can't understand why Richard is throwing away his future by not giving the speech he's been assigned. He's not the only one who can't understand.

Two days later, Richard's Uncle Tom pays him a visit. He wants to know why his nephew rejected the headteacher's speech. After reading both speeches, Uncle Tom says the headteacher's speech is better.

'I don't doubt it,' Richard agrees. 'But why did they ask me to write a speech if I can't deliver it?'

Standing his ground, Richard resolves to stick to his own speech. He and Griggs, who's accepted a speech from the headteacher, practice every day, orating to the trees, the sky and the clouds of the American South, until Richard knows his words so well that he could've recited the speech in his sleep. All the while, he wades through the stream of hostility and incredulity from his classmates and family.

Richard makes himself one last promise before the speech. That he's going to graduate wearing long pants instead of being the only boy in his class to wear short pants. So, borrowing money from his employer, he buys a pearl-grey suit.

On the night of graduation, nerves wrack Richard. But he speaks his own words, not caring whether the audience or the school likes them or not. When it's done, he vaguely remembers some applause and handshakes. Had someone invited him to a party too? He can't remember. He doesn't *want* to remember. Richard dislocates himself so thoroughly from the situation that when he tries recalling all the details later in life, he feels they belong to someone in another time and place. What he does remember was the final straw of his living in the South. The North, with all its hazy potential of a black man being able to live with dignity, called to him. And he did everything in his power to get there.[1]

This harrowing situation, described by the writer Richard Wright in his autobiography *Black Boy*, wasn't the first time he'd be forced into making a decision that tested his principles. It wasn't the first time he'd suffered racist abuse. It wasn't the first time he'd questioned what it felt to be treated as a human being. His life would be filled with the same feelings of oppression and search for meaning that compelled him to leave the South and fulfil his calling to become a novelist.

In time, he would become one of the earliest best-selling black authors in American history with his unapologetic critiques of the African American experience in works like *Native Son*, *The Man Who Lived Underground* and many other books that capture alienation, struggle and the most fundamental rights of a people to live free.

Born hungry

Born in 1908 in the town of Roxie, Mississippi, Wright came into the world hungry. Hungry for food. Hungry for understanding. Hungry for meaning. Hungry for a way to live in an environment that felt unliveable from his earliest days. His father Nathan was a sharecropper, while his mother Ella was a schoolteacher. They came out of a post-Civil War world where their parents had been freed from slavery. Wright's paternal grandad had served in the Southern 28th United States Coloured Troops. His maternal grandad had escaped slavery and served in the US Navy.

An early memory of Wright's came from when he was 4, living in a cramped apartment with his mother, father, brother and grandma. In the winter, Wright felt bored, neglected and curious in front of a fire. So, he plucked a few straws from a broom and tossed them in to see what would happen.

> My idea was growing, blooming. Now I was wondering just how the long fluffy white curtains would look if I lit a bunch of straws and held it under them ... I pulled several straws from the broom and held them to the fire until they blazed; I rushed to the window and brought the flame in touch with the hems of the curtains.[2]

Accidently setting the house on fire, Wright ran outside and hid inside a brick chimney, terrified of what might happen to his family. Luckily, no one was hurt. But as punishment, Wright was lashed by his mother, an experience that stuck with him for years as he grew up in a space of seeking wonder among the violence and hard living that he and his family were trapped in. Wright found wonder in the desire to imitate sparrows on dusty country roads, the languor of leaves rustling like rain, the thirst of watching sugarcane get chopped, the dreamy flow of the Mississippi River, the endless feeling of hunger when he breathed in the smell of new-cut grass.

Wright's father left the family when he was 6 – an event the boy found difficult to comprehend. On one hand, Wright associated his father with the person who would provide food for him. On the other, he associated him with deep bitterness and fear that seemed unfathomable as a boy. Twenty-five years later, Wright and his father reunited and he forgave the man who'd walked out on him and his mother, reflecting 'from the white landowners above him there had not been handed to him a chance to learn the meaning of loyalty, of sentiment, of tradition. Joy was unknown to him as was despair'.[3] Their experiences had long set them adrift from each other, worlds away from the home that had never really felt like home.

Without her husband in the picture, Wright's mother took a job as a cook in the homes of white people to support her children. When not accompanying his mother on her jobs, Wright roamed and wandered, gravitating towards a saloon that attracted and repelled him. Loitering outside soon turned to begging for pennies and being taught how to drink and curse by the patrons of the bar who were entertained by the wild little boy from the streets. By his own admission, 'I was a drunkard in my sixth year, before I had begun school. With a gang of children I roamed the streets … I saw more than I could understand and heard more than I could remember. The point of life became for me the times which I could beg drinks.'[4]

After intervention from his mother and neighbours, Wright stopped drinking and began his formal education, though it became increasingly difficult for his mother to cope with raising him. Wright would get used to being taken out of school several times in his childhood – one of those earliest experiences involved him being sent to an orphanage. He recalled being terrified, running away and being brought back by the police. But some relief seemed to be on the horizon – Wright's mother told him they were moving to live with his aunt in Arkansas.

Sated with words

On the way to Arkansas, Wright entered the home of his grandmother in Jackson. A big house filled with religious expectation, Wright and his brother found enjoyment outside in the green fields and conversations they had with boys and girls their own age, children who they thought were less worldly, who'd never ridden on a train, who'd never seen or felt the sleepiness of the Mississippi River, who'd never known the fear and bravery of running away from an orphanage. All these experiences paled in comparison to a conversation he had with a young schoolteacher who boarded with his grandmother. Ella was her name and Wright begged her to share what she was reading with him. Back in Roxie, Wright had jumped onto any book he could get his hands on, most of them being left behind on the street by kids in the neighbourhood.[5] He *needed* to know what the words meant and now Ella could unlock more secret knowledge with a story he'd never encountered before.

Finally agreeing to share, Ella told Wright the novel she was reading was *Bluebeard.* And as she told him the fable, Wright's world changed. He saw a world tinged with magic and his imagination blazed. Before the story could be finished, Wright's grandmother interrupted, demanding Ella stop filling the boy's head with the Devil's work. No matter how Wright protested, she slapped him. But that slap, or any future punishment, wouldn't be harsh enough to beat out the magic that Wright had experienced that day, magic that he'd bring to the world in due time.

Wright's experiences of being near his grandparents dredged up other sensations he couldn't understand. His grandmother looked lighter-skinned than others in the family and he remembered feeling 'the bitter amusement of going into town with Granny and watching the baffled stares of white folks who saw an old white woman leading two undeniably Negro boys in and out of stores on Capitol Street.'[6] He asked his mother about this and she explained exactly what their family's heritage was – that grandma had been a slave and that when Wright grew up he'd be called a coloured man. Up to this point, Wright had felt a 'vague uneasiness' about the stories he'd heard 'that coloured people were killed and beaten, but so far it had all seemed remote'.[7]

In Elaine, Arkansas, that uneasiness became a close-to-home threat, as his Uncle Hoskins was killed by white men greedy for his successful liquor business. That terrible experience drove Wright's mother to pack up again and move the family to West Helena. Racism, fear and anxiety were never far away. Wright's aunt Maggie dated and housed a fugitive for an undisclosed crime, bringing cops to the door. Stories of black men being lynched by mobs, of white women slapping black women infested Wright's thoughts and feelings as the First World War ended and sparked more racial tensions in the South.

When his mind wasn't filled with dread or the stifling religion of his family, Wright was either studying or getting into fights:

> The roundhouse was the racial boundary of the neighbourhood, and it had been tacitly agreed between the white boys and the black boys that the whites were to keep to the far side of the roundhouse and we

> blacks were to keep to our side … our battles were real and bloody; we threw rocks, cinders, coal, pieces of iron and broken bottles.[8]

Through these battles both mental and physical, Wright aged beyond his years, doing jobs around the neighbourhood to support his sick mother, constantly bouncing around new homes when the rent got too much. Eventually, Wright's mother suffered a stroke and he and his brother were raised by their grandmother, aunts and uncles.

By the time he was 12, Wright had vowed to himself that he would endure. That he would seek experiences that kept him alive, he would question and gravitate towards people whose feelings and thoughts were like his own, an attitude to reinforce his love of books, art, learning and writing. He resisted all attempts by his grandmother to join the Seventh-day Adventist Church, which brought her own life so much meaning, a religion he felt made her disregard others so callously while giving her an all-consuming love for humanity. It baffled and repelled her grandson, even as he tried so hard to understand what she *saw* in it. For Wright felt that he'd find the answers he sought *in* the world, not in the world after: 'Religion as such never deeply interested me; I have never felt deeply enough to be swayed to believe … from the earliest time I can remember, I longed for happiness here and now, in the form of feeling with the feelings of my body.'[9]

Unable to be saved in his grandma's eyes, Wright felt the freedom to live life on his own terms. Even if that freedom came with complications, such as having to navigate a new public school and new ways to find work. Wright settled on selling papers, only to realise later that he'd been selling papers that preached the hateful speech of the Ku Klux Klan. This was pointed out to him by a black man who told him to examine the racist art and Wright stopped selling the papers immediately.

Another early job that forced him to confront the realities of race relations in the South came when he worked as an insurance agent. He would accompany a former janitor called Brother Manc out to plantation shacks where he'd handle figures and write claims. In these shacks, he encountered black children who'd never read a book, while he fretted over running out of books to read. The hard travelling ground Wright down and he felt guilty watching Brother Manc bamboozle people as he delivered sales talk like he was preaching to a congregation.

Through all the menial jobs and the drudgery, Wright held onto the desire that he'd become a writer. And so when he was in year nine (eighth grade), he wrote his first fiction story called *The Voodoo of Hell's Half-Acre* about a villain who wanted to take over a widow's house. Finishing it in three days, he took the story to the local black newspaper and spoke to the editor about publishing it. Wright left, feeling like the editor wouldn't bother reading it. Still, he went back the next day and found out his story had been published. The editor encouraged Wright to keep on writing, the first person who'd ever told the budding young author that he should do such a thing.

Wright's classmates and family couldn't believe he'd written the story and that it was being published in a newspaper. Some thought he'd copied it out of a book. Others questioned why on earth he'd want to write in the first place. His family poured further damnation on him. Wright's dream of heading North and writing novels only became stronger. He took more jobs, determined to save up enough money so that he could escape the South. Porter, optician apprentice, hotel bellboy. Every occupation came with more abuse and Wright soldiered on, doing whatever he had to do to change his reality. This drive led him to delivering bootleg liquor and getting involved in a dodgy ticket-selling scheme at a movie house. Wright took no pleasure in crime – it was a means to an end. With $50 in his pocket, he gathered up his clothes and before he left, he told his mother he was running away. He promised he'd send for her when he was settled and then got on a train to Memphis. As he moved closer to his destination, the unfathomable tension that Wright had been feeling bubbled to the surface and he cried: 'I understood the pain that accompanied crime and I hoped that I would never have to feel it again. I never did feel it again, for I never stole again … Well, it's my life, I told myself. I'll see now what I can make of it.'[10]

In Memphis, he made the most of his situation. He boarded with a mother and daughter and found work as a dishwasher. Living with the family was a source of relief and awkwardness for him. On one hand, it felt like they accepted him far more readily than his kin. On the other hand, the mother pushed for Wright and her daughter to get married. Wright didn't want to be forced into anything. His focus remained fixed on two things: to keep on heading North and to bring his mother and brother with him. To do this, he put his previous experience to work and got a new job in an optician's office. Here Wright could save as he needed, while also being able to buy magazines like *Harper's Magazine* and the *The Atlantic*.

As his white co-workers tried to make fun of him and other black employees, Wright continued to turn to books for an idea of how to forge a path forward. At one point, he asked a colleague if he could forge his signature so he'd be able to take books out of the local library. Specifically, Wright wanted to read the works of the journalist H.L Mencken, which opened a new world of words and meanings that pulled him further down the writing rabbit hole. In 1926, he made good on his promise to bring his mother and brother to Memphis and they all started planning to leave for Chicago. Tentative dates were set, with the catalyst being an unannounced visit from Wright's aunt Maggie, who'd been abandoned by the criminal 'uncle' that'd brought trouble to the Wright family's door years before. Something had to give and so it was decided that Wright and his aunt would go to Chicago first.

To get a clean break from his job, Wright told his boss he had no choice but to go to Chicago so he could look after his paralysed mother. His plan worked. At last, he was leaving the 'southern darkness' that had always told him he had a 'place in life'. But he wasn't leaving the South to forget the South. He was leaving 'so that some day I might understand it, might come to know what its rigours had done to me, to its children … I headed North, full of the hazy notion that life could be lived with dignity, that the personalities of others should not be violated'.[11] If only it would be that easy.

Promised lands

Coming to Chicago in 1927, Wright soon got a job as a postal clerk. One night, while eating with co-workers and debating the state of the world, Wright found that many of them were members of the Communist Party. Not long after that, a Jewish acquaintance, Sol, mentioned to Wright that he'd had a short story published in a magazine called *Anvil.* The magazine was published through a revolutionary artist group known as the John Reed Club.

Sol convinced Wright to attend a meeting, though Wright remained sceptical about any Communist having a legitimate interest in the plight of black people. When he arrived at the John Reed Club, Wright was introduced to several artists, all of whom were courteous and respectful. Again, Wright was dubious. Were they treating him so well because of the colour of his skin? But try as he might, he couldn't find any condescension in them. He was asked to contribute to a magazine called *Left Front* and dived into some reading material from the club. What he found in the magazines was a passionate call to tell the stories of the disenfranchised and give marginalised communities a voice. So, he wrote a poem that linked black and white experiences together.

The editor of *Left Front* accepted the poem and other pieces from Wright and from that moment forward, Wright committed himself fully to the John Reed Club. He admired the mission of demanding the government create jobs for unemployed artists. This desire to support fellow writers, to have his voice heard and get other voices heard, led him to join the Communist Party.

As a member, he held onto his aim to promote other creatives and operated within a unit inside of the John Reed Club. He was tasked with reporting everything he did with the club and despite his best efforts to fit in, there were many party members who labelled him as an intellectual bourgeois. Even though Wright had been forced to cut his education short, he'd taught himself to learn through books, a fact that singled him out even to other black Communists. 'I learned, to my dismay, that the black Communists in my unit had commented upon my shined shoes, my clean shirt, and the tie I had worn. Above all, my manner of speech had seemed an alien thing to them.'[12]

Nevertheless, he persisted with his party work and became interested in writing about the experiences of his people. He met a man called Ross, who'd also come up North to escape the brutalities of the South. Wright stayed with Ross and his wife, where he interviewed the man for details of why he wanted to become a Communist. Word got around and other members began to question Wright about what he was doing, continuing to brand him as an intellectual and that they tended not to do well in the party.

'But I'm *not* an intellectual,' Wright insisted. 'I sweep the streets for a living.' By this time, he'd been let go from his postal job and put on relief. It made no difference. The mantra of 'you don't understand, comrade' became a wall that Wright could never break through no matter how much he protested and defended his position. Consequences be damned, Wright carried on his work of interviewing people and eventually used the profiles to write short stories. One of these stories, 'Big Boy Leaves Home', was published in an anthology.

While the constant suspicion from fellow Communists strained his patience and faith in politics, Wright could still make a living, being placed by the relief authorities in the South Side Boys Club. He found this work engrossing. Every day, he saw young black boys swim, draw and read, homeless, wild youths who found solace in their tough talk of women, guns, politics and crime. Wright kept detailed notes of these experiences, crafting a blueprint that would inspire perhaps his most famous work, *Native Son.*

If he could have gone on writing in peace, he'd have been happy. But party duties forced him away from his expression and he butted heads with Communist leaders. With each fresh confrontation, Wright became more disillusioned. One traumatic experience happened in 1935 when he attended a writer's conference in New York and the white Communists that had promised him a place to stay went back on the offer when they found out the colour of his skin. When Wright finally got to the conference, he was the only one to argue that John Reed Clubs across the country stay open because they helped young writers. His plea fell on deaf ears and with that knowledge, Wright knew his time with the Communist Party was at an end. Back in Chicago, Wright tried to cut ties with the party amicably. In no uncertain terms, he was told that no one resigns from the party but Wright wouldn't be intimidated. He reflected that his former comrades could never fathom the individuality that ruled him.

From that point on, he inhabited a kind of purgatory whenever he was around members of the party. They expected him to jump when they called on him and ostracised him when he was working on creative projects, like his time at the Federal Writers' Project, where he tried to earn a living by writing guidebooks. Several of his co-workers were Communists and they gave him the silent treatment. To them, he was a 'traitor of the working class'. But this wasn't the worst of it.

Once, he was threatened at knifepoint in a theatre by Communist sympathisers. Another time, he arrived for a May Day public protest. A white Communist told him to get out of the ranks, even though Wright had been invited by a (black) friend who didn't defend him and he was manhandled out of the crowd and thrown roughly onto the street. 'I had suffered a public, physical assault by two white Communists with black Communists looking on … But I did not feel belligerent. I had outgrown my childhood.'[13]

Breakthroughs

Despite all the hardship he faced on many fronts, Wright continued to write and came to national attention with his novella collection *Uncle Tom's*

Children in 1938. Readers were confronted with the haunting question of how a black person could live as a human being in America. In the same year, he established a friendship with another influential black author Ralph Ellis and Wright used the acclaim from the novellas to finance a move to New York, where he worked on *Native Son* in Harlem.

Releasing in 1940, *Native Son* put Wright on the map as a polarising figure. In one sense, his protagonist Bigger Thomas distilled all the collective trauma of a people alienated from a society that refused to accept them. A street kid, Bigger is employed by a wealthy white family but ends up killing the daughter of the family by accident. In the act of murder, Bigger feels freedom for the first time in his life. On creating Bigger, Wright wrote of the difficulty he had with how such a character would be received by white and black communities. 'I knew that I could not write of Bigger convincingly if I did not depict him as he was; that is, resentful towards whites, sullen, angry, ignorant, emotionally unstable ... which American oppression had fostered in him.'[14] He also wrote, 'I knew from long and painful experiences that the Negro middle and professional classes were the people of my own race who were more than others ashamed of Bigger and what he meant ... never did they want people, especially white people, to think that their lives were so much touched by anything so dark and brutal as Bigger.'[15] But Wright pushed all hesitation aside and created a character whose brutal actions he never glorified, but showed how a culture and a country can shape the lives of people like Bigger.

The reaction to *Native Son* was extraordinary. Wright became the first African American author to be championed by the Book of the Month Club and his novel became a bestseller. Others condemned it for the violence which seemed to confirm white people's worst fears of the black community. Yet Wright's literary star shone brightly nonetheless and publishers were eager to capitalise on the runaway success of America's leading black author. Marrying his pregnant wife Ellen and moving from Harlem to Brooklyn, Wright wrote prolifically into the early 1940s.

A standout novel from this period, *The Man Who Lived Underground*, depicted a black man wrongly accused by the police of a crime he didn't commit and fled underground. Wright's publishers had been expecting him to finish a novel called *Black Hope*, yet Wright had never felt an idea for a book come to him so clearly.

In writing *The Man Who Lived Underground*, Wright was inspired by his grandmother's religious experiences and the unfortunate realities that his community had to deal with in relation to the police. When submitted for publication, the book was rejected, perhaps because it was *too* provocative, *too* real for the sensibilities of 1940s America. So, Wright shelved the novel and it was later reworked into a short story (and finally published in full length in the 2020s). A writer's writer, the author of *Native Son* understood that not everything created would make it into the public arena. He focused on producing a play of *Native Son*, which was released on Broadway to positive reviews and later completed his autobiography *Black Boy* in 1945.

Even with Wright's successes, the spectres of racism and suspicion would never be vanquished. For one thing, his former ties to Communism would never be forgotten by people in the party and organisations trying to shut the party down. For another, he and his Polish wife constantly felt scrutinised for being a mixed couple in New York.

Wright had had enough. He wanted to go to somewhere he and his family could live without fear. In 1946, the Wrights packed up and left the US for Paris.

I choose exile

The post-Second World War world of France was a world of liberation. Citizens of Paris were hungry for new ideas, experiences and literature. The philosophy of Existentialism was all the rage and literary powerhouses Jean-Paul Sartre, Simone de Beauvoir and Albert Camus were changing the world, one argument at a time. Wright had befriended the three during their time in New York and found their European sensibilities enthralling. As Sarah Bakewell writes in her book *At the Existentialist Café*,

> one element of American life unequivocally horrified Sartre, Beauvoir and Camus: its racial inequalities, and not only in the South … many black Americans who found themselves in Paris after the war appreciated being treated with basic human respect. They were more than respected; they were often idolised, as French youngsters so loved black American music and culture.[16]

After a few months, Wright knew he'd found a place like nowhere else on earth and with difficulty, he finally managed to get a visa for his family and became a permanent expat in 1947. He fell in love with his adoptive home instantly, gushing over the fact that the French people had 'no illusions, life is accepted for what it is, the grim along with the beautiful'.[17] Here, at last, was a place where he could feel free, with Sartre, Beauvoir and Camus helping him bring his voice to a new audience. Publishers courted his attention, while Ellen became De Beauvoir's literary agent, embedding the Wrights into the high society of the Parisian literary scene.

Naturally, American publishers were curious to know the details of what a life of freedom looked like for a black man overseas. The magazine *Ebony* commissioned Wright to write about his experiences. Expecting uplifting stories in line with the content of the magazine, the director John H. Johnson was horrified when he found out Wright intended to pull no punches. In an essay called *I Choose Exile*, Wright skewered the American treatment of the black community, stating that he never intended to come back to the US. In his own words, 'there is nothing in the life of America that I miss or yearn for. Barring war or catastrophe, I intend to remain in exile. I shall, of course, keep my American citizenship … but I prefer to live out my days among a civilised people.'[18] Johnson believed the essay would ruin the magazine and rejected it.

Meanwhile, Wright embraced a form of Existentialism that he applied to the black experience in the 1953 novel *The Outsider*. The main character, Cross Damon, finds himself on the wrong side of the law and is confronted with the task of reinventing himself, doing whatever it takes to achieve his version of freedom. In the writing of the novel, perhaps Wright was trying to recreate and preserve freedom and escape the constant suspicion of the FBI, who'd been monitoring him since 1943 because of his Communist past. Because in the 1950s, his work was criticised as being out of touch with the growing call for civil rights back home. Wright lost friendships because of these arguments, the most public being his falling out with his protégé James Baldwin. The younger man had sought out Wright when he'd settled in Paris and their father–son relationship seemed to have nourished them both for a while. Yet Baldwin attacked Wright's stance and themes in works like *Native Son* in his essay *Everybody's Protest Novel*.[19] Wright and Baldwin were never able to reconcile. Another author, Chester Himes, accused him of giving information to the CIA about Communists he'd known so he could keep his French visa.[20] These attacks may have caused Wright to steer his writing in a different direction and he turned to crafting non-fiction and travel writing.

Wright's travels took him to Indonesia and the Gold Coast of Africa, where he lectured and immersed himself in the cultures, collecting these experiences in *Black Power* and *The Colour Curtain*. Other works in the latter half of the decade included *White Man, Listen!* and a return to his roots with the novel *The Long Dream*. By 1958, Wright's books had lost their appeal to mainstream audiences. Even he felt pessimistic about his work being accepted, especially his follow-up to *The Long Dream*, *Island of Hallucinations*. *The Long Dream* hadn't done well. Again, Wright had been accused of being out of touch with the times and when he submitted the first draft of *Island of Hallucinations* to his agent, the author lamented, 'I can readily think of a hundred reasons why Americans won't like this book.'[21]

Paris no longer held the same magic it once did either. Feeling that the once liberal atmosphere had become oppressive and dominated by American politics, Wright tried to move his family to London but was unsuccessful.

Contributing to the difficulty of moving was Wright's illness. He suffered a crippling attack of dysentery that he might have contracted during his travels. Could illness have been a part of his premature death? Because abruptly in 1960, at the age of 52, Wright died of a heart attack in Paris. His friends and daughters weren't convinced. They wondered if he'd been assassinated by the CIA and to this day, the mystery remains.

What *isn't* a mystery is the enduring impact Richard Wright had on American literature, philosophy and civil rights. Ferociously and proudly independent, he forged a path for himself and other black creatives to explore new opportunities and refuse to be put into boxes by culture and society. As his grandson Malcolm Wright put so eloquently, Wright

> poetically distilled the rewarding and dangerous condition of Otherness (dwelling on the periphery of society) ... *Otherness.* All members of oppressed minorities hold an innate understanding of it. The pain and violence of being othered can engender insights and freedoms of a kind not easily shared with those who have never left the bosom of comfortable belonging. Standing outside, looking in, The Other sees our relationship to the world in ways those not estranged from society simply cannot.[22]

Chapter 12

The Lady of Truth and the Fight for Freedom

There are many moments where history is made with the rallying cry of one person. A voice that cuts through the din of prejudice, violence and the darkest impulses of humanity, that makes people stand up and question themselves. The voice that rang out during 28th–29th May 1851 in Akron, Ohio, was a voice that shattered barriers at the Ohio Women's Convention. It belonged to a black woman called Sojourner Truth and in front of men and ministers staunchly opposed to women having the right to vote, she preached for black people, black *women* to be treated with the same decency as everyone else,

> That man over there says that women need to be helped into carriages and lifted over ditches, and to have the best place anywhere. Nobody ever helps me into carriages, or over mud-puddles, or gives me any best place! And ain't I a woman? Look at me! Look at my arm! I have ploughed and planted and gathered into barns and no man could head me! And ain't I a woman? I could work as much and eat as much as a man – when I could get it – and bear the lash well.[1]

A lifetime of oppression, of battling to be heard shuddered in every syllable. She was the mother of thirteen children. All who'd been sold into slavery. And who had heard her when she'd poured her grief to the world? Jesus. Sojourner turned to another man in the crowd. 'That man in black there, he says women can't have as much rights as men because Christ wasn't a woman! Where did your Christ come from? Where did your Christ come from? From God and a woman! Man had nothing to do with Him.'[2]

Several versions of this speech have been recorded, but the content and message remain the same: A black woman speaking up for the rights of her gender, identity and heritage. In the years to come, it lit a spark for more voices to shout into the darkness of inequality and illuminate a path towards deeper conversation. For Truth, it was all about faith and it propelled her through a painful life and into the role of a great activist and abolitionist.

An unjust childhood

Born Isabella Baumfree, all she knew in her childhood was the lash of slavery. She was the daughter of James and Elizabeth Baumfree, slaves of a Dutch man called Colonel Ardinburgh in Ulster County, New York. When Ardinburgh died, ownership of the Baumfrees fell to his son Charles. In her biography, Isabella recalled the terrible living conditions to which she and her family were subjected – a claustrophobic cellar beneath the hotel of her master with all the other slaves of the household.

> She carries in her mind, to this day, a vivid picture of this dismal chamber; its only lights consisting of a few panes of glass, through which she thinks the sun never shone … the space between the loose board of the floor … was often filled with mud and water, the uncomfortable splashings of which were as annoying as its noxious vapours must have been chilling and fatal to health.[3]

Down in the dark, Isabella learned that many of her brothers and sisters had been sold to other masters and she listened to her mother cry for their loss. She listened alongside her only remaining brother, Peter. She listened to beautiful, warming tales that her mother told them of God and his protection. That when they were beaten and treated cruelly, they must pray to him for help. Isabella took the teachings to heart, holding them sacred for the rest of her life. She would need her faith like a shield in the turbulence to come, as she was sold to a new master, John Nealy, for $100 and a flock of sheep. Nine years old at the time, Isabella had to face the decline of health for both parents too. Her father had become crippled, blind and sickly, while her mother died from palsy. James passed away not long after and Isabella was left alone with a cruel master and haughty mistress. Isabella could only speak Dutch and the Nealys only English. In one instance, Nealy bound her hands and whipped her so viciously that she was scarred for life, physically and mentally.[4]

Isabella prayed regularly to God to be put somewhere else, somewhere safer and kinder. One day, a fisherman named Scriver came to the Nealy's and asked to buy her. Seeing this as her prayers being answered, Isabella agreed and she was sold to him for $105. The work she did for the Scrivers was wild and outdoorsy – she carried fish, hoed corn and searched for herbs and roots beyond their farm. To her, this was an improvement, though she was sold again a year and a half later to the Dumont family in 1810.

Dumont made Isabella's life a living hell, raping her and lording his power over her in the guise of a more enlightened slaveowner as if such a thing could ever exist. Needing to survive, Isabella did everything she could to make herself compliant and attentive to the Dumonts. Looking back, she saw how injust and inhumane it all was, 'the false position they were all in, both masters and slaves … the absurdity of the claims so arrogantly set up by the masters, over beings designed by God to be as free as kings; and at the perfect stupidity of the slave, in admitting for one moment the validity of the claims.'[5]

Seeking solace in her faith again, Isabella found truth in God, meaning she developed a character of always searching for truth and honesty, that detested lies and grasped for sincerity wherever it was to be found. She also found love with a slave called Robert, a union banned by her master and his. (Robert's master didn't want his slave to have children with another slave because he wouldn't be able to own them.) Yet love could never be chained and both continued to see one another in secret, until Robert was discovered and beaten badly for his transgressions. There were no more secret meetings after that and Isabella was soon married off to Thomas, another Dumont slave.

With her husband, Isabella had several children, who became her whole world, a reason to hope for something better. She recalled how when she'd go to the field to work she used to put her children in a basket, tie a rope to each handle and hang it above a tree and then have one of their siblings rock the basket gently as a way to distract, entertain and calm them.

Hope seemed to be on the horizon for them all. Slave emancipation was to be decreed in the state of New York on the 4th of July 1827 and her master Dumont had promised Isabella that he would free her, so long as she would do well and be faithful to him for another year.

That promise was fickle. When Isabella asked Dumont to be a man of his word and free her, he refused to grant her freedom because her hand was badly diseased and he claimed it stopped her from being productive. Infuriated, Isabella decided that she'd stay with Dumont and spin 100 pounds of wool until she'd completed what she believed was her sense of obligation to him. Even so, Isabella couldn't ignore the hunger for freedom that burned inside of her and later in 1826, she decided to take matters into her own hands.

Freedom on her own terms

Isabella long pondered on how she could escape her fate. She prayed to God for clarity, telling him she was afraid to go in the night and that everybody would see her in the day. The thought came to her that she should leave at sunrise. Thanking God for the thought, she acted on it. As the sun came up, she carried her baby daughter Sophia in one arm and a cotton handkerchief filled with clothes in the other away from the Dumont house. How must it have felt to be forced to leave her other children behind? For as much as she would have wished to bring them with her, the law prevented her. Until they'd served as bound servants into their twenties, her children would remain in bondage.

She ran towards the home of a man, Levi Rowe, who she knew would shelter her. Rowe did exactly that and guided her towards the home of Mr and Mrs Van Wagener, a couple with a sympathetic ear and a willingness to help her. Of course, it wasn't long before Dumont tracked Isabella down.

'Well, Bell, you ran away from me. But you didn't get very far.' Dumont said.

'No. I didn't *run away*. I *walked away* by daylight and all because you'd promised me a year of my time.' Isabella countered.

When Dumont realised she wouldn't come back with him, he threatened to take away her daughter. Then, Mr Van Wagener stepped in and said although he'd never engaged in the buying of slaves he would buy Isabella's services, rather than see her taken away by force. Also, he would pay to house the girl as well. Dumont agreed to the sum of $25 and the deal was struck. And like that, Isabella, in her heart, finally belonged to no master, for Van Wagener insisted that he call him and his wife by their first names.[6]

In the year she stayed with the Van Wagners, Isabella engaged in her next fight for freedom – the freedom of her son Peter, who'd been sold illegally out of New York state into Alabama. As soon as she heard this news, Isabella walked alone back to the Dumonts and in the face of Mrs Dumont's racism and ranting, Isabella stood firm and said, 'I have no money, but God has enough and I'll have my child again.'

With help, Isabella found a lawyer to take on her case against Solomon Gedney, the man who'd bought her son. The lawyer arranged Gedney to bring the boy to New York on a bond of $600. The lawyer advised his client that she would have to wait for the law to take its course over the next few months. Isabella couldn't fathom such a wait. She wanted Peter back in her arms *now.* She wouldn't be convinced of anything that her counsel told her and so she went to another lawyer called Demain.

When she showed up at Demain's doorstep, the lawyer was dazzled and confused by the passion and zeal of the black mother who would do everything in her power to get her son back. Isabella told him she had no money to pay him so Demain instructed her to gather $5 from a Quaker organisation in a nearby town. They would surely donate the money to her and once she'd given him the $5, Demain would have her son in twenty-four hours. So, Isabella walked ten miles into town, gathered more than $5 and walked all the way back to give Demain the money.

Some called her a fool for giving the lawyer all the money. She ought to have at least bought some shoes for herself, given all the walking she'd done. 'I don't want money or clothes right now,' Isabella answered. 'I only want my son and if five dollars will get him, more will surely get him.'[7]

Demain repeated his promise that he'd get her son within twenty-four hours. Isabella returned several times in a day, hoping for good news. She returned in the morning while Demain was sleeping. Demain informed her that Peter would be with her before noon, as he'd sent a man he trusted most highly to bring Peter and Gedney to her, dead or alive. Making good on his promise, Demain told Isabella that her son was nearby. But she had to go and identify him, for the boy refused to say that he had a mother. Isabella went to the office where Peter was being held where he denied her and screamed that she was some terrible thing who wanted to try and take her away from the kindness of his master. Isabella persisted, fighting to break through the brainwashing and abuse Gedney had inflicted upon her child.

Finally, she and Demain were able to calm Peter and make him see that his mother had come to take him home. A court official ruled in Isabella's favour and her son was placed into her custody. She was the first black woman in history to win a case against a white man.

Mother and son relocated to New York City, where Isabella faced new trials of supporting her family and providing for her children. Her search for work led her to the homes of wealthy businessmen, doing menial jobs.

While his mother toiled and searched for meaning in God, Peter fell into the earthly vices of New York, dancing and carousing with layabouts and street toughs. Two years Isabella spent in the dark about her son's affairs and when she found out, she tried to steer him onto a more righteous path. Peter shrugged off school and education. He regularly found himself in trouble and Isabella pulled him out of it until she couldn't do it anymore. Once, during a bad run-in with the police, Isabella refused to get him out of the situation. He needed to learn from his mistakes.

Peter turned to a local barber he respected and this intervention made Peter reassess his path. He decided to go to sea and serve on a whaling ship, a decision that Isabella found hard to believe at first. On meeting the barber, Isabella saw her son's repentance was genuine and they wrote each other letters as Peter travelled. Unfortunately, they lost touch with each other. Some letters were never delivered and Isabella never knew what happened to her son out at sea.

Perhaps to cope with her son's disappearance and her own uncertain position in the world, Isabella continued to explore new ways to worship God. At one point, she joined the Methodist Church and worked to spread its message across New York by visiting some of the worst places in the city. But the religious fervour of the Methodists became too much for Isabella because in her eyes they failed to make the connections that the body was as much a part of God's home as the spirit. This became clear in a meeting where members of the church were whipped up into ecstasy and stood on her cloak. In the frenzy, she was knocked to the ground and 'thinking she had fallen in a spiritual trance, they increased their glorifications on her account ... rejoicing so much over her spirit, and so entirely overlooking her body, that she suffered much, both from fear and bruises'.[8]

Seeking answers elsewhere, Isabella then fell into the orbit of Robert Matthews aka the Prophet Matthias. Matthews was the leader of a religious cult called the Kingdom of Matthias that preached a doctrine inspired by the God-fearing dogma of Calvinism. Isabella worked as Matthews' housekeeper while he held court and pontificated in the mansion of one of the businessmen he'd conned into following him. Matthews was eventually charged, along with Isabella, with the murder of one of his followers. But her testimony was key in acquitting them both and with a lack of evidence, they avoided harsher punishment. Matthews only spent a few months in prison for the repeated beating of his daughter.[9]

Isabella managed to get away from the cult, though it left her questioning so many things. Any savings she'd built up through the years had been subsumed into the Kingdom and it'd left a bitter taste in her mouth and of the opinion that the rich robbed the poor and the poor robbed each another. She felt guilty over her own actions, for in her mind, she'd stolen work from other disadvantaged people.

But we shouldn't confuse Isabella's time with the Kingdom for blindness or complacency. Her open-mindedness made her search for her *own* answers in the expression of her faith. While she never learned to read or write, she would still look to the Bible for guidance. She preferred to have children read passages for her so she could make up her own decisions about its teachings. This was preferable to having adults read to her because they would often explain their version of the Bible. This wasn't enough for her. Most of all, Isabella looked for the *truth,* both subjective in how others experienced religion and objective in how it impacted their choices in relation to her as a black woman.

She settled on living by the simple principles of do unto others as you would have them do unto you and love thy neighbour as you love yourself. With those principles etched into her mind, it was time to leave New York. The Holy Spirit was calling her. Before she could start her journey, she had to be reborn with a new name to match her new mission. On the 1st of July 1843, she changed her name to Sojourner Truth and set out to do God's work.

Crusading for equality

Truth headed North, making her way through Connecticut, where she became a part of the Second Advent movement of the immediate return of Jesus. This community was headed by the charismatic William Miller and Truth was welcomed into the camp, drawing big crowds for her singing and preaching. But experience had taught her well and eventually she became disillusioned with Miller's promises and stepped away from the group when the second coming of Christ failed to happen as he claimed it would.

Taking to the road again, she was encouraged by friends to find the Northampton Association of Education and Industry (NAEI) in the town of Northampton. Here, there were no false promises or the power-hungry scheming of cult leaders. The NAEI had been founded by abolitionists and progressive thinkers who were against the inhumanity of slavery. They supported radical causes like women's rights and pacifism. The community lived on a farm with a working silk mill and other amenities that allowed them to work the land and support each other.[10] Truth's eyes were opened to the anti-slavery movement and she met other influential abolitionists like Fredrick Douglass. She and Douglass had many inspiring debates and conversations, with him describing her 'as a strange compound of wit and wisdom, of wild and flintlike common sense'.[11]

Truth stayed in Northampton for the next ten years, even after the NAEI disbanded in 1846. She bought a house and worked on her memoirs, dictating her early life to her friend Olive Gilbert, which became *The Narrative of Sojourner Truth*. However, her experiences had taught her that material possessions were fleeting and that there was more good to be done on the road than on staying in place. The 1850s involved Truth speaking out against inequality far and wide, selling her property and moving to Battle Creek, Michigan, to rejoin the Seventh-day Adventist Church.

When the Civil War broke out, Truth was called to arms like so many others. She was a pacifist but believed that the war was God's just punishment against slavery and she helped to recruit many black soldiers for the Union Army. She worked at the National Freedman's Relief Association in Washington while still finding the time to ride in the capital's streetcars in refusal of segregation while the war blazed around her.[12]

After the war, Truth, now in her late sixties, showed no signs of slowing down. She lobbied for a programme where former slaves could have land granted to them, a cause she fought as hard as any she'd fought for before. Unfortunately, this dream was never realised, as Congress refused to enact it. She spent her final days in Battle Creek, being cared for by her daughters. Despite being nearly blind and deaf, she was in good spirits when a reporter from the *Grand Rapids Eagle* came to the house to interview her. A few days later, one of the brightest lights of the abolishment movement was snuffed out on the 26th of November 1883. Frederick Douglass captured the essence of Truth's character in his eulogy of her: 'Venerable for age, distinguished for insight into human nature, remarkable for independence and courageous self-assertion ... she has been for the last forty years an object of respect and admiration to social reformers everywhere.'[13]

The light of Sojourner Truth wasn't extinguished. It continued to shine in all the people she inspired, in every person who took up her crusade for giving women the right to vote, in rallying against the injustices of slavery, in celebrating the agency of black women who pushed the abolitionist movement forward and who continue to break new ground in business, politics and life today.

Chapter 13

The Philosopher of Signs and the Mythology of Pop Culture

Signs are all around us. Signs carved into popular culture that we take at face value without questioning how they got to be a part of popular culture. These signs can be made of ideologies and presented as the way the world should be, which are then taken up by the people who see them without realising the original meaning. For example, let's look at the image of the revolutionary, an image associated with Che Guevara.

Guevara has become a symbol for rebellion and counterculture because of the signs that have been projected onto him by society. His 'cool rebel' mystique has nothing to do with his actual qualities because as a political revolutionary, Guevara was willing to kill people to achieve his goals. The society he 'rebelled' to create was just as oppressive as the society he brought down and his public speeches were only rhetoric.

After his death, Guevara's image became an image to be moulded by corporations. His face was printed on T-shirts to appeal to a consumer's desire to identify with the perceived qualities of the rebel – youth and anti-authoritarianism. Guevara's image has now lost all its real meaning and become appropriated as a new symbol. So, when someone wears that T-shirt with Guevara's face, they could think they are making a statement about individuality and raging against the machine. In truth, they have bought the T-shirt and bought into conformity. This is accepted in popular culture because the image of a person with dangerous ideas has been turned into a myth.[1] This was the opinion of the French philosopher Roland Barthes. To him, myths were popular ideas drained of their meaning and repackaged to mean something new. He said as much in his famous work *Mythologies*, where he examined different aspects of French life and pulled them out of context to see how signs become a part of popular culture. This habit of breaking down myths, of learning to look beyond the veneer of advertising, made Barthes one of the leading thinkers of his day. His ground-breaking ideas contrasted with his turbulent personal life and desire to hide his identity as a gay man. And it's in examining every aspect of Barthes' myth that we find useful lessons – whether that's how to interpret the messages of mass media or confronting the treatment of LGBT communities around the world.

Language trembles with desire

Coming from a middle-class background, Barthes grew up in Cherbourg, Normandy. The family fell on dire times before Barthes was a year old. His father Louis, a sub-lieutenant in the French Navy, died in the First World War. His mother, Henriette, struggled to provide for her son and so moved them to the village of Urt in south-western France. There they were supported by Henriette's in-laws and Barthes was raised by his mother, aunt and grandma.

The early years within his feminine family were fulfilling for Barthes. He learned to play the piano and consumed books and poems. When he was 11, his mother took him to Paris to be closer to her mother. Of this time, Barthes recalled,

> my childhood and adolescence were spent in poverty. There was often no food in the house. We had to go buy a bit of paté or a few potatoes at a little grocery on the rue de Seine, and this would be all we'd have to eat. Life was actually lived to the rhythm of the first of the month, when the rent was due.[2]

Barthes status as a war orphan provided access to state benefits, which helped with the complicated financial situation. Henriette slaved away at a bookbinding job to make ends meet, while having another mouth to feed with her second son Michel, who joined them in 1927. Henriette's mother refused to provide any financial support, even though she came from a not unwealthy background.

Even with these setbacks, Barthes managed to go to school in Paris and showed a good head for learning. But in 1934, a case of tuberculosis interrupted his education and he was placed in a sanatorium. While he missed out on important exams, Barthes could rely on an endorsement from the famed poet Paul Valery, a family friend, to get him a scholarship. He went to the Sorbonne University to study classical literature and got involved in theatre. Perhaps it was here that his love of language truly started to take shape and build the foundation for his semiotic theory – the process of reading signs and messages across different cultures. Because at times language for Barthes was 'legislation, speech is its code. We do not see the power which is in speech because we forget that all speech is a classification, and that all classifications are oppressive'. Other times, it was downright seductive. 'Language is a skin: I rub my language against the other. It is as if I had words instead of fingers, or fingers at the tip of my words. My language trembles with desire.'[3]

Barthes' illness continued to make life difficult and unfit for military service in the Second World War. From 1941–1944, he lived at the Saint-Hilaire-due-Touvet sanatorium in the French Alps. His stay was made harder by the depression he felt at the death of his first lover, Michel Delacroix, who died of TB.

Barthes' sexuality has a wide discourse about it, with some scholars arguing that he remained a closeted gay man all his life and never revealed his preferences publicly. Yet he would later build his lifestyle on spending nights cruising Parisian gay bars and Tunisian brothels like it was going out of style, while also declaring his love for women like the philosopher Julia Kristeva, once claiming, 'she's the only person I'm really in love with.'[4] Historian Jeanne Willette commented that Barthes 'was unfortunate enough to come of age at a time when homosexuality was not a public matter … living with his only parent, his mother, his entire life. As he got older and became less attractive to the young men he desired, he declined to impose himself upon them.'[5]

To view Barthes as being stuck in the closet is limiting, as Nicholas de Villiers deconstructs in *Opacity and the Closest*. Focusing on the idea of queer opacity, De Villiers explains that the concept is neither about the transparency of being 'out' or the concealment of being 'in'. He casts Barthes as a practitioner of queer opacity, living a life that defied the expectation that LGBT identity is something obligatory that must be shown. De Villiers praises Barthes and his friend Michel Foucault as providing new means of queer expression.[6]

Indeed, there are many sensual, secret nods that Barthes referenced in his writing. In his essay *The World of Wrestling*, Barthes wrote about the spectacle of French wrestling, capturing vivid details of 'the flaccidity of tall white bodies which collapse with one blow or crash into the ropes with arms flailing, the inertia of massive wrestlers rebounding pitiably off all the elastic surfaces of the ring, nothing can signify more clearly and more passionately the exemplary abasement of the vanquished'.[7] Barthes and Foucault would attend these matches, wrestle each other afterwards and entice other men to take part in their activities too.[8]

Returning to Barthes' student years, he was able to move past his depression and pursue his creativity at Saint-Hilaire-du-Touvet. He contributed to the student magazine *Existences* and gave presentations and lectures on music and poetry. In 1945, he was transferred to a sanatorium in Switzerland, where he would really meet the rest of the world at last through his friendship with the activist Georges Fournie. Nearly 30, Barthes had been wrapped in cottonwool all his life, first by his mother, then by the institutions and hospitals that looked after him. Fournie was a man of the world, an active member of the French Resistance and Trotskyist group. Both would spend hours talking and debating, learning from each other. Barthes discussed theatre and literature. Fournie talked about Marx and Trotsky, educating his friend in a 'happy kind' of Marxism that didn't involve dogmatic support for the Soviet Union and Stalin. In 1947, Fournie introduced Barthes to the publisher Maurice Nadeau, leading to Barthes writing for the anti-establishment paper *Combat* (which chapter 10's Albert Camus had helped to legitimise). From here, he took on a series of short-term teaching positions in France, Rome and Egypt and into the 1950s, he began to make his mark on the French literary scene.

Mythologising provocateur

1953 saw the release of Barthes' first book *Writing Degree Zero*, a book of critical essays inspired by Jean-Paul Sartre's *What is Literature?* He developed the idea that literature as a phenomenon is a modern concept, part of a bigger system of property owned by the author and publisher.[9] A transitionary book, *Writing Degree Zero* would be a good testing ground for later works like Barthes' more famous *The Death of the Author.*

The essay collection that put Barthes on the map came in 1957's *Mythologies.* Between 1954 and 1956, he wrote fifty-four essays about French popular culture and laid out his philosophy of signs, messages and myths. The subject matter is discordant, veering from steak and chips and ornamental cooking to strip teases and Citroën cars. In each essay, Barthes skilfully picks apart every motif and association that comes with the objects he writes about. *The New Citroën* is a fantastic case study, with Barthes demythologising the futuristic Citroën DS 19, comparing cars to 'great gothic cathedrals' and the mystique of the DS 19's design: 'Speed here is expressed by less aggressive, less athletic signs, as if it were evolving from a primitive to a classical form.'[10] Other essays like *Ornamental Cooking* are prophetic in their discussion of mass media presentation. In this essay, Barthes describes how ornamentation makes food look more appealing and sellable to consumers in photography:

> Ornamentation proceeds in two contradictory ways ... on the one hand, fleeing from nature thanks to a kind of frenzied baroque (sticking shrimps in a lemon, making a chicken look pink, serving grapefruit hot), and on the other, trying to reconstitute it through an incongruous artifice (strewing meringue mushrooms and holly leaves on a traditional long-shaped Christmas cake, reflecting the head of crayfish around the sophisticated bechamel which hides their bodies).[11]

This brings to mind the exaggerated gloss of food photography on social media, the filters and hyperbole of Instagram.

Mythologies turned Barthes into an intellectual rockstar and by 1960, he'd gained a permanent teaching position at the Ecole Pratique des Hautes Etudes at the Sorbonne. He was considered a leading figure of the French structuralism and semiology movements, which focused on decoding mass culture and looking beyond the surface level of objects to reveal the deceptive truths of what Barthes saw as bourgeois society. Big advertisers, like the Publicis advertising agency in Paris, took notice of his work and hired him to analyse the semiology of the Renault company.

With this new fame, Barthes travelled and lectured throughout the 1960s. And a place that had a lasting effect on him was Japan. During 1966–1967, Barthes visited the country three times. It began with an invitation from the director of the Franco-Japanese Institute in Tokyo for Barthes to lead a seminar on the structural analysis of narrative.

Japan was a place of wonder and freedom for Barthes, a place where he could be himself without fear of hiding. He flocked to Kabukicho in the Shinjuku region of Tokyo, the city's bustling gay district that he provided a map of in his Japan-centric text *Empire of Signs*. Barthes' visit to Japan came at a time when the underground *gei boy* culture was thriving. *Gei boy* was a blanket term for transvestites who worked in entertainment venues like tea houses and played the role of the female *geisha*.

In the archive dedicated to the text, there are many photos that Barthes took of his time in the city, from men enraptured by pachinko parlours to male *bunraku* (puppet play) actors dressed in feminine roles to highlight erotic subtext. Barthes also showed a fixation with the dramatic flair of *bunraku* and masks, like the kind popularised by queer Japanese novelist Yukio Mishima in his *Confessions of a Mask*. Mishima, like Barthes, was forever masquerading behind a mask of heterosexuality,[12] according to Benjamin Hiramatsu Ireland in his *Memoirs of a Gaysha: Roland Barthes' Queer Japan*.

1967 became another watershed year for Barthes when he penned his influential *The Death of the Author* essay, writing, 'a text is not a line of words releasing a single "theological" meaning (the "message" of the Author-God) but a multi-dimensional space in which a variety of writings, none of them original, blend and clash. The text is a tissue of quotations drawn is from the innumerable centres of culture.'[13]

Barthes explains that all books have been inspired by ideas that have come before. More importantly, he suggests that the author isn't a divine being who creates meaning out of nothingness but a collage-maker, piecing together ideas in new and interesting ways, that within Western societies, people who create stories are more often celebrated for their articulation of ideas instead of the meanings behind them.

Also, readers shouldn't look too deeply into the intention behind an author's work, believing 'the explanation of a work is always sought in the man or woman who produced it, as if it were always in the end, through the more or less transparent allegory of the fiction, the voice of a single person, the author "confiding" in us.'[14]

What this encouraged in Barthes' view was that a reader would then look at a text from a biographical point of view and that it was an extension of an author's flawed set of values.[15] That's not to say he thought it was a bad thing to look for the personal meaning an author put into their work, but you can never arrive at a definitive conclusion. It's always a two-way street because the reader creates their own meaning in a book.

After this, Barthes continued to experiment with literary deconstruction into the 1970s. He wrote *S/z*, pulling apart the narrative codes he saw in Balzac's novella *Sarrasine*. He wrote several essays for the French Communist magazine *Tel Quel* and even visited China with other editorial members after the magazine had dissociated from the party and declared support for Maoism. However, Barthes was disappointed with the country's lack of foreignness. He'd hoped for a different kind of Communism than in the West and he and his colleagues were left disillusioned. Foreignness, otherness – these concepts meant a great deal to Barthes, always seeking to escape his cultural lens and how he saw himself. He seemed to find what he was looking for in photography, developing a distinction between what he called the studium and the punctum. The studium is the cultural habit of studying a photo, while the punctum is the subjective experience a person feels when they look at a photo.[16]

By the mid-1970s, Barthes appeared to have more reason than ever to want to study himself. He wrote his autobiography, writing in the third person and examined family photos. This self-reflection was likely made more severe by the death of his beloved mother, whom he'd lived with for sixty years. She passed away at age 85.

It led Barthes to create *Camera Lucida*, an essay on the nature of photography and a meditation of a son losing his mother. But before it was published, Barthes was run over by a laundry truck in Paris on his way home. He died of his injuries in March 1980 and was buried beside his mother in the village of Urt, where his love of creativity and words had first blossomed. In his lifetime, Barthes challenged the traditional structure and meanings of language and writing. He brought new insights to the worlds of academics, advertising and philosophy. He simultaneously created his own myth and demythologised himself with every new literary project. He left behind an inspiring and troubling legacy for the LGBT community and didn't create any specific school of thought for people to subscribe to. But his influence is felt in individualistic thinking, of going against the grain with cultural norms. Barthes pulled ideas from everywhere and that is the basis for all philosophies. Testing and trying perspectives, opening new conversations and searching for wisdom in places both familiar and unfamiliar.

Interviews

Stoic Parenting, Transcendence and Being a Citizen of the World With Brittany Polat

Stoicism has played a big role in your life, which you've shared in works such as Tranquility Parenting: A Guide to Staying, Calm, Mindful and Engaged and it'd be interesting to know how you think Stoicism can help in the context of parenting.

Every parent knows how difficult it is to raise another human being, especially in the context of a global pandemic. I actually came to Stoicism as a result of having three children and realising that I needed some kind of operating system to do a good job as a parent. If you read parenting books, you see that some of them recommend developing a 'parenting philosophy' for how you want to raise your kids.

But what Stoicism offers is a whole life philosophy, which sets your goals as a person, your goals as a family, and your specific ways of interacting with your kids. I think it's important to define the big picture of your character and your life first, and then your goals as a parent will flow naturally from that. Stoicism helps us to be consistent across all our roles: as a parent, as a professional, as a community member, and of course as a good person. This way we can model to our kids how to stay calm amidst frustration, how to interact effectively with other people and how to deal with adversity.

What techniques do you think can be used to promote Stoicism to children and encourage them to think in a philosophical way?

Although young children are not ready to do philosophy in the same way adults do philosophy, we can start introducing many Stoic concepts from a young age. Teaching children how to regulate their desires and aversions, deal with emotions, share and cooperate with others – these are all things parents do already.

We can give them a Stoic twist as we help our kids develop these lifelong skills, so our kids will grow up with a Stoic outlook on life. As your kids get older, you can then introduce more technical concepts (like *eudaimonia* and *prohairesis*). But I think it's important not to lecture your kids about Stoicism. There's no faster way to make an older child or teenager stop listening than to start lecturing. Instead, we want to focus on being a good role model and building a good relationship with our kids. When you do this, you will find plenty of teachable moments as you live and learn alongside your child – little opportunities to explain how a Stoic would do things. But the most effective teaching tool is always to lead by example.

Your work has a strong focus on the concept of transcendence. What does transcendence mean through a Stoic lens?
I use the word in its psychological sense of self-transcendence, which is actually a term coined by Viktor Frankl. Frankl (an Austrian psychiatrist who survived multiple concentration camps during the Holocaust) thought that we find meaning in life by connecting with something outside ourselves: doing meaningful work, loving someone, suffering for a noble cause.

If we get too stuck on ourselves and our own small concerns, our sense of proportion gets all out of balance, and we become petty and miserable. But when we expand our boundaries and connect with the wider universe and other people, we feel that we are part of something grand and meaningful.

Stoics expounded very similar ideas two thousand years before Frankl. When you read Seneca, Epictetus and especially Marcus Aurelius, you see them constantly reminding us to get over ourselves. The famous 'view from above' exercise is really about self-transcendence, connecting with the totality of the cosmos and giving our little egos a rest. We need this sense of perspective to be psychologically healthy, and Stoicism offers a rational and practical way of seeing the big picture.

There's a misinterpretation of Stoics being indifferent to others and not caring and it struck me in a past interview you did with Modern Stoicism when you mentioned Stoics are meant to care wisely. What does it mean to care wisely?
I think this stereotype of unemotional and indifferent Stoics developed over the centuries because so many of the original Stoic teachings were lost. Later readers just didn't have enough context to interpret the school's doctrines appropriately. Thanks to a lot of scholarly work in recent decades, we are

in a much better position now to understand what the ancient Stoics were trying to tell us.

The ancient Stoics want us to care about other people – because it's natural for humans to care about other humans – but they want us to do so without making our happiness depend on other people. There are many ways our happiness could be shattered by another person: people annoy us, insult us, reject us, leave us.

Stoicism says that we find our happiness by living in agreement with nature and developing an excellent character for ourselves. We don't become happy by getting everything we want in life, and that includes other people. If we want to find a rich and lasting happiness (*eudaimonia*), we need to focus on our inner resources, not on what other people are doing. We will never be happy if we make our happiness dependent on being loved by a certain person or on gaining social approval.

So, Stoicism is not about *not caring*. It's about learning to care wisely, in the right way and about the right things.

In your writing, you've mentioned the 4 Cs of flourishing and I think it's a great way to explain the outcomes of applying Stoicism to any situation. For those who are unfamiliar with the 4 Cs, what are they and why are they important to flourishing?

I developed the 4 Cs as a mnemonic device to help us stay Stoic in any situation: Character + Cosmos + Control = Choice. When facing a challenge, the first thing to think about is maintaining your *good character*. If you start screaming at someone or otherwise react negatively, you are harming yourself by damaging your own character. You want to always remember your goal of being an excellent person.

Next, think about your connection to the cosmos. This will help you zoom out from the immediate situation and put things in perspective. Whatever is happening to you is a normal part of life; many other people are probably experiencing the same thing.

The famous dichotomy of control is also essential, as you remember what is within your power and what isn't. If the stressor you're dealing with is outside of your control, you can shift your mindset from frustration or hostility to acceptance. If the stressor is under your control – or even if you can partially influence it – then focus on taking action, not on being upset.

All these factors combine to help you make your choice about what to do. If you have thought about your character, the cosmos, and what is within your control, you will be able to make a good decision. Of course, it takes a lot of practice to be able to do this on a regular basis. Preparation is your best ally: during your morning meditation, try to spend time reflecting on how you will handle upcoming challenges. That way you will be ready to respond with the 4 Cs whenever a difficult situation arises.

In addition to your written work, you've also launched Stoicare with fellow Stoic Eve Riches. What are you hoping to achieve with Stoicare in the coming years?
Yes, we're excited about Stoicare and how it highlights the caring/community side of Stoicism. We hope to draw more attention to all the ways Stoics can care about other people and the planet.

Breaking down the technical terms of Stoicism is something I find fascinating and two ideas that stand out are prohairesis and eudaimonia. What do those terms mean to you?
Let's tackle *eudaimonia* first. This was the ancient Greek term for deep, rich flourishing – living your best life, we might say today. It definitely does not correspond to the twenty-first-century understanding of happiness, which usually means a fleeting emotion based on receiving external goods.

Eudaimonia is a stable condition that results from the development of wisdom. I love A.A. Long's definition (from *Epictetus: A Stoic and Socratic Guide to Life*): 'Philosophical *eudaimonia* is a condition in which a person of excellent character is living optimally well, flourishing, doing admirably, and steadily enjoying the best mindset that is available to human beings.' It's a condition that's worth working your whole life to achieve.

Epictetus's favourite term, *prohairesis,* is much harder to pin down. Although it means 'choice' in a basic sense, it means so much more in a philosophical sense. In my interpretation, *prohairesis* is more like your moral self: it's the character you've built for yourself over time, the accumulation of your past choices. Each choice we make in the present paves the way for all our future choices.

Each choice shapes who we are, how we see ourselves, and how likely we are to take certain actions in the future. So, when Epictetus says, 'You are your *prohairesis*,' this is true on many levels. You create your self – your character – through your past and present choices. Thinking about our *prohairesis* can inspire us to make good choices today to create the future self we want to be.

Ethical Leadership and Philosophical Training at Work With Ben Wilber-Force Ritchie

Great to chat, Ben, and to see all the work you're doing with philosophy. What were your earliest experiences with philosophy and has your perspective changed over time?

It's changed a lot throughout my life. I studied philosophy at school, starting back when it was called theology and philosophy for GCSE, and then at A level and what captured me was the philosophical aspect.

So, we ran through things such as Plato, Socrates, Aristotle, Epicurus. The big hitters of the time. It was very much Western philosophy and that interest then flowed naturally into my university degree.

The real reason why I ended up doing it at university was because, at that time, I didn't know what to study. My background was military, so my intention was to join the Royal Marines. But I wanted to get a degree and enjoy university at the same time.

My perspective was that philosophy, because there are no right or wrong answers, would be perfect. I thought: 'I basically can't get it wrong! I just have to argue really well.' That was my illogical teenage reasoning for choosing philosophy. Thankfully, I got really into it as I realised how well it teaches you to think.

When you're sitting in a room discussing something as abstract as why a chair is a chair, and someone is keeping the pressure on your brain with complex thought exercises such as: 'Okay, define it with four legs – but a table has four legs. Define it as something you sit on – but you also sit on a horse, which also has four legs – so now we need to differentiate further.'

When I engaged in exercises like that it opened a new world for me where our initial perceptions don't need to be right or wrong. It's about the quality of the discussion. How has my perception of philosophy changed over time? I'm even more interested in the topic now because I've had more life experience and am subsequently sharper in my approach to discussing and applying it.

I agree with you there about having life experience and philosophy. I never studied it academically myself and am interested in applying practical philosophy. So, which schools of thought and philosophers have inspired you day to day?
I'm not one for just quoting philosophers as if that's the only thing that matters. It's the reasoning they have behind a great quote that means something to me. But there are a few Western philosophers that have impacted my life. Plato is a natural choice because his approach to redefining the political and social state of his time is crucial to how I approach my work and my life. I think we teach a lot of people about repetition. We give them something to learn and then teach them how to turn the handle over again and again. In my mind, philosophy isn't that. It's not about creating repetition; it's about creating novel concepts. And that's what Plato was saying.

His one key aspect that I resonate with, especially in business, is the idea that leaders should be the people that don't want leadership or power. His idea of a philosopher king being in control because they have a passion for learning, a real interest in something other than power, cuts to the heart of who would make a great leader.

It might seem counterintuitive when we think about all the people that do want to be leaders. Surely we should put them in those positions? But Plato's concept is that we need passion and interest more than we need power and the intent to wield it. In business today I think we can do better on that.

I try to live my life in a way that says follow your passion and if you happen to be put in a position of leadership, then do it. But I'm not living my life wanting a position of leadership or wanting power and practising philosophy to get there.

That's a powerful way of looking at leadership. It reminds me of the idea that power doesn't corrupt, it only reveals the person who you always were inside. You wear a couple of business hats and I'm interested to hear more about what you do as an ethics manager and through your platform Phicilitate.
Both roles are complementary. My ethics manager role is that I work for a large aerospace and defence firm. Within that firm I help individuals to think better by being the ethical voice in a room.

So, in a meeting room, it's discussing how we recruit, how we treat our staff, what sort of training programmes we need, how we deal with things going wrong etc. All of those are ethical discussions and it's thinking about an ethical box within which to operate.

We could take a utilitarian stance i.e. look at the outcome having the greatest good for the greatest number of people. That is a decision to be made by a business, but that's an ethical method to make a decision. Or you could take a Kantian approach by using rules and asking questions such as: 'Could we turn this into a universal law? If we ensure that we train one person on this, could we train all our people on this?' And if the answer is no, maybe that's unfair. Again, it's a business decision, but from an ethical standpoint.

I like to try to use those two methods to balance out Aristotle's virtue ethics along with feminist care ethics. The idea that being a caring businessperson in the past was seen as the female role as opposed to the male role. (If we're going to use gender binaries.) But what if being caring isn't a gendered characteristic? What if in business we say: 'Let's think about the greatest care for our employees? How will that help us make a decision?'

The ethics manager role complements the work I do through my own company Phicilitate because it allows me to understand the real world of business and what the current workplace challenges and opportunities are. I have practical experience using philosophy in organisations, which helps me train and advise other businesses in how to do the same thing.

You also partner with Philosophy At Work. How did that partnership happen and how does that complement what you do?

It came about through contributing to an article in a talent magazine. My goal for that was based on my love of philosophy and its practical applications, as I was interested in talking about the idea of companies appointing a Chief Philosophy Officer. This role can be used to direct the character of a business towards being more ethical.

The founder of Philosophy At Work, Dr Brennan Jacoby, also contributed to this article and reached out to me. We had a discussion about philosophy in business and then I brought him into my company to deliver a week-long selection of workshops and we partnered from there.

We have similar mantras. Brennan wants to help businesses think better and is great at taking a philosophical concept, putting it into a business format and then training people on how to do that.

My approach with philosophy is to be a thinking partner. So, the difference there is that you'd invite me in and you'd have your meeting as normal. But I'd be a part of that and I'd help you to think using the techniques that I've developed given my practical experience in business. So, if you pair Brennan's brilliant application of philosophy in a practical way and my knowledge of how to be in a room and apply the techniques in a collaborative way, that's a brilliant partnership.

You've already mentioned philosophy can help from a leadership perspective. Are there any other ways the subject can make a positive change in business?
Leadership is definitely a key aspect with Plato's reluctant leader idea. Then you have the Stoic leadership approach of someone like Marcus Aurelius of not getting worried by things that happen to you and dealing with it as best you can in the present moment. There's also the concept of role modelling that can be taken from Plutarch's work. He compared characters throughout history e.g. Julius Caesar and Alexander the Great and looked at what made them successful and what made them fail.

Alexander the Great is a brilliant example because he's one of the most successful, undefeated leaders the world has ever seen. But he also killed one of his best friends when he was drunk. And Plutarch asks how was able to master his enemies so well but not his own emotions.

Going back to Plutarch's idea of role modelling, it's a strong basis for coaching and mentorship. But it's not about venerating people or putting them on a pedestal. It's about finding characteristics you admire in your colleagues, manager or business partners and being honest about the things you don't like. You learn to lean towards the qualities that resonate with you and have a positive impact and away from those that don't.

Focusing on mental health, what practical philosophy techniques can people use as part of their routine?
One exercise comes from Epicurus, as his approach to mental health was to reach a state of *ataxaria,* or contentedness. That doesn't mean to focus on happiness or increasing the things that you think will make you happy.

In his example, happiness is like wine. If you get a taste for the most expensive stuff, your average day-to-day wine will no longer satisfy you. So, you should limit your intake of expensive wine and re-baseline yourself on the everyday varieties. His focus was to remove unnecessary anxiety, the sort of anxiety that results from no longer being satisfied with little daily pleasures. So, he would advise removing any worries in your life and troubles that are on your mind. Focus on reaching a zero state of contentedness and then, when you have a normal glass of wine, this will give you far more satisfaction than usual.

Put another way, this could take the simple form of building a list of things you need to do today and ticking them off one by one. Consider which tasks will remove the most anxiety and prioritise those first. This can get us into a much better head space.

You've also mentioned you're interested in exploring more Eastern philosophy. What fascinates you about schools of thought from that part of the world?
I'm interested in the idea of harmony and balance, represented well by the concept of yin and yang as the sunny side and shady side of a hill. So, the side you call yin and the side you call yang will change throughout the day as the sun moves across the sky and that is how I picture Eastern philosophy.

It's aligned far more to Eastern cultures, societies and their way of life. Philosophy is part of it, not apart from it. Whereas in the West, we look at philosophy in a more structured and rule-based way. While I appreciate that view, I prefer philosophy for the sake of philosophy. Not to see it as a tool for winning an argument.

I've been reading Confucius lately and find a lot of humaneness in his perspective. When he uses the term gentleman, I see it as a well-meaning individual who understands the duties they have in society. It's the responsibilities we have for ourselves and others.

To bring it back to mental health, with Western philosophy we'd provide a rulebook to find a good mental health routine. With the East, it's giving you a feeling and if you reach that feeling then you'll be able to find greater balance.

If you could go back in time to talk to any philosopher, who would it be and why?
A philosopher that interests me and who I think would be a great dinner guest is Albert Camus. The reason for this is that although he grew up in Algeria, he spent his early life in France during the Nazi occupation. His focus at the time was on using philosophy to make a change. To him, it wasn't about talking behind closed doors and not going out into the real world to use philosophy. His books *The Myth of Sisyphus* and *The Plague* are great commentaries on the current state of society.

Camus didn't write philosophy books. He wrote books which had loads of philosophy in them, and that's where I'm trying to get to in my approach to business, and through my historical fiction novels such as *Furze: Sweethearts* and *Swan Songs.* I don't just want to be seen as a businessperson who uses philosophy; I want to be able to show that philosophy has always had, and continues to have, an essential practical use personally and professionally.

To have Camus at a dinner table would be a catastrophe of ideas. He'd challenge me in a way that I've never been challenged before and while many philosophers would do that theoretically, he lived what he preached at a dangerous time when his country was overrun by what he viewed as a plague. That is something I can't help but admire.

Montaignian Perspectives and the Philosophy of Survey Research With Sam McNerny

What's your background and how did you get to where you are now?
I do polling and customer surveys for small- and medium-sized e-commerce brands. Typically, they're trying to solve the problem of driving organic growth and spending less on performance marketing and budgeting efficiently. As for how I got here, it's hard to delineate a clear starting point. I've always been interested in the behaviour of people and that manifested itself in doing a philosophy major in college. This led me to learn more about behavioural science and popular psychology.

From there, my first real job was at a big ad agency in New York, and I was there for five years doing strategy and insight work. While I was there, I learned how to do online surveying and run polling experiments. Around the pandemic, I went solo and started working with e-commerce brands that have a variety of customer questions that need to be answered by surveys and polls. That's how my career manifested into market research.

You mentioned you did a philosophy major and when we first met, we had a great conversation about the practical benefits of philosophy. How has the subject impacted your life?
I've thought about this a lot. I could tell you a romantic story about how I fell in love with the topic and use it to inform my decisions every day. But really, it's just about me appreciating underdogs. And I think that's what a lot of memorable philosophers were – underdogs who ended up changing culture in a meaningful way. Socrates is a good example of this. So is Bob Dylan.

So, my understanding of philosophy came from it being taught to me chronologically from the ancients up to the modern philosophers. It was seeing it as a story of people one-upping each other.

A philosopher that stands out to me is Michel de Montaigne because he did something that no one had done before. Back in the sixteenth century, he examined himself by starting the genre of the essay and there were a couple of things that were innovative about his approach. One is he commented on everyday living. There are essays where he talked about taboo subjects like farting and burping, which went unaddressed by other philosophers up to that point. When I read an essay, I feel like Montaigne is right there with me.

The second thing he does is have a very interesting relationship with the truth. Montaigne never bullshits in the Harry Frankfurt sense of the word, who made a great distinction between bullshitters and liars. This line of thought is that liars respect the truth. They have to because they're shielding the truth, whereas bullshitters are indifferent towards the truth. They're engaging in a different enterprise. Montaigne valued the truth, but he was content to make an observation and explore a few different perspectives. Then let it go without having to prove the truth in the Socratic tradition.

In his writing, there's also a sense of Montaigne being along for the ride as much as the reader with philosophy. That's how I feel when I'm learning philosophy and that's down to Montaigne's meandering and easy-to-follow tone.

My intuition from Montaigne's work is that you can draw a line from him to standup comedians. I don't think you could necessarily make that comparison with any other philosopher in terms of observing daily life. Now, Montaigne wasn't trying to make you laugh. But he was trying to make you think.

I do agree with you about Montaigne's ability to make it feel as if he's talking directly to the reader. Moving into your role as a market researcher I imagine there must be lots of details you have to sift through day to day. So, I'd love to hear more about your research philosophy and how it impacts your approach to surveys.
When people think of surveys, prosaic or ham-handed questions might come to mind, e.g. would you recommend this product to a friend? But I'd like to offer a defence and context for survey. The concept of the survey emerged in the late nineteenth century with the British social reformer Charles Booth. Between 1890 and 1900 he and a team of researchers walked the streets

of London collecting personal income data, which you can imagine to be gruelling in that time. After ten years of asking people how much money they made, Booth collated the data and published it in some beautiful maps. We could compare these maps to modern data visualisations. Booth's survey led to the Old Age Pensions Act passing, which was the first welfare law ever passed in the West. So, this case study is a great lesson in how progress can only really come from measuring the thing that you're trying to change.

Another personal survey hero of mine is George Gallup. In the 1930s, he upended the go-to-approach for polling voters. This was magazines with large readerships polling their readers. Gallup scaled the stats of representative sampling. He'd go out and make sure his sample reflected the census on the grounds of age, gender, ethnicity, income and geography. His big moment came in the 1936 election where he correctly forecasted Roosevelt winning when popular newspapers were saying Roosevelt wouldn't win. Fast forward and the survey today is maligned as a market research relic. But you really can't write the history of the twentieth and twenty-first centuries without a survey.

I find when I'm using surveys, clients have questions about their total addressable market. So, that would be things like age, gender and income distribution. There's a lot of science behind making this data work for you in understanding a market. I see surveys as an interface. Think of a theatre stage or a TV screen. What's on that stage or screen is deliberately trying to influence an audience. Surveys can be used in the same way with the right sequence of questions to draw out certain opinions and preferences from an audience. Specifically, I'm talking about asking people if they find a brand relevant or not to them and if they intend to purchase from the company or not. Then using their responses to challenge them.

There are always people who'll say, 'This brand is relevant to me but I wouldn't consider making a purchase.' And I love asking those people why not and using their previous answers to set it up.

Their next response could be, 'I don't intend to buy right now.' And my survey answer might be, 'Well, what's stopping you? You just said this product is relevant to your needs.' It's getting the customer to explain themselves and create some tension. There's an argument to be made that I'm leading the witness or customer in that context. But in that situation, I'm not using a survey like a scientific tool. I'm using a survey as a creative tool to get people to react in a certain way.

That's some fascinating history around surveys. Digging deeper, what kind of tactics would you recommend to make a survey engaging to people?
When I think engaging, I don't mean in the way that platforms like Reddit engage readers. I mean making it as easy as possible for the customer to answer. That will make the results more insightful.

I was recently reviewing a client survey where they asked the question, 'When choosing products within our categories, which of these benefits is most important to you?' If you think about it, that's a leading question because it assumes that assessing the category and finding a product with the right benefits is something you actually do.

When reading the question, I struggled to imagine a situation where people would choose a product within this particular category. The question only provided a vague mental state. You don't want to put a customer in a vague mental state with any question you ask. My suggested change was, 'Since consuming this product, which of these benefits has been most important to you?' That's a lot easier to answer.

Another thing that makes surveys engaging in this sense is good writing. It's about using simple words over complex language. And when the writing is done, it's important not to get too close to the words. It's always worth having a second set of eyes and asking for the questions to be read aloud. If any questions sound weird or are hard to answer, then you'll want to edit them. I do think in my research philosophy there's some Montaigne lurking in the background. He's easy to read so it's about making everything I write easy to read too.

Lots of great practices for survey creation. I'm also curious to know what your process is like for survey research.
It starts with understanding the client's problems and their objectives, e.g. driving organic growth or building certain segments. I might begin by chatting with the founder or VP of marketing and then learning as much as I can about the product. This will take different forms.

It may be speaking with current users, asking more in-depth questions with the marketing team, looking at online reviews etc. The closer you can get to the customer, the better because you come to appreciate what they like and what they don't like.

When designing a survey, I normally field it with a group of ten to fifteen respondents which takes an hour or less. I get the results, see what works and adjust as necessary. I typically do that between ten and twenty times before pressing go on the main data collection. I do this to mimic the fail fast, fail early approach to products that come out of Silicon Valley.

This approach differs from big research agencies that will labour over a questionnaire for weeks or months. This also requires a lot of stakeholders and debating, whereas my strength as a solo consultant is to iterate rapidly.

What's your opinion on AI regarding market research or surveys?
I'm really excited about it and I've embraced it and have ChatGPT open most days. That said, there's a lot of talk about this kind of technology being overrated in the short term and underrated in the long term. I'll give you a few short-term things that have helped me personally.

First, ChatGPT is good for analysing text data. I've included more open-text responses in my surveys than I normally would because I can throw the results into it. I've done this with old surveys that I've analysed and it's better. There's a decent-sized market for text analytics that I think AI really disrupts, if not renders completely useless. I've also found it useful when it comes to pointing me in the right direction for sampling resources. So, if I have questions about census data or if I can use zip codes to infer income, I find ChatGPT better than Google. This is because you're having a dialogue with the tool and asking it to try different things.

In the long term, I think people are underestimating how dramatically ChatGPT will change things. For me, surveys are the most enduring kind of market research tool simply on the grounds that they've been around for the longest. Other than conducting interviews, which has to be the original form of market research.

So, a lot of contemporary tools that seem sophisticated like social listening or analysing transactional data via credit cards will likely die a lot faster than surveys. But it wouldn't surprise me in ten years if technologies like ChatGPT have transformed how people are doing surveys.

Making Philosophy Great Again With Classical Wisdom's Anya Leonard

Great to chat, Anya. What were your first experiences with philosophy and has your perception of it changed over the years?
Thank you for having me and taking the time to speak to me too. Great question. I think people often mistake philosophy to be an academic subject

but it's about a lifestyle and a way of thinking. For me, it started in what might sound like a bizarre place. As a kid, I used to spend my summers in Kazakhstan and my father had studied astronomy originally in college. So, we would go up to this observatory in the Tian Shen mountains and spend the night literally sleeping on concrete slabs.

I would go with my brother and as a teenager I wasn't concerned with deep subjects. But I remember my brother being like 'you've got to think about why we're here, what's the purpose, where we're going' etc. It was these experiences that opened me to the bigger picture of how to contemplate the world. Later, I went to St John's College in Annapolis, Maryland, and studied philosophy properly.

Following on from that perspective, what are your thoughts on philosophy being a way of life rather than just something to study?
I think you can be a philosopher and never have studied a single philosopher in your life. I think that's always valuable because people from different backgrounds and walks of life will have had different levels of exposure to thinkers that have existed or not had that much exposure. That doesn't mean that we can't have a love of wisdom or can't think about what it means to live a good life. The very act of thinking about that makes you a philosopher. Thinking about those things leads to a more contemplative life for the individual and provides the tools for making good decisions.

How did Classical Wisdom get started and how has the organisation evolved over time?
Classical Wisdom was originally co-founded between me and a man named Bill Bonner in 2010. Bill is the owner of a large, multibillion-dollar financial publication company called Agora and they have branches throughout the world. One of his subsidiaries is a French publishing house and it's the last publishing house to do critical translations. We've still got thousands of documents that have never been critically translated from the ancient world and as you can imagine the Classics is not as profitable an industry as one might wish. So, Classical Wisdom was created to see if we could find a self-sustainable way of promoting and preserving the classics because relying on grants and government funding has disadvantages. Primarily, you never know when the politics change and who's going to be empowered.

I left the Agora umbrella amicably about five years ago and then partnered with another website called Ancient Origins and Classical Wisdom has evolved from there. It's the same mission of promoting and preserving the classics.

I think we're at a point where ancient philosophy is due for renewal because there's a lot going on in the world right now. People feel the instability with wars, pandemics and on a personal level we get distracted online with attention deficit causing activities that leave us unfulfilled. We need to find a way to reintroduce the purpose of a meaningful life and I think a Classics-based community is a good way to do it.

That's definitely a cause I can believe in. On that note, which philosophers have inspired you in your own life?
There have been many. In the past, I've done events with Stoic practitioners like Donald Robertson, Karen Duffy and Nancy Sherman and I loved preparing for those because I was rereading a lot on the Stoics. In particular, Karen cites Epictetus a lot and I was reading Epictetus in between looking after a little kid. I was having trouble sleeping for a while and at 4 a.m. I'd go to the kitchen and read Epictetus and it was like a balm for the soul. It was wonderful.

I find modern philosophy is fascinating but less relatable. What I love about ancient philosophers is that they are so human. I'm also a big fan of Epicurus and like most people there have been times in my life where I've worried about death and felt anxious about it.

Right after university, I lived in Dubai and every day I'd have to drive down Sheikh Zayed road and there were always huge traffic jams. I used to go to my commute every day and wondered if was going to come home again because a car accident was bound to happen. I found going through Epicurus helpful for releasing that fear and anxiety. Because if you live your life in anxiety and fear, you're not going to live life.

I totally agree. It reminds me of a line from Marcus Aurelius when he said something about not escaping from anxiety. He'd chosen to discard it and it's crucial to do that even on a small scale. What kind of mental health benefits do you think certain schools of thought can have?
There is a lot of benefits and Stoicism has a lot of great mental health techniques. The View From Above and seeing the big perspective is

wonderful. I also think reading any ancient philosophy or literature can also give you that huge perspective on where we are in history.

Aristotle also has a lot to contribute. One of the things I like in his *Nicomachean Ethics* is his ideas about moderation and finding a way to decide between being brave and cowardly and not being overly cautious or excessive. Aristotle has some wonderful things to say about friendship. It's realising the kind of relationships we have with people, identifying them correctly and how they affect our lives. If they're true friendships, it's important to nurture them and realise how important those friendships are for being a good person.

If you could hang out with any ancient philosopher, who would it be and why?
I like Aristotle a lot but I don't think I would necessarily want to hang out with him because it would be exhausting trying to read his work, let alone talk to him. I can imagine having him at a dinner party though and I'd also invite Zeno of Citium, Diogenes the Cynic and the Pre-Socratics. I call them the first philosophers rather than assign them the category of pre-Socratic because I feel like that's putting them down. Thales of Miletus would be an interesting person to hang out with and so would Heraclitus. So many of his thoughts about change read like poetry.

In terms of the concept of suffering, I try to see it from a Stoic perspective of voluntary hardship. Though I understand that concept might be difficult for people to see. What are your thoughts on suffering through a philosophical lens?
I've talked about the beauty of suffering at an event before and would agree with the Stoic perspective. I wouldn't necessarily agree with the Christian view that you need to suffer. The reality is that we'll all suffer at some point in our lives. It's inevitable that some things happen on a personal, public or societal level and that acknowledging suffering as a natural process is helpful for seeing what kind of perspectives it brings. When I did the last event about chronic pain and anxiety, there was an idea that you can grow through trauma. I don't wish people to have to suffer trauma to reach enlightenment. But if you're going to suffer, trying to learn from it and become a better person is a good thing.

I was reading an interview you did with the Plato Academy and you mentioned you think Scepticism has some merits in today's world. What is your understanding of Scepticism and how do you think it can be helpful today?
It's the idea of suspending judgement, and to tie it back to Stoicism there's a great line from Epictetus I was reading the other day and he was like, 'You've got to seek the truth, you got to reject the falsehood and suspend judgement on those that you don't know.' It's such an easy solution and yet people really don't employ it enough. I think it's one of those things that we're seeing right now on social media with the next big cause. Socially, we seem to be pressured to always have a definitive answer or standpoint on complex issues. It's almost like a mob mentality that if you don't put a flag or a badge or sticker on your profile then you're somehow immoral or wrong, even though most people don't understand even a fraction of the issues.

So, the idea of people admitting that they don't know things and suspending judgement would be hugely valuable. To quote Socrates, people like to think it's, 'I know that I know nothing' but it's really, 'I do not claim to know that which I do not know.'

Putting ourselves into an honest and vulnerable position to say, 'I don't know and I'm going to suspend judgement until I do know' would give great pause to everybody for resolving conflict and handling the polarisation of politics.

I think we could all stand to do more of that. On that train of thought, how relevant do you think ancient philosophical devices such as rhetoric and filibustering are for today's world. Do you think they can be used for good?
I think they are essential. It's a real shame that as a society we've not prioritised the way we learn how to speak and address and converse and persuade into the proper structure of how to do speech and discourse. It's also essential for us to realise when it's being used on us. When you see these devices being used, if you know what they are, they lose their power, and you can watch political rallies on both sides.

There can be a perception of philosophy only being used in the academic world. What are some ways that people can make it accessible and who are some people you see doing a great job of making philosophy more accessible and fun?
Making philosophy more enjoyable and conversational has always been a mission for me with Classical Wisdom. The stories of ancient history and

philosophy are genuinely fantastic. I've done a presentation on the Battle of Actium, deep-diving into the relationship between Cleopatra, Mark Antony and Octavian. I mean that stuff is crazy and it's better than a movie!

It's the same with ancient philosophy. Look at Diogenes the Cynic. He was throwing chickens at people and doing all this other stuff and it's hilarious. So, it's about showing people the fun side of philosophy, and podcasts, TV shows and books are doing a good job. I wrote a children's book about the Greek poetess Sappho and I've got a few other ideas about making the subject fun for kids. Donald Robertson is also doing great things around Marcus Aurelius with *How to Think Like a Roman Emperor*, his graphic novel and the reconstruction of Plato's Academy.

As mentioned, I think we're in a time where people are seeking something more substantial. If someone is going through a difficult time, it's wonderful to be able to peer through thousands of years of history and see that everybody's problems are the same. Books and other mediums can be a guide.

How to Bring Philosophy Into the Workplace With Dr Brennan Jacoby

What's your background in philosophy?

I grew up in a religious and philosophical home. My parents were both musicians and they were interested in the big ideas of life. So, I digested a lot of those ideas about philosophy through trying to make sense of religion and spirituality.

I ended up doing a BA, MA and a PhD in philosophy. This started when I went to a liberal arts university and the way that works is you have to do a bit of everything. So, I sat in on an intro to philosophy and loved it. I'd been doing my major in radio communications at the time and decided that if I learn how to think in a philosophical way that I can come back to radio and have more to say. So, I switched my major from communications to philosophy and religion.

Out of the philosophy and religion courses I did, I was more drawn to philosophy. This was because they were focusing on questions that felt more expansive and appealed to my curiosity. I whittled my major down to just philosophy and eventually completed my MA with a focus on ethics. After that, I did a PhD on the philosophy of trust and betrayal.

What kind of philosophers or philosophies inspire you in your day-to-day life? Three philosophers come to mind. The first is Plato and his Allegory of the Cave, which is an incredibly engaging story. I think the idea of imagining that you're a person chained up and can only see shadows against a cave wall, and then someone comes in and frees you to show you how the world really is makes for a compelling thought. I found that resonated with me at the time of my life when I was leaving home and becoming more of my own person and exploring my identity. Even now, Plato's Allegory of the Cave sticks with me. Sometimes I ask myself whether I'm on a treadmill just going through the motions when I'm busy, or if I'm really living. Thinking in that way helps me get back to what really matters.

The second philosopher that's impacted my life is the Danish thinker Soren Kierkegaard, who's sometimes called the father of existentialism. He gels with my personal story because he was writing and thinking in a religious context. In Kierkegaard's Copenhagen, art and philosophy were flourishing while nominal Christianity existed in society. Kierkegaard thought we should do whatever we're doing with more authenticity. He didn't want people to just say what they were (e.g. a particular religious identity or otherwise) without critically engaging with things. So, what drew me to him was his pursuit of the real and what's good and not wanting to be pretentious. Not only was Kierkegaard a brilliant philosopher, but he would really try to live his philosophy. In this society where everyone was marching to church on a Sunday, he would sit outside a café where he knew everyone would have to walk by to go to church and make a stand. This meant he'd drink wine on a Sunday and not go to church. Despite being a Christian himself he had a more authentic sense of his own faith and beliefs. He has these great quotes where he talks about going through the motions of a religion because he thinks it's so far from the authentic form of belief that he had. He said it's like trying to make tea with a piece of paper that once sat next to some used tea leaves – it's incredibly far removed from something real. With Kierkegaard, I'm reminded that we can get to grips with our angst and fears. It's important to grapple with them, rather than trying to assuage them by going through the motions.

The third person is Annette C. Baier. She was a feminist philosopher whose work in the 1980s on trust influenced me. She was a Kantian in terms of ethics and wrote a paper called *Trust and Antitrust* that kicked off a whole literary genre on the philosophy of trust. But she wasn't trying to do the philosophy of trust really. She was doing ethics by saying that throughout the history of ethics most of the big Western schools of thought have been written by men. Her critique of that tradition was that those approaches to ethics assume a view of humanity as inauthentically autonomous. Those accounts forget that we're all born as connected beings. In her writings, Baier recorded that, as a woman, she was more connected to the idea of childbirth. And if we take the feminist perspective we have to start with the belief and recognition that we aren't islands. We're linked up as relational beings. If that's the view, then trust, reliance and collaboration are important moral concepts. Baier's work made me more aware of my own biases in the philosophical education I'd had that was analytical, Western and male-focused. So, based on the influence that Baier kickstarted in me, I'm always trying to push beyond my received canon of philosophy. I want to learn about thinkers and truths that go beyond my bias.

What's the mission behind Philosophy At Work and how did it get started?

Philosophy At Work was born out of a recognition that businesses are impacted by the quality of their thinking. I was working specifically on the topic of trust and consulting with two businesses that had lost the public's trust or were wanting to collaborate better internally. At the same time, the leaders I was working with expressed a need for quality thinking across their organisations. Trust is part of that, since we don't think our best if we don't feel safe. But there is so much more that philosophy can offer to help individuals, teams and businesses think well.

So, I started Philosophy At Work to help businesses think their best. We're a collective of people with philosophy backgrounds who deliver training workshops on strategic thinking, decision-making, navigating change, self-awareness, creative thinking and psychological safety. We don't go around quoting Plato and Kierkegaard. We aim to deconstruct the moves that philosophers have made in their thinking and translate them into thinking tools that apply to work. I don't want people to come away from our workshops talking about philosophy. I want them to do their own good thinking and then turn that thinking into good action.

That's great to hear. What has struck me about your business is applying philosophy as a practical endeavour and its real-life implications. That said, what practical benefits do you think philosophy has in a business context?
First, it's useful for the mechanics of professional thought, i.e. how to be strategic and carve out the time needed to make sense of a difficult project. The business case for philosophy is that if you're thinking well, your work is going to be better formed and meaningful to you as an individual. Because good thinking leads to greater effectiveness, philosophy is positive for work culture and employee retention. But it's also helps build an environment for meaningful work. It's also good for how an organisation can have a true impact on society and the environment. This is because 'good thinking' is not value-neutral. When you're thinking your best, you're not just optimising some kind of cognitive machine. You're also coming to good conclusions in the ethical sense too. When a business is thinking its best, then it's more likely to make decisions that are good for the bottom line, the environment and for the society stakeholders are involved in.

What challenges have you seen with introducing philosophy to different businesses?
Language and framing. When I first started doing this work, I had a framing of philosophy as academic, and in that system I'd received the view that what's most important is defining terms and considering what other philosophers had said about those things. I'd bring that thinking into a workshop setting and the feedback was that although it sounded interesting, the people I was talking to didn't know what to do with the thinking I'd shared with them. So, getting the framing right was key and that meant being less academic and more business focused.

Now, I start workshops by finding out the business challenge, which might be that a brand needs all its people to get better at navigating change. I'm not going to quote philosophers who've said something interesting about change. Instead, I'm going to provide structures to help the group understand their own relationship with change and pick up practical tools to help them move forward in their own times of change.

How we approach language in this work has been the second key learning for me. Philosophers are great at using careful language and complicated words to try and articulate a nuanced point. For example, with trust there are 'predictive expectations' and there are 'normative expectations'. The former is about predicting how someone will behave and the latter is what you think they ought to do.

I find those words helpful, but in workshops they are just words that don't have much meaning to workshop participants. So, we have to break terms down and use everyday language. Most importantly, we have to remember that the whole point is to help the participants in our sessions learn and grow, not just be able to articulate insights.

As a collective, Philosophy At Work is always bringing in new ideas and perspectives. So, what does the journey look like for the business in the next five to ten years?
Philosophy At Work has always been responsive to what the business world needs in terms of output. But the interesting space for me is continuing to define what we mean by 'thinking your best'. I have the view that it's about well-formed thinking with the right skills and mechanics.

I'd like us to get even braver with that concept and lean into good thinking as a way that informs ethical products. When I first started the business, I did not want to create an ethics think tank because the world already has a lot of them. But the more we do this work, the more I think philosophy is essential to help organisations address social and environment challenges. It should be able to say something and help people cultivate their character in an ethical direction. We are still not an ethics think tank, but I now see that the practical thinking tools we teach help businesses do 'good' work in every sense of that term.

Sustainability, Ethics and Virtue Signalling With Vikas and Rachael Shah

What does philosophy mean to you both in business and how does it tie into the mission of your company Swiscot?

Vikas: So, I had a tech company years ago called Ultima Group and after the first dot-com bubble when I got out of that business and I was looking for what to do next. My dad was trading fabrics on his own and he said to me, 'Son, whatever you do, don't get involved in textiles.' I had the naive thought of 'Well, why do you say that?' There was a big generational change happening in textiles becoming more professional and so I bought the business off him. Since day one, I've had the underlying aim of textiles delivering the same type of service you'd get in professional services. It's replicating the best of what's going on in the digital world and applying it to the industry.

Rachael: I'm newer to the textile industry. The first ten years of my career were working for technology companies, charities and at the Co-op. And over the last decade, I've seen a human-centred philosophy that I've taken on board. It's about trying to understand people, what their problems are and how technology helps. I've been inspired to bring that into the textiles industry and look at everything from a sustainability perspective. So, with that in mind, my philosophy has been about finding the best ways to work with people and that they are satisfied in their jobs.

Vikas: For me, I've always tried to read as much as I can about philosophy as a discipline. Especially with how philosophy changes between cultures and nations. That has been instrumental in helping to understand our international customers and suppliers. If you understand philosophy, you can understand the context of a culture and why someone behaves a certain way.

Philosophy is also good for asking the question of 'why do I bother?' in business. Because you have to make sure your philosophy and values align with partners and stakeholders and we can look at that in a motivational context too. Stoicism is helpful here. The focus of dealing with the unknown and all the different things that could happen. Stoicism is good for thinking about how you cope with the kind of adversity that comes along in business on a day-to-day basis. It's a misunderstood philosophy in that people often think the Stoics ignored things. They didn't ignore things; they just knew how to deal with them. In a business like ours, where there is so many moving parts, Stoicism is good for managing the unknown and managing anxiety.

Following on from that Stoic point of view, are there any other schools of thought that have inspired your journeys as business owners?

Rachael: I like to think that my and Vikas's different philosophies and inspirations are complementary. I'm inspired by the principles of the Co-operative Movement that I learned while working at the Co-op. It's getting people around a table, discussing ideas and building a community where people work together for good.

I also like to apply principles of Buddhism, which I think are a good contrast to Stoicism. It reminds me to have a compassionate mindset. On one hand, you're trying to be resilient and you offer yourself and others kindness. Especially if you're going through a tough time because of redundancy or team disbandment.

Lastly, nature-based philosophies and animism is appealing for me. In the sense of seeing how we're all a part of nature's science. It's celebrating the seasonality of life and linking that to the motion of a fast-moving business across the year. Ultimately, nature is good for grounding myself.

Rachael, it'd be great to get your opinion on the subject of greenwashing and how businesses can genuinely implement good sustainability practices.

Rachael: I think it starts with a business being in tune with its own philosophy. Companies have historically been focused on the optimisation of shareholder value. But there's now been a shift with B-Corps towards stakeholders and thinking about what your mission and role as a business is in society, beyond making money. So, ask if your values fit with the world you want to operate in and lead with radical transparency.

There's a lot of things now around how you're calculating your carbon footprint or what you're reporting on. You aren't just saying a message for the sake of it. You could argue that there's a lot of existentialism going on in the sustainability world. In the sense that there's so much to be done that people feel free to try anything but might be overwhelmed by that fact at the same time. So, it's starting with the things you can absolutely change. Apply whatever philosophy works for you and your business and make the change step by step.

Vikas, in your book Thought Economics, you interviewed people with various philosophies on business. What common threads did you pick up from those conversations?

Vikas: The broad conclusions were the self-evident ones. But people assume they aren't. I'll give you a practical example where there's this huge hustle culture in business and lots of people who follow pseudo-intellectual gurus of business and do the whole 4 a.m. club nonsense. The reality is that of all the people I interviewed who made a lot of money and sold businesses, not one of them subscribed to that kind of attitude. Ultimately, they tended to make their business and the values align with themselves, rather than joining a tribe.

So, one of the big disconnects often is the people who haven't figured out what they want to do and they're playing at it, versus the people who have a deep commitment to what they want to do. They know what and why they are going to do something. I spoke to a lot of tech entrepreneurs who were motivated by aesthetics as a movement. They were motivated by beauty, form and structure because they wanted to simplify things. Jony Ive, Apple's chief designer, was a great example of this. A desire for simplicity was one of the most important traits that came across in all interviewees.

Another element was how those individuals intellectually distanced themselves from their peers in a healthy way because they realised they were different. They'll try to take in as many different types of input and information as they can. You'd assume that's the way that most people would be, but then it was great to be able to confirm that from 500 interviews.

Thanks for sharing that. It reminds me of a saying from the Stoic Epictetus on first knowing who you are, then adorning yourself accordingly. Moving to mental health, I know that's an important topic for both of you. What are your thoughts on how exec and non-exec directors can provide genuine mental health change in an organisation?

Vikas: The first thing is not to overdo it. Because the companies who go in for wellbeing washing are undermining the amount of fight that's required to achieve change. What I mean by that is a lot of wellbeing programmes will encourage people to shelter from the storm as opposed to facing into it. And if you want to be successful in any discipline, you need to understand how to face into the storm. That's not to dismiss elements of a programme that directly relate to people who're going through something extraordinary at the time or need support for neurodiversity. But there's a massive problem with a lack of resilience as a result of building shelters and not giving people the ability to face things.

Rachael: One of the tangible things we like to do is provide people with the means to move their minds and bodies about. So, we're focused on building initiatives that promote going out and getting fresh air, being in nature, etc. And adding some healthy competition to the mix, e.g. we have a treadmill in the office and we encourage people to track their steps with each other. Other practices that can help are encouraging journaling and free writing. Because a lot of people like to find answers for themselves and journaling can give you the space and time to think and question.

What's your perspective on the crossovers between philosophy and philanthropy?

Vikas: To me, this relates to the relationship between wealth and identity. For example, there's a lot of people who have the goal of wealth accumulation and want to signal how they've done. That's okay, by the way. Because as long as you're honest then that's a value to you, and you're living your value.

If you have a different approach to wealth and reject that kind of materiality, you'll have an interest in philanthropy. That can also relate to your view of faith and the soul. Because if you believe in the extermination of being at the point at which you die, then why would you care what you're leaving? Why would you want to take anything with you? Why not distribute it in your lifetime and enjoy doing it?

What grates on me is the disconnect where you'll see people who have the capacity to give. They'll make extraordinary statements about what they want to change but never cut the check. That's a misalignment of values.

What trends do you see in your industry in the next decade and how do you think philosophy can navigate them?

Rachael: There's a greater drive towards transparency with customers and bringing shady behaviour into the light. More data is also being gathered and I think this will help to foster better supply chain collaboration. We see this data gathered in the measuring of carbon footprints and reducing emissions. Because once everyone has measured their energy and knows what their footprint is, it'll inevitably force businesses to question suppliers and collaborate and reduce emissions consciously.

This data will also help to inform new sourcing and forecasting models. Some emerging brands are already making the exact quantity of product that they need to fulfil an order. While historically in retail, you'd buy 100,000 pieces and hope to sell 100,000 pieces.

Vikas: UK clothing retailer Boohoo is an interesting example in relating to the philosophical concept of truth. You can split truth into two components, which is objective and subjective. So, if we think about the truth of how a business operates objectively vs subjectively that's where you have a dissonance in fast fashion. (We're not in fast fashion, but the dissonance there is the truth of how a market operates.)

To sell clothes at a certain price, the truth would mean you have to use slave labour and break rules. But as a consumer, do you care? Or are you going to virtue signal the hell out of it? The way to unpick that is to look at Boohoo's sales and share price. The subjective truth is that consumers don't care because they keep buying.

What I think is happening is both sides have forgotten the truth. This means Boohoo will virtue signal about their credentials and the consumer accepts the signal and lives in an untruth. Occasionally, there is some discomfort, which is exposed in the media and then everything goes back to normal. Personally, I think it almost be better if a fast fashion business said, 'Look, you can buy this fabulous item for £4. Please have your eyes open as to what that means, but there you go.'

What's your perspective on the reasons why people virtue signal?

Vikas: Virtue signalling comes from a place of insecurity. If you don't deeply understand the topic, you'll virtue signal because you want to be seen to be a part of or know about something. The reality is that when you understand something in depth, you cease to want to do that in the same way as people who can genuinely afford nice watches tend to not have them in the same way as people who can't really afford them, and need to put them on finance and so on. Because the minute something becomes known, it tends to be less impactful. From a business perspective, that's transparency. If we're negotiating with a customer, we'll tell them here's our price and if you want it cheaper, then a corner will have to be cut. Then it's up to them to feel out how comfortable they are with that.

There's an argument to say that consumerism is the ultimate manifestation of nihilism. When society became secular, the more nihilistic people became. All of a sudden, there's no meaning anymore. So, you look for more meaning and correlate it with celebrity and influence culture. When a society becomes nihilistic, it's easy to manipulate people and capitalism feeds on that. People need to decide for themselves what they want to be and what you value is the beginning of how you navigate through business and life.

Stupid Ideas and the Philosophy of Direct Response Copywriting With Glenn Fisher

Who was Glenn Fisher before he was a copywriter?
I was an accountant/auditor. I was going through life writing reports about the financial systems of places in the local council. And then something broke in my head and I decided I didn't want to do that anymore. I wanted to write in some form or another. Since I liked creative writing, I decided to do a degree locally. Flash forward, I needed a writing job and knew I didn't want to be a journalist. So, I applied for every job that had the word 'writer' in it and by pure chance I applied for an Agora job in London. The role was for a junior copywriter and I didn't know what copywriting was at the time. It seemed cool and I got to learn about direct-response copywriting. I spent ten years at Agora being mentored by people like Mark Ford and Bill Bonner. I was very lucky to do that and learned how to write, persuade and sell. After that, I went freelance and wrote a copywriting book called *The Art of the Click*. I've been freelancing for several years and started The Fix with Nick O'Connor, whom I worked with at Agora. We used to talk about copy all the time and lived near each other too. Our discussions became what The Fix is now.

What I appreciate about your perspective on copywriting, Glenn, is that you're philosophical in your approach. I think there are a lot of practical benefits to bringing philosophy into copywriting and would love to hear your thoughts on that.
Yeah. I remember first meeting you in Manchester and you said you were a philosophical copywriter. I was like, 'Oh, that's interesting.' I like that idea. So, the way I think about that topic is starting with the schism in my mind when I realised I didn't want to do auditing anymore. I started doing a lot of reading and really got into a lot of comedy stuff. I strongly believe in comedy and silliness without it undermining things. So, I had that strand.

I also had an artistic literature strand where I liked reading classics but never really connected with them. But that moved into modern literature from authors like Paul Auster. I like the art of experimental literature. The manipulation of structure and language.

The third arm I discovered was from writers like Alain de Botton who'd taken the core of original philosophical work that would be difficult to understand on its own. So, taking works like Jean-Paul Sartre's *Being and Nothingness* and diluting them to be more digestible. Once I'd connected all these strands I started digging further.

It might sound like trite copywriting advice but when I read something I'm always looking for that intertextuality. What's the thing that the author references that I don't know so I can go and find out. When I read works from guys like Nietzsche and Schopenhauer, I find them harder to understand.

But all those ideas apply to understanding people and ultimately that's what your job as a copywriter is. It's persuading people to do something. And to persuade them you have to understand what makes people do things. I think there's such a close tie between the work that's been done in philosophy to understand the mind and behaviour.

I see this in how we make decisions in life and the way we can't help but do certain things. An example is Nietzsche's idea of eternally repeating the same mistakes and going the same route. I'm the same. But the difference is I understand what I'm doing and why I'm doing it. When it comes to copy, understanding the fact that the reader is thinking ,'Oh, I really don't want to do that but I'm going to have to do that' is a very helpful thought. It's why I tend to go through a cycle of reading a funny book, a literary book and a philosophy book. Because if you just did philosophy, you'd become a boring person very quickly. Those other elements make it good. For anyone interested in a philosophy gateway drug, I'd recommend de Botton's *The Consolations of Philosophy.*

I can always do with more philosophy gateway drugs. That's great insight. And I do agree philosophy should be paired with other things like creativity and art to be able to understand people on a deeper level. You're also a big rhythm guy when it comes to writing. I remember you telling me a story in the pub about how your partner Ruth caught you doing specific motions when you write and you're not always aware you're doing it. Let's unpack that. What does rhythm mean to you in copywriting?

Yeah. Like I was telling you when we saw each other recently. Ruth told me, 'You're doing that thing again when you're writing!' And I was like, 'Oh, Jesus. That again …' I think there are two things that people would find interesting about rhythm in copywriting. First, it's the sense of musicality in the act of writing. So, that's when we're talking about me bouncing along when I write. It's an abstract concept but I believe there's a vitality and energy that comes across in the written word when that person has written in an engaging way.

You can sense it if someone doesn't want to write what they're writing. I'll use Ruth as an example. She was doing email marketing and she doesn't like doing it. I could recognise it because her character wasn't coming out in what she was writing. It was staid copy. So, I said, 'Well, what do you want to say?' She explained. I said, 'Write that.' And then she was able to write it and do it in a more musical way that reflected her in the words that were on the page.

So, I think when you're trying to write, you should imbue yourself with the excitement that you want your reader to have. By doing that, you should physically feel like 'we're all here and nodding. We're trying to buy this thing. We're excited by this thing'. If you've got that, it's going to naturally come across in your copy. You feel excited. You're going to miss words. You're going to write in a clipped way.

The second thing is the rhythm of language and the way words appear on the page. I've been convinced for a long time that good writing has a natural swing to it. And a swing can have lots of different rhythms. If you just have 1,4,4 all the time it's going to be boring. You want to have different rhythms that come out of genres like jazz. Or bands like Radiohead with weird timings. Johnny Greenwood is a genius and he's doing all these little weird things in his music.

Going back to copy, let's say you have an email sequence. The opening paragraph needs to be short and clipped to get your attention. But then if you just did that all the way through then it would be boring and staccato. So, you might then use a long-flowing Proustian sentence that leads you in and brings you out. It's not wrong or bad to use only one kind of rhythm. It's just not for me personally. A great example is I've read a book recently by a popular author. And I'm not going to say who it actually is because that's just being bitchy. But it was all short, clipped sentences. And I was like, 'Hmm. I'm really struggling with this. But I'll carry on anyway.' Then I realised I couldn't go on reading it because the writing felt overstylised.

Putting that back onto copy, if you're persuading someone to take action and you stop the reader's natural rhythm, you've lost your prospect. They aren't going to keep reading. It's why Nick and I always read our copy reviews aloud on The Fix to test rhythm. Getting rhythm right isn't hard. You just need to read the copy aloud and follow the natural rhythms of your own voice. Then it's being honest and saying to yourself, 'I've run over there. I can't do that. That word doesn't flow.'

And there you have it. The rhythm of rhythm in copywriting. So, I'd like to transition into the rhythm of ideas now. I was watching a Fix video where you and Nick were explaining the write-and-delete method with headlines. And something that got my attention was your idea of Mr Frinzinky. Where did that idea come from and what're your thoughts about idea generation in general?

Ah ha! Well, that idea is going deep within the indulgent mind space of Glenn Fisher, which Nick would tell me off for. But it might be interesting to see where my mind is when I came up with that character.

I've got an idea for a novel about the small town I grew up in. Basically, the main premise is that elephants start appearing in the town, causing some kind of disruption. But everyone learns to live with it because it's the elephant in the room metaphor blown up massively. Then I was thinking about how the council would react and they'd blame the circus on the edge of town. Maybe they think the elephants are coming from that circus. Then I imagined the circus master. So, I need someone who is like the foreign outsider. The name Frinzinky came to mind. But actually, he'll just be called something really boring like Paul. He wants to give the illusion that he's interesting.

I guess the lesson here is that it's okay to let your imagination flow without worrying about how stupid it sounds. Most of my ideas are stupid. But it's having the confidence to like the ones that stick. I like the idea of Frinzinky because I've kept it in my head enough times and written it down so I don't forget.

But when ideas fail, that's okay too. I attribute that perspective to being taught by the old-school Agora elite like Bill Bonner and Mark Ford. It's about failing fast and not being worried when it happens. It's good life and good idea generation advice.

Great stuff. So, transitioning into your book The Art of the Click, I found the interviews in it to be really useful copywriting advice. The one you did with Mark resonated in particular. I was struck by your discussion with him about the paradox of authentic copy. That the idea of writing in someone else's voice sounds like the

most inauthentic thing ever but copywriters have to make it authentic. What're your thoughts on what makes authentic copy?
When I think of authenticity and writing in the same sentence, I think of Hemmingway. He said something like you have to write one true sentence. For most of my life, I've been like, 'What're you on about?' I didn't get what Hemmingway was saying. And then I was writing some fiction a few years back and something clicked in my head about writing a sentence that was true. Not in the made-up sense of a character like Mr Frinzinky.

It's not the same in copy either if you're writing a sales letter about a topic like being a gold mining expert. I've never mined an ounce of gold in my life. So, I'm not going to be writing the truth in the sense that it's my personal truth. But I realised that the one true sentence in copywriting comes from having all the information, research and idea generation behind what you're writing. There's a feeling of authenticity down to the sentence level. There are certain words that follow on from each other and there are certain rhythms. I think you have to be able to write those kinds of sentences honestly. There's a natural flow that works on the page. I'm aware this sounds all very amorphous. If we could recreate the feeling of authenticity, then we'd all be millionaires.

That's probably what AI is trying to do and what it fails to do. You need that unknown human element, and the rhythm will always change. You can't just add adjectives and superlatives. Every sentence has its own inherent natural syntax and structure. So, an authentic voice to me is being able to understand what you really want to say and express that with the most clarity you can.

I think you expressed the concept of authenticity in copy well. Now, seeing as AI is one of the biggest topics in copywriting right now what's your opinion on it?
On a philosophical level, I think AI will be here forever. There are ways to use it for good and for bad. But in regard to things like ChatGPT, I'm not interested to the extent that I've got too much on my plate to worry about it. I have used it a couple of times like when I wrote a promotion recently about AI. Nick and I have also used it for writing a skit. Another way I can see it working is when writing a privacy policy for a website because it saves time.

While ChatGPT is interesting I can see through the flaws and limitations. And on the question of whether it'll replace copywriters, I think the bigger problem is what the definition of a copywriter is. Because if all someone did was write then ChatGPT could definitely replace that. But that's not what copywriters do. We're ideas people and ChatGPT may be able to come up with original ideas one day. But not right now. I think in our industry it's a distraction and another reason not to focus on the stuff you should do like work on copy and use principles that have been around for decades. An example that comes to mind is *Scientific Advertising* by Claude Hopkins which came out in 1923. A hundred years later and most of the advice is still the same. Advice that people are now selling at an incredibly high price when you can get a PDF version of Hopkin's principles for free.

What're your plans for The Fix and the personal goals you'd like to achieve? Maybe join Nick in his idea to open a craft beer brewery?
I'll follow the man as far as I can so we'll see if we can make that happen eventually. When we started The Fix, it was us just talking about copy and it's quickly become something that's expanding around us. Ultimately, we're focusing on cutting through the noise about the amount of nonsense out there about copywriting. Not in a holier-than-thou crusader kind of way. But where we can have a laugh and be a bit frivolous.

Awesome. My last question is what does waffy mean?
I think it came out of my peer group when someone missaid Daffy Duck. I used to say Waffy Duck. (I don't know if I invented it but it's possible I said it first.) I like to use it to describe weird, silly things. My editor for *The Art of the Click* saw waffy in the book and I was adamant that it was the only word that needs to stick. It's become my personal philosophy – Get comfortable with being waffy.

Tyler Paytas on the Practical Wisdom of the Stoics, Kant and Sidgwick

To kick things off, I'm interested in hearing about your first experiences with philosophy and how it helped to shape your formative years.
I was interested in philosophical questions long before I knew much about philosophy as an academic discipline. Growing up, my friends and I would debate topics like the existence of God and various ethical questions. I was fortunate to be surrounded by thoughtful and reflective friends who enjoyed lively discussions. I fell in love with the formal study of philosophy when I was a university student. The realisation that one could make a career out of

thinking about and discussing the most interesting and important questions was mind-blowing.

However, during my postgraduate years, I became overly focused on professional achievement and career advancement. While the work I was doing in moral philosophy had some positive influence on me, I fell into the common trap of seeing philosophy primarily as an intellectual competition and an opportunity to 'win' rather than as a vital tool for self-development.

This began to change in 2017 (two years after completing my PhD). I read a book by Massimo Pigliucci called *How To Be a Stoic* after seeing it on a published list of popular new books. I already had some familiarity with the Stoics from graduate school, but I hadn't gone in-depth before. The main benefit I derived from the book was learning about Epictetus. A few months later while I was visiting a friend in Perth, I saw a copy of Epictetus's *Discourses and Selected Writings* (Penguin Classics edition – the best translation!) in the philosophy section of a local bookshop. I decided to buy it, and the next morning I read the *Enchiridion* for the first time. That was the moment when I realised that philosophy had much more to offer than what I had taken from it during my academic career. I now utilise Stoic philosophy as my basic ethical framework and guide to living. While I am still vulnerable to anxiety, anger and misguided desires, I am slowly but surely becoming less vulnerable than I used to be.

Through your philosophy work you focus on figures such as Plato, Epictetus, Kant and Sidgwick. What is it about these philosophers that resonate with you personally?
I consider Plato to be the greatest thinker in history. While I enjoy engaging with his metaphysical views, my favourite dialogues are those that emphasise the ethical teachings of Socrates and the example that he set. The *Crito* and the *Apology* provide perfect illustrations of integrity, fearlessness, and a proper understanding of what is truly good and bad for human beings.

Regarding the title of greatest thinker in history, a strong case can also be made for Kant. My favourite parts of Kant's philosophy are his ethics and philosophy of religion. I find Kant's discussion of virtue and moral motivation deeply moving and inspiring. My main critique of Kant's ethics is his view that pleasure is necessary for a good life (I share the Stoic view that pleasure is merely a preferred indifferent). I am a huge fan of Kant's approach to religion. His argument that religion must be grounded in moral principles rather than the other way around seems absolutely right.

What I love about Sidgwick is his willingness to directly address the most fundamental questions of human existence and the relentless spirit with which he attempts to find the answers. I'm especially fond of his moral epistemology, which is based on the idea that our intuitions about abstract principles are more reliable than our immediate 'gut reactions' to particular situations. As with Kant, my main disagreement with Sidgwick concerns his value theory, specifically his belief that pleasure is the sole source of human well-being.

Epictetus is my favourite philosopher. The best characterisation of his teachings that I've heard is 'soul-stirring'. When I read the *Discourses*, I get the sense that he is speaking directly to me with clear awareness of all my shortcomings. And yet, his arguments and admonitions still leave me feeling inspired rather than ashamed. One of the passages that hits especially close to home is from Book 2: 'But please stop representing yourself as a philosopher, you affected fool! You still experience envy, pity, jealousy, and fear, and hardly a day passes that you don't whine to the gods about your life. Some philosopher!' (2.17.26–27)

You're the co-author of two books called Plato's Pragmatism: Rethinking the Relationship between Ethics and Epistemology and Kantian and Sidgwickian Ethics: The Cosmos of Duty Above and the Moral Law Within. Can you explain what each of these books focuses on and what the writing process was like for each?
I wrote *Plato's Pragmatism* with my friend and former classmate, Nich Baima. Conventional interpretations of Plato attribute to him the view that the ultimate rational aim is believing what is true and avoiding what is false, consequences be damned. Nich and I argue that Plato prioritises ethical commitments above epistemic concerns. Sometimes the goal of being a good person requires that we relax our commitment to certain epistemic norms. For example, in the *Phaedo*, Plato has Socrates engaging in motivated (i.e. biased) reasoning regarding the fate of his soul after the death of his body. On our interpretation, this is because having certain beliefs about the afterlife will make it easier for Socrates to conduct himself with the utmost virtue during his final moments and thus solidify his teachings and allow him to serve as an exemplar for his friends and future generations.

Writing this book was a lot of work but co-authoring with a close friend made the process enjoyable. Academic writing can often be lonely and stressful, and having a teammate who is equally invested in the project is a great source of support and motivation.

Kantian and Sidgwickian Ethics is a collection of essays that I co-edited with my friend and mentor Tim Henning. The collection aims to examine the ethical systems of Kant and Sidgwick side by side to gain a deeper understanding of both while also searching for potential points of convergence that might help reconcile long-standing disagreements within philosophical ethics. The essays are written by leading Kant and Sidgwick scholars, and they cover a range of topics including moral epistemology, metaphysics, and free will. I authored one of the essays, which is on Kant's and Sidgwick's respective views on the moral necessity of God.

In short, both philosophers believe that there is something intolerable about a universe where happiness and virtue can come apart, and only God can ensure that the virtuous experience the happiness they deserve (in the afterlife). I suggest that the Stoic view on these issues – that virtue is sufficient for happiness – represents a more inspiring ideal.

You've stated that you share Sidgwick's belief that as rational beings we're bound to aim at good generally. What does this perspective mean specifically?
That phrase comes from one of Sidgwick's foundational ethical intuitions presented in the *Methods of Ethics*: 'And it is evident to me that as a rational being I am bound to aim at good generally, not merely at a particular part of it.' There are different ways of interpreting this claim, but I take Sidgwick to mean that one ought to be equally concerned with equal portions of the good regardless of where it happens to be located. In other words, if someone is struggling, it doesn't ultimately matter whether it's me, a family member, or a distant stranger. I don't have any ultimate reason to care more about myself, my intimates, or my compatriots. This is similar to the Stoic idea that we should view the entire human race as close kin and view ourselves as citizens of the world.

You've also spoken about the connection between philosophy and animal welfare. What perspectives and practices do you think need to be brought into this area?
There's been a lot of great work done by philosophers to make progress on the issue of animal welfare. Peter Singer comes to mind as someone who has done an incredible job of getting people to think more carefully about the treatment of animals and what sort of ethical consideration they are owed.

At this point, the most pressing concern is the practice of factory farming. I think reasonable people can disagree about the ethics of bringing an animal into existence for the purpose of consumption if that animal has a high quality of life and a minimally painful death. However, I don't think there's much room for debate about the ethics of factory farming. While most people quickly acknowledge the problem when presented with the relevant facts, it is easy to forget about it and resume one's normal habit of purchasing factory-farmed meat.

The main difficulty is the prevalence of meat consumption in society. It's difficult to keep the horrors of factory farming in mind when one sees the vast majority of others carrying on as if nothing is wrong. And even for those who remain mindful of the issue and attempt to revise their practices, it can be disheartening and demotivating to witness so many people (including friends, family, and co-workers) continuing to participate.

I'm not sure what the solution is. One reason for optimism is the development of cultured meat. If people are one day able to purchase affordable meat grown in a lab that is indistinguishable from conventional meat, I suspect that factory farming will become a thing of the past.

What type of teaching methods do you employ to make philosophy more accessible to a younger audience?
I pride myself on being able to explain difficult concepts in plain language. I also try to illustrate complex points using relatable examples. This was a bit easier earlier in my career when the generational gap between me and my students wasn't as substantial—my references to '90s pop culture might as well be about the 1890s at this point. Still, I've found that the key to making philosophy enjoyable and accessible to a younger audience (or any audience for that matter) is to teach with energy and enthusiasm.

If you could go back in time and speak to any philosopher, who would it be and why?
It would have to be Epictetus. I can't imagine anything more exhilarating and beneficial than hearing one of his lectures in person.

What kind of philosophy-based projects are you working on in the future?
My current research focuses on virtue and emotions. I'm especially interested in negative emotions like fear, envy, and anger. I'm currently working on a paper challenging the present orthodoxy among academic philosophers

that anger is rational and justified so long as it is 'fitting' in the sense that it involves an accurate appraisal of wrongdoing. I argue that even if one's anger is in response to genuine wrongdoing or injustice, that's not enough to vindicate it because there are alternative responses available that have all the advantages of anger without the drawbacks. As one of my favourite Stoic authors Donald Robertson puts it, 'Anything anger can do, reason (and positive emotions) can do better.'

Notes

Chapter 1

1. Marcus Aurelius, *Meditations*, Book 2, p.12
2. Lee Clarke, *Marcus Aurelius' Meditations: Inside the Mind of the Philosopher Emperor*, www.thecollector.com/marcus-aurelius-meditations/
3. *What is Roman Stoicism?*, https://study.com/learn/lesson/roman-stoicism-beliefs-philosophers.html
4. Donald Robertson, *How to Think Like a Roman Emperor: The Stoic Philosophy of Marcus Aurelius* (St Martin's Publishing Group, 2019), p.49
5. Robertson, p.67
6. *Meditations*
7. *The Letters of Fronto,* www.attalus.org/info/fronto.html
8. Ryan Holiday, *Lives of the Stoics: The Art of Living from Zeno to Marcus Aurelius* (Profile Books, 2020), p.271
9. Cornelis J. Kooiker, *The Fatal Illness of the Roman Emperor Antonius Pius*
10. *The Chief Ancient Sources on Marcus Aurelius*, https://onlinelibrary.wiley.com/doi/pdf/10.1002/9781444311075.oth1
11. *Meditations*
12. Max Frenzel, *Cultivating Your Inner Citadel*, https://medium.com/the-ascent/cultivating-your-inner-citadel-1036023dcd32
13. *Roman Empire, Marcus Aurelius: The Rain And Lightning Miracles*, www.romanumismatics.com/historicarticles?view=article&article_id=556&dateFilter=0
14. Robertson, *The Metaphor of the Sun in Marcus Aurelius*, https://donaldrobertson.name/2017/12/06/the-metaphor-of-the-sun-in-marcus-aurelius/
15. Robertson, *Why Did Marcus Aurelius Allow Commodus to Succeed Him?*, https://donaldrobertson.name/2018/01/19/why-did-marcus-aurelius-allow-commodus-to-succeed-him/

Chapter 2

1. Rosemary Black, *Glossophobia (Fear of Public Speaking): Are You Glossophobic?*, www.psycom.net/glossophobia-fear-of-public-speaking
2. Brian Leggett, *History of Classical Rhetoric: An overview of its early development (1)*, https://blog.iese.edu/leggett/2012/10/16/history-of-classical-rhetoric-an-overview-of-its-early-development/
3. *Why Did Plato Hate the Sophists?*, https://ivypanda.com/essays/why-did-plato-hate-the-sophists-philosophy/
4. *Aristotle's Rhetoric*, https://plato.stanford.edu/Archives/Win2004/entries/aristotle-rhetoric/
5. Plutarch, *The Parallel Lives*, http://penelope.uchicago.edu/Thayer/e/roman/texts/plutarch/lives/cicero*.html
6. Cicero (Translated by James. M. May), *How to Win an Argument: An Ancient Guide to the Art of Persuasion* (Princeton University Press, 2016), p.28
7. *Cicero: Academic Skepticism*, https://iep.utm.edu/cicero-academic-skepticism/
8. Cicero, p.31
9. Holiday, p.127

10. Cicero, p.74
11. Cicero, p.107

Chapter 3

1. Musonius Rufus (Translated by Cora E. Lutz), *That One Should Disdain Hardships: The Teachings of a Roman Stoic* (Yale University Press, 2020), p.11
2. *That One Should Disdain Hardships,* Introduction, p.xxvii
3. Holiday, p.216
4. Rufus, p.23
5. Introduction, p.vii
6. Rufus, p.39
7. Rufus, p.83

Chapter 4

1. H.G. Moeller, *Taoism*, www.sciencedirect.com/topics/social-sciences/taoism
2. *Taoism: Cultivating Body, Mind and Spirit*, www.taoisttaichi.org/taoism-cultivating-body-mind-spirit/
3. Elizabeth Reninger, *Taoism for Beginners: Understanding and Applying Taoist History, Concepts and Practices* (Rock Ridge Press, 2020), p.26
4. *Overview of Internal Alchemy in Taoism*, www.learnreligions.com/internal-alchemy-in-taoism-an-overview-3182918
5. Reninger, pp.30–31
6. Reninger, pp.27–28
7. John Minford, *Did Lao-Tzu and Confucius Know Each Other?*, https://lithub.com/did-lao-tzu-and-confucius-know-each-other
8. Joshua J. Mark, *Lao-Tzu*, www.worldhistory.org/Lao-Tzu/
9. Reninger, p.88
10. *Tao Te Ching Quotes*, www.readthistwice.com/quotes/book/tao-te-ching
11. Hans Qu, *Star Wars: The Force and Taoism*, https://filmschoolrejects.com/star-wars-force-taoism/
12. Reninger, p.28
13. Lu Yan, *The Living Method of Turning the Light Around*, www.dailyzen.com/journal/the-living-method-of-turning-the-light-around/
14. Reninger, *The Taoist Altar*, www.learnreligions.com/the-taoist-altar-3182504

Chapter 5

1. Christine De Pizan, *The Book of the City of Ladies*, p.7
2. De Pizan, p.239
3. De Pizan, *The Book of Fortune's Transformation*, in *Selected Writings*, pp.101–102
4. Charlotte Cooper-Davis, *Christine De Pizan: Life, Work, Legacy* (University of Chicago Press, 2021), pp.10–11
5. Cooper-Davis, p.45
6. Cooper-Davis, p.47
7. Cooper-Davis, p.69
8. Cooper-Davis, p.76
9. De Pizan, p.239
10. De Pizan, p.70
11. De Pizan, p.101
12. De Pizan (Translated by David Hult), *The Debate of the Romance of the Rose* (University of Chicago Press, 2010), p.60
13. Cooper-Davis, p.98
14. Cooper-Davis, p.104

15. De Pizan, (Translated by Sarah Lawson), *The Treasure of the City of Ladies* (Penguin Books, 2003), p.60
16. De Pizan, *The Treasure of the City of Ladies*, p.40
17. Cooper-Davis, p.133

Chapter 6

1. Zhang Guodong, *A Critical Interpretation of Leo Strauss' Thoughts on Machiavelli*, https://philarchive.org/archive/ZHAACI-3
2. Richard Christopherson, *Old Nick and His Traducers*, www.jstor.org/stable/41204805
3. Niccolo Machiavelli, *The Prince*, www.online-literature.com/machiavelli/prince/18/
4. Dr Alexander Lee, *Machiavelli: His Life and Times* (Picador, 2020), pp.11–12
5. Lee, p.11
6. *Florence in the Renaissance*, www.historycrunch.com/florence-in-the-renaissance.html
7. Lee, pp.12–18
8. *Lorenzo The Magnificent*, www.florenceinferno.com/lorenzo-the-magnificent/
9. Lee, pp.35–36
10. Taryn Smee, *The Rise and Fall of the Medici: Renaissance Italy's Most Powerful Family*, www.thevintagenews.com/2018/11/17/the-medici/
11. Lee, p.52
12. Lee, p.76
13. Lee, pp.85–90
14. Lee, p.133
15. Machiavelli, *The Prince*
16. Dragos Moldoveanu, *The Downfall and the Death of Cesare Borgia*, https://elsborja.cat/blog/the-downfall-and-the-death-of-cesare-borgia/
17. Lee, p.358
18. Lee, p.458
19. Lee, p.469
20. Lee, p.570
21. Machiavelli, *The Prince*
22. Machiavelli, *The Prince*
23. Thomas Osborne, *Machiavelli and the liberalism of fear*, www.ncbi.nlm.nih.gov/pmc/articles/PMC5731607
24. *Reason Why Tupac Changed His Name to Makaveli*, https://tupacuncensored.com/reason-why-tupac-changed-his-name-to-makaveli/
25. *Niccolo Machiavelli on Reading as a Cure for Boredom*, https://fs.blog/niccolo-machiavelli-on-reading/

Chapter 7

1. Sarah Bakewell, *How to Live: A Life of Montaigne in One Question and Twenty Attempts at an Answer* (Vintage Books, 2011), p.18
2. Bakewell, p.21
3. Bakewell, p.64
4. *Montaigne's Rule for Reading: The Promiscuous Pursuit of Pleasure*, https://fs.blog/what-did-montaigne-like-to-read/
5. Hazel Smith, *In the Footsteps of Montaigne*, https://francetoday.com/learn/history/in-the-footsteps-of-montaigne/
6. Bakewell, p.92
7. Bakewell, p.104
8. Bakewell, p.159
9. Bakewell, p.24

10. Bakewell, p.175
11. Bakewell, p.237
12. *Biography examines political motivations of Montaigne*, https://news.uchicago.edu/story/biography-examines-political-motivations-montaigne
13. Bakewell, pp.252–253
14. *Marie le Jars De Gournay*, www.enotes.com/topics/marie-le-jars-de-gournay
15. Bakewell, p.296
16. *What is Epicureanism?*, https://kinnu.xyz/kinnuverse/philosophy/the-timeless-wisdom-of-great-greek-philosophers/epicureanism/
17. Bakewell, p.115
18. *Montaigne and skepticism*, www.cambridge.org/core/books/abs/cambridge-companion-to-montaigne/montaigne-and-skepticism/6CC36484C0ACE24758BD360A8F39E0FA
19. Bakewell, p.136
20. Montaigne (Translated by M.A. Screech), *The Essays: A Selection* (Penguin Classics, 1993), p.206

Chapter 8

1. Mary Wollstonecraft, *A Vindication of the Rights of Woman*
2. Emma Raymond, *The Early Life of Mary Wollstonecraft*, https://eastendwomensmuseum.org/blog/2021/4/30/the-early-life-of-mary-wollstonecraft
3. *Mary Wollstonecraft Family Troubles*, www.shmoop.com/study-guides/biography/mary-wollstonecraft/bio/family-troubles
4. Janet Todd, *Ascendency: Lady Mount Cashell, Lady Moira, Mary Wollstonecraft and the Union Pamphlets*, www.jstor.org/stable/30070996
5. Wollstonecraft, *Thoughts on the Education of Daughters*, www.gutenberg.org/files/67466/67466-h/67466-h.htm
6. *Thoughts on the Education of Daughters*
7. Simon Court, *William Godwin: Political Justice, anarchism and the Romantics*, https://wordsworth.org.uk/blog/2015/10/04/william-godwin-political-justice-anarchism-and-the-romantics/
8. Nancy Means Wright, *A Fiery Female Meets the Devil: Mary Wollstonecraft and Henry Fuseli*, www.elizabethkmahon.com/2011/09/fiery-female-meets-devil-mary.html
9. Edmund Burke, *Reflections on the Revolution in France*, p.61
10. *Mary Wollstonecraft: Finding Feminism in the French Revolution*, https://radicalteatowel.co.uk/radical-history-blog/mary-wollstonecraft-finding-feminism-in-the-french-revolution
11. Wollstonecraft, *Vindications of the Rights of Men*, p.80
12. *A Vindication of the Rights of Woman*, p.135
13. *A Vindication of the Rights of Woman*, p.288
14. Wollstonecraft, *Letters Written in Sweden, Norway, and Denmark*, www.gutenberg.org/files/3529/3529-h/3529-h.htm
15. Wollstonecraft, *Letters*
16. Maria Popova, *The Original Marriage of Equals: The Love Letters of Feminism Founding Mother Mary Wollstonecraft and Political Philosopher William Godwin*, www.themarginalian.org/2018/10/15/romantic-outlaws-mary-wollstonecraft-william-godwin-love-letters/
17. Richard Holmes, *How a Husband's Loving Biography Ruined His Wife's Reputation*, https://lithub.com/how-a-husbands-loving-biography-ruined-his-wifes-reputation/
18. *Romantic Outlaws: The Extraordinary Lives of Mary Wollstonecraft & Mary Shelley*, www.youtube.com/watch?v=7WJdOM2kgDs&t=1081s

Chapter 9

1. Suzanne Fagence Cooper, *To See Clearly: Why Ruskin Matters* (Quercus, 2019), p.55
2. Cooper, p.60
3. John Ruskin, *The Storm-Cloud of the Nineteenth Century*, www.gutenberg.org/files/20204/20204-h/20204-h.htm

4. *Ruskin and Byron*, www.lancaster.ac.uk/fass/ruskin/empi/notes/fbyron02.htm
5. Cooper, p.15
6. Carmen Casaliggi, *Towards the Study of Ruskin's Water*, https://victorianweb.org/authors/ruskin/casaliggi1.html
7. Cooper, pp.124 –125
8. *Ruskin and Turner*, www.lancaster.ac.uk/fass/ruskin/empi/notes/gsturnerz02.htm#:~:text=(See%20also%20Ruskin%2C%20Turner%2C,and%20two%20important%20oil%20paintings
9. *Ruskin and Turner*
10. Cooper, p.35
11. Ryan Roark, *The Afterlife of Dying Buildings: Ruskin and Preservation in the Twenty-First Century*, https://courtauld.ac.uk/research/research-resources/publications/courtauld-books-online/ruskins-ecologies-figures-of-relation-from-modern-painters-to-the-storm-cloud/14-the-afterlife-of-dying-buildings-ruskin-and-preservation-in-the-twenty-first-century-ryan-roark/
12. Cooper, p.85
13. *John Ruskin's Seven Lamps of Architecture*, https://moniquerblog.wordpress.com/2014/12/19/john-ruskins-seven-lamps-of-architecture/#:~:text=Finally%20the%20seventh%20lamp%2C%20the,and%20Religious%20Faith%20of%20nations.
14. Cooper, p.92
15. Cooper, p.134
16. Cooper, p.209
17. *The History of the Guild*, www.guildofstgeorge.org.uk/about/the-history-of-the-guild
18. Cooper, p.154
19. Elizabeth K. Helsinger & John Matthews Manly, *The Structure of Ruskin's Praeterita*, https://victorianweb.org/authors/ruskin/helsinger3.html
20. Cooper, p.136

Chapter 10

1. *Dialogue from Film – Monty Python & the Holy Grail – Black Knight*, https://thingsthatmadeanimpression.wordpress.com/2012/07/25/dialogue-from-film-monty-python-the-holy-grail/
2. *The History of The Pied-Noirs*, www.algeria.com/blog/the-history-of-the-pied-noirs/
3. M.M. Owen, *How Albert Camus Found Solace in the Absurdity of Football*, www.mmowen.me/camus-absurd-love-of-football
4. *Albert Camus and football*, https://camus-society.com/2017/11/29/albert-camus-and-football/
5. Matthew Lamb, *On the Influence of tuberculosis on Camus' early life and work, 1931–1941*, https://publicthings.substack.com/p/7-on-the-influence-of-tuberculosis
6. Maria Popova, *Albert Camus on Writing and the Importance of Stubbornness in Creative Work*, www.themarginalian.org/2023/08/22/albert-camus-writing/
7. Clayton Paul Kyles, *The Unapologetic Algerian: The Position of Albert Camus within the Algerian Situation*, https://repository.lib.ncsu.edu/bitstream/handle/1840.20/38465/etd.pdf?sequence=1&isAllowed=y
8. Anakaren Cervantes, *Albert Camus: Journalist at Heart, Scholar by Profession*, https://stanfordfreedomproject.com/multi-media-essays-on-freedom/albert-camus-journalist-at-heart-scholar-by-profession/
9. Alice Kaplan, *Paris from Camus's Notebooks*, www.theparisreview.org/blog/2016/09/19/paris-camuss-notebooks/
10. Kaplan
11. Albert Camus, *The Stranger*
12. Camus, *The Myth of Sisyphus* (Penguin Books, 2005), p.119

13. Ronald Aronson, *An excerpt from Camus and Sartre, The Story of a Friendship and the Quarrel that Ended It*, https://press.uchicago.edu/Misc/Chicago/027961.html#:~:text=Jean%2DPaul%20Sartre%20and%20Albert,of%20Sartre%27s%20play%20The%20Flies
14. *Camus at Combat: From the Revolution to the Republic*, https://intellectualsandthemedia.org/2018/12/05/camus-at-combat-from-the-revolution-to-the-republic/
15. *Camus & The Barbarity of Capital Punishment*, www.outlookindia.com/website/story/camus-the-barbarity-of-capital-punishment/294945
16. Sarah Bakewell, *At the Existentialist Café: Freedom, Being and Apricot Cocktails* (Vintage, 2006), p.257
17. Jeffrey Meyers, *Malraux, Camus and the Nobel Prize*, https://thelondonmagazine.org/article/malraux-camus-nobel-prize/
18. *Albert Camus' speech at the Nobel Banquet at the City Hall in Stockholm, December 10, 1957*, www.nobelprize.org/prizes/literature/1957/camus/speech/
19. Bakewell, p.246
20. Robert Zarestsky, *The Logic of the Rebel: On Simone Weil and Albert Camus*, https://lareviewofbooks.org/article/logic-rebel-simone-weil-albert-camus/
21. *Camus and his women*, www.theguardian.com/books/1997/oct/15/biography.albertcamus
22. Jean-Paul Sartre, *Tribute to Albert Camus*, http://faculty.webster.edu/corbetre/philosophy/existentialism/camus/sartre-tribute.html
23. Camus, p.65

Chapter 11

1. Richard Wright, *Black Boy* (Vintage Classics, 1945), pp 175–180
2. *Black Boy*, p.2
3. *Black Boy*, p.33
4. *Black Boy*, p.20
5. *Black Boy*, p.20
6. *Black Boy*, p.43
7. *Black Boy*, p.47
8. *Black Boy*, p.81
9. Wright, *Memories of My Grandmother*, collected with *The Man Who Lives Underground* (Vintage Classics, 2023), p.169
10. *Black Boy*, p.209
11. *Black Boy*, pp.261–262
12. Wright, *I Tried to Be a Communist*, www.theatlantic.com/magazine/archive/1944/08/richard-wright-communist/618821/
13. *I Tried to Be a Communist*
14. Wright, *How Bigger Was Born*, https://archive.org/details/in.ernet.dli.2015.499539/page/n5/mode/2up
15. *How Bigger was Born*
16. Bakewell, p.171
17. Philip Quarles, *Richard Wright's Love Letter to Paris*, www.wnyc.org/story/192767-richard-wright/
18. Wright, *I Choose Exile*, www.artofsunday.com/logs/i-choose-exile
19. Lauren Michele Jackson, *What We Want From Richard Wright*, www.newyorker.com/books/under-review/what-we-want-from-richard-wright
20. James Campbell, *The Island affair*, www.theguardian.com/books/2006/jan/07/featuresreviews.guardianreview25
21. Campbell
22. Malcolm Wright, *Afterword, The Man Who Lived Underground*

Chapter 12

1. Sojourner Truth, *Ain't I a Woman?*, www.nps.gov/articles/sojourner-truth.htm#:~:text=At%20 the%201851%20Women's%20Rights,and%20after%20the%20Civil%20War.
2. Truth
3. Truth, *The Narrative of Sojourner Truth*, https://digital.library.upenn.edu/women/ truth/1850/1850.html
4. *The Narrative of Sojourner Truth*
5. *The Narrative of Sojourner Truth*
6. *The Narrative of Sojourner Truth*
7. *The Narrative of Sojourner Truth*
8. *The Narrative of Sojourner Truth*
9. *Robert Matthews (Profit Matthias)*, www.litcharts.com/lit/kingdom-of-matthias/characters/ robert-matthews-prophet-matthias
10. *A Utopian Community in Florence, MA*, https://davidrugglescenter.org/northampton-association-education-industry/
11. *Northampton Dedicates Sojourner Truth Statue*, www.massmoments.org/moment-details/ northampton-dedicates-sojourner-truth-statue.html
12. *Life Story: Sojourner Truth (ca. 1797–1883)*, https://wams.nyhistory.org/a-nation-divided/ antebellum/sojourner-truth/
13. Dick Russell, *Black Genius: Inspirational Portraits of African-American Leaders* (Skyhorse Publishing, 2009), p.419

Chapter 13

1. *An Introduction to Roland Barthes's Mythologies: A Macat Literature Analysis*, www.youtube. com/watch?v=6GCzq8we-bI
2. *Roland Barthes French Philosopher, Social Theorist and Semiotician*, www.theartstory.org/ influencer/barthes-roland/
3. www.theartstory.org/influencer/barthes-roland/
4. Ben Rogers, *Death of the author ROLAND BARTHES: A Biography by Louis-Jean Calvet, trs Sarah Wykes*, www.independent.co.uk/arts-entertainment/books/death-of-the-author-roland-barthes-a-biography-by-louisjean-calvet-trs-sarah-wykes-polity-press-163-25-1567120. html
5. www.theartstory.org/influencer/barthes-roland/
6. Chase Dimock, *Opacity and the Closest: Queer Tactics in Foucault, Barthes and Warhol by Nicholas De Villers*, https://lambdaliterary.org/2012/08/opacity-and-the-closet-queer-tactics-in-foucault-barthes-and-warhol-by-nicholas-de-villiers/
7. Roland Barthes, *Mythologies* (Vintage Classics, 2009), p.9
8. Magali Nachtergael, *Barthes, Queer Before Queer?: A Journey Into Barthes' Visual Culture*, https:// oa.ici-berlin.org/repository/doi/10.25620/e180625-1
9. Jeanne Willette, *Roland Barthes: Writing Degree Zero*, https://arthistoryunstuffed.com/roland-barthes-writing-degree-zero/
10. Barthes, pp.101–102
11. Barthes, p.90
12. Benjamin Hiratmasu Ireland, *Memoirs of a Gaysha: Roland Barthes's Queer Japan*, /https://sites. cardiff.ac.uk/barthes/files/2018/11/HIRAMATSU-IRELAND-Memoirs-of-a-Gaysha.pdf
13. Barthes, *The Death of the Author*, https://sites.tufts.edu/english292b/files/2012/01/Barthes-The-Death-of-the-Author.pdf
14. *The Death of the Author*
15. Tom Nicholas, *The Death of the Author: WTF? Roland Barthes Death of the Author Explained*, www.youtube.com/watch?v=B9iMgtfp484
16. *The Foreignness of Self*, https://memoryphotographyliterature.wordpress.com/2012/02/16/ the-foreignness-of-self/

Bibliography

Albert Camus and football, https://camus-society.com/2017/11/29/albert-camus-and-football/

Albert Camus' speech at the Nobel Banquet at the City Hall in Stockholm, December 10, 1957, www.nobelprize.org/prizes/literature/1957/camus/speech/

An Introduction to Roland Barthes's Mythologies – A Macat Literature Analysis, www.youtube.com/watch?v=6GCzq8we-bI

Aristotle's Rhetoric, https://plato.stanford.edu/Archives/Win2004/entries/aristotle-rhetoric/

Aronson, Ronald, *An excerpt from Camus and Sartre, The Story of a Friendship and the Quarrel that Ended It*, https://press.uchicago.edu/Misc/Chicago/027961.html#:~:text=Jean%2DPaul%20Sartre%20and%20Albert,of%20Sartre%27s%20play%20The%20Flies

Aurelius, Marcus, *Meditations*

A Utopian Community in Florence, MA, https://davidrugglescenter.org/northampton-association-education-industry/

Bakewell, Sarah, *How to Live: A Life of Montaigne in One Question and Twenty Attempts at an Answer* (Vintage Books, 2011)

Bakewell, Sarah, *At the Existentialist Café: Freedom, Being And Apricot Cocktails* (Vintage, 2006)

Barthes, Roland, *Mythologies* (Vintage Classics, 2009)

Barthes, *The Death of the Author*, https://sites.tufts.edu/english292b/files/2012/01/Barthes-The-Death-of-the-Author.pdf

Biography examines political motivations of Montaigne, https://news.uchicago.edu/story/biography-examines-political-motivations-montaigne

Black, Rosemary *Glossophobia (Fear of Public Speaking): Are You Glossophobic?*, www.psycom.net/glossophobia-fear-of-public-speaking

Burke, Edmund, *Reflections on the Revolution in France*

Campbell, James, *The Island affair*, www.theguardian.com/books/2006/jan/07/featuresreviews.guardianreview25

Camus, Albert, *The Stranger*

Camus, Albert, *The Myth of Sisyphus* (Penguin Books, 2005)

Camus At Combat – From The Revolution To The Republic, https://intellectualsandthemedia.org/2018/12/05/camus-at-combat-from-the-revolution-to-the-republic/

Camus and his women, www.theguardian.com/books/1997/oct/15/biography.albertcamus

Camus & The Barbarity Of Capital Punishment, www.outlookindia.com/website/story/camus-the-barbarity-of-capital-punishment/294945

Casaliggi, Carmen, *Towards the Study of Ruskin's Water*, https://victorianweb.org/authors/ruskin/casaliggi1.html

Cervantes, Anakaren, *Albert Camus: Journalist at Heart, Scholar by Profession*, https://stanfordfreedomproject.com/multi-media-essays-on-freedom/albert-camus-journalist-at-heart-scholar-by-profession/

Cicero: Academic Skepticism, https://iep.utm.edu/cicero-academic-skepticism/

Cicero (Translated by James. M. May), *How to Win an Argument: An Ancient Guide to the Art of Persuasion* (Princeton University Press, 2016)

Clarke, Lee, *Marcus Aurelius' Meditations: Inside the Mind of the Philosopher Emperor*, www.thecollector.com/marcus-aurelius-meditations/

Christopherson, Richard, *Old Nick and His Traducers*, www.jstor.org/stable/41204805
Cooper, Suzanne Fagence, *To See Clearly: Why Ruskin Matters* (Quercus, 2019)
Cooper-Davis, Charlotte, *Christine De Pizan: Life, Work, Legacy* (University of Chicago Press, 2021)
Court, Simon, *William Godwin: Political Justice, anarchism and the Romantics*, https://wordsworth.org.uk/blog/2015/10/04/william-godwin-political-justice-anarchism-and-the-romantics/
De Pizan, Christine, *The Book of Fortune's Transformation*, in *Selected Writings*
De Pizan, Christine, *The Book of The City of Ladies*
De Pizan, Christine, (Translated by Sarah Lawson), *The Treasure of The City of Ladies* (Penguin Books, 2003)
De Pizan, Christine, (Translated by David Hult), *The Debate of the Romance of the Rose* (University of Chicago Press, 2010)
Dialogue from Film – Monty Python & The Holy Grail – Black Knight, https://thingsthatmadeanimpression.wordpress.com/2012/07/25/dialogue-from-film-monty-python-the-holy-grail/
Dimock, Chase, *Opacity and the Closet: Queer Tactics in Foucault, Barthes and Warhol by Nicholas De Villers*, https://lambdaliterary.org/2012/08/opacity-and-the-closet-queer-tactics-in-foucault-barthes-and-warhol-by-nicholas-de-villiers/
Florence In the Renaissance, www.historycrunch.com/florence-in-the-renaissance.html
Frenzel, Max, *Cultivating Your Inner Citadel*, https://medium.com/the-ascent/cultivating-your-inner-citadel-1036023dcd32
Guodong, Zhang, *A Critical Interpretation of Leo Strauss' Thoughts on Machiavelli*, https://philarchive.org/archive/ZHAACI-3
Helsinger, K, Elizabeth & Matthews, Manly John, *The Structure of Ruskin's Praeterita*, https://victorianweb.org/authors/ruskin/helsinger3.html
Holiday, Ryan, *Lives of The Stoics: The Art of Living from Zeno to Marcus Aurelius* (Profile Books, 2020)
Holmes, Richard, *How a Husband's Loving Biography Ruined His Wife's Reputation*, https://lithub.com/how-a-husbands-loving-biography-ruined-his-wifes-reputation/
Ireland, Benjamin Hiratmasu, *Memoirs of a Gaysha: Roland Barthes's Queer Japan*, https://sites.cardiff.ac.uk/barthes/files/2018/11/HIRAMATSU-IRELAND-Memoirs-of-a-Gaysha.pdf
Jackson, Lauren Michele, *What We Want From Richard Wright*, www.newyorker.com/books/under-review/what-we-want-from-richard-wright
John Ruskin's Seven Lamps of Architecture, https://moniquerblog.wordpress.com/2014/12/19/john-ruskins-seven-lamps-of-architecture/#:~:text=Finally%20the%20seventh%20lamp%2C%20the,and%20Religious%20Faith%20of%20nations.
Kaplan, Alice, *Paris from Camus's Notebooks*, www.theparisreview.org/blog/2016/09/19/paris-camuss-notebooks/
Kooiker, Cornelis J., *The fatal illness Of the Roman Emperor Antoninus Pius*
Kyles, Clayton Paul, *The Unapologetic Algerian: The Position of Albert Camus within the Algerian Situation*, https://repository.lib.ncsu.edu/bitstream/handle/1840.20/38465/etd.pdf?sequence=1&isAllowed=y
Lee, Alexander, *Machiavelli: His Life and Times* (Picador, 2020)
Leggett, Brian, *History of Classical Rhetoric – An overview of its early development (1)*, https://blog.iese.edu/leggett/2012/10/16/history-of-classical-rhetoric-an-overview-of-its-early-development/
Life Story: Sojourner Truth (ca. 1797–1883), https://wams.nyhistory.org/a-nation-divided/antebellum/sojourner-truth/
Lorenzo The Magnificent, www.florenceinferno.com/lorenzo-the-magnificent/
Machiavelli, Niccolo, *The Prince*, www.online-literature.com/machiavelli/prince/18/
Marie le Jars De Gournay, www.enotes.com/topics/marie-le-jars-de-gournay

Mary Wollstonecraft Family Troubles, www.shmoop.com/study-guides/biography/mary-wollstonecraft/bio/family-troubles

Mary Wollstonecraft: Finding Feminism in the French Revolution, https://radicalteatowel.co.uk/radical-history-blog/mary-wollstonecraft-finding-feminism-in-the-french-revolution

Mark, Joshua J., *Lao-Tzu*, www.worldhistory.org/Lao-Tzu/

Meyers, Jeffrey, *Malraux, Camus and the Nobel Prize*, https://thelondonmagazine.org/article/malraux-camus-nobel-prize/

Minford, John, *Did Lao-Tzu and Confucius Know Each Other?*, https://lithub.com/did-lao-tzu-and-confucius-know-each-other

Moeller, H.G., *Taoism*, www.sciencedirect.com/topics/social-sciences/taoism

Moldoveanu, Dragos, *The Downfall and the Death of Cesare Borgia*, https://elsborja.cat/blog/the-downfall-and-the-death-of-cesare-borgia/

Montaigne and Skepticism, www.cambridge.org/core/books/abs/cambridge-companion-to-montaigne/montaigne-and-skepticism/6CC36484C0ACE24758BD360A8F39E0FA

Montaigne's Rule for Reading: The Promiscuous Pursuit of Pleasure, https://fs.blog/what-did-montaigne-like-to-read/

Montaigne (Translated by M.A. Screech), *The Essays: A Selection* (Penguin Classics, 1993)

Nachtergael, Magali, *Barthes, Queer Before Queer?: A Journey into Barthes' Visual Culture*, https://oa.ici-berlin.org/repository/doi/10.25620/e180625-1

Niccolo Machiavelli on Reading as a Cure for Boredom, https://fs.blog/niccolo-machiavelli-on-reading/

Nicholas, Tom, *The Death of the Author: WTF? Roland Barthes Death of the Author Explained*, www.youtube.com/watch?v=B9iMgtfp484

Northampton Dedicates Sojourner Truth Statue, www.massmoments.org/moment-details/northampton-dedicates-sojourner-truth-statue.html

Osborne, Thomas, *Machiavelli and the Liberalism of Fear*, www.ncbi.nlm.nih.gov/pmc/articles/PMC5731607

Overview of Internal Alchemy in Taoism, www.learnreligions.com/internal-alchemy-in-taoism-an-overview-3182918

Owen, M.M., *How Albert Camus Found Solace in the Absurdity of Football*, www.mmowen.me/camus-absurd-love-of-football

Plutarch, *The Parallel Lives*, http://penelope.uchicago.edu/Thayer/e/roman/texts/plutarch/lives/cicero*.html

Popova, Maria, *The Original Marriage of Equals: The Love Letters of Feminism Founding Mother Mary Wollstonecraft and Political Philosopher William Godwin*, www.themarginalian.org/2018/10/15/romantic-outlaws-mary-wollstonecraft-william-godwin-love-letters/

Quarles, Philip, *Richard Wright's Love Letter to Paris*, www.wnyc.org/story/192767-richard-wright/

Qu, Hans, *Star Wars: The Force and Taoism*, https://filmschoolrejects.com/star-wars-force-taoism/

Raymond, Emma, *The Early Life Of Mary Wollstonecraft*, https://eastendwomensmuseum.org/blog/2021/4/30/the-early-life-of-mary-wollstonecraft

Reason Why Tupac Changed His Name to Makaveli, https://tupacuncensored.com/reason-why-tupac-changed-his-name-to-makaveli/

Reninger, Elizabeth, *Taoism for Beginners: Understanding and Applying Taoist History, Concepts and Practices* (Rock Ridge Press, 2020)

Reninger, Elizabeth, *The Taoist Altar*, www.learnreligions.com/the-taoist-altar-3182504

Roark, Ryan, *The Afterlife of Dying Buildings: Ruskin and Preservation in the Twenty First Century*, https://courtauld.ac.uk/research/research-resources/publications/courtauld-books-online/ruskins-ecologies-figures-of-relation-from-modern-painters-to-the-storm-cloud/14-the-afterlife-of-dying-buildings-ruskin-and-preservation-in-the-twenty-first-century-ryan-roark/

Robert Matthews (Profit Matthias), www.litcharts.com/lit/kingdom-of-matthias/characters/robert-matthews-prophet-matthias

Robertson, Donald, *How to Think Like a Roman Emperor: The Stoic Philosophy of Marcus Aurelius* (St Martin's Publishing Group, 2019)

Robertson, Donald, *The Metaphor of The Sun in Marcus Aurelius*, https://donaldrobertson.name/2017/12/06/the-metaphor-of-the-sun-in-marcus-aurelius/

Robertson, *Why Did Marcus Aurelius Allow Commodus To Succeed Him?*, https://donaldrobertson.name/2018/01/19/why-did-marcus-aurelius-allow-commodus-to-succeed-him/

Rogers, Ben, *Death of the author ROLAND BARTHES: A Biography by Louis-Jean Calvet, trs Sarah Wykes*, www.independent.co.uk/arts-entertainment/books/death-of-the-author-roland-barthes-a-biography-by-louisjean-calvet-trs-sarah-wykes-polity-press-163-25-1567120.html

Roland Barthes French Philosopher, Social Theorist and Semiotician, www.theartstory.org/influencer/barthes-roland/

Roman Empire, Marcus Aurelius – The Rain And Lightning Miracles, www.romanumismatics.com/historicarticles?view=article&article_id=556&dateFilter=0

Romantic Outlaws: The Extraordinary Lives of Mary Wollstonecraft & Mary Shelley, www.youtube.com/watch?v=7WJdOM2kgDs&t=1081s

Rufus, Musonius, (Translated by Cora E Lutz), *That One Should Disdain Hardships: The Teachings of a Roman Stoic* (Yale University Press, 2020)

Ruskin and Byron, www.lancaster.ac.uk/fass/ruskin/empi/notes/fbyron02.htm

Ruskin and Turner, www.lancaster.ac.uk/fass/ruskin/empi/notes/gsturnerz02.htm#:~:text=(See%20also%20Ruskin%2C%20Turner%2C,and%20two%20important%20oil%20paintings

Ruskin, John, *The Storm-Cloud of the Nineteenth Century*, www.gutenberg.org/files/20204/20204-h/20204-h.htm

Russell, Dick, *Black Genius: Inspirational Portraits of African-American Leaders* (Skyhorse Publishing, 2009)

Sartre, Jean-Paul, *Tribute to Albert Camus*, http://faculty.webster.edu/corbetre/philosophy/existentialism/camus/sartre-tribute.html

Smee, Taryn, *The Rise and Fall of the Medici – Renaissance Italy's Most Powerful Family*, www.thevintagenews.com/2018/11/17/the-medici/

Smith, Hazel, *In the Footsteps of Montaigne*, https://francetoday.com/learn/history/in-the-footsteps-of-montaigne/

Taoism: Cultivating Body, Mind and Spirit, www.taoisttaichi.org/taoism-cultivating-body-mind-spirit/

Tao Te Ching Quotes, www.readthistwice.com/quotes/book/tao-te-ching

The Chief Ancient Sources on Marcus Aurelius, https://onlinelibrary.wiley.com/doi/pdf/10.1002/9781444311075.oth1

The Foreignness of Self, https://memoryphotographyliterature.wordpress.com/2012/02/16/the-foreignness-of-self/

The History of the Guild, www.guildofstgeorge.org.uk/about/the-history-of-the-guild

The History of The Pied-Noirs, www.algeria.com/blog/the-history-of-the-pied-noirs/

The Letters of Fronto, www.attalus.org/info/fronto.html

Todd, Janet, *Ascendency: Lady Mount Cashell, Lady Moira, Mary Wollstonecraft and the Union Pamphlets*, www.jstor.org/stable/30070996

Truth, Sojourner, *Ain't I a Woman?*, www.nps.gov/articles/sojourner-truth.htm#:~:text=At%20the%201851%20Women's%20Rights,and%20after%20the%20Civil%20War

Truth, Sojourner, *The Narrative of Sojourner Truth*, https://digital.library.upenn.edu/women/truth/1850/1850.html

What is Epicureanism?, https://kinnu.xyz/kinnuverse/philosophy/the-timeless-wisdom-of-great-greek-philosophers/epicureanism/

What is Roman Stoicism?, https://study.com/learn/lesson/roman-stoicism-beliefs-philosophers.html

Why Did Plato Hate the Sophists?, https://ivypanda.com/essays/why-did-plato-hate-the-sophists-philosophy/

Willette, Jeanne, *Roland Barthes: Writing Degree Zero*, https://arthistoryunstuffed.com/roland-barthes-writing-degree-zero/

Wollstonecraft, Mary, *A Vindication of the Rights of Women*

Wollstonecraft, Mary, *Letters Written in Sweden, Norway, and Denmark*, www.gutenberg.org/files/3529/3529-h/3529-h.htm

Wollstonecraft, Mary, *Thoughts on the Education of Daughters*, www.gutenberg.org/files/67466/67466-h/67466-h.htm

Wollstonecraft, Mary, *Vindications of The Rights of Men*

Wright, Malcolm, *Afterword, The Man Who Lived Underground*

Wright, Nancy Means, *A Fiery Female Meets the Devil: Mary Wollstonecraft and Henry Fuseli*, www.elizabethkmahon.com/2011/09/fiery-female-meets-devil-mary.html

Wright, Richard, *Black Boy* (Vintage Classics, 1945)

Wright, Richard, *How Bigger Was Born*, https://archive.org/details/in.ernet.dli.2015.499539/page/n5/mode/2up

Wright, Richard, *I Choose Exile*, www.artofsunday.com/logs/i-choose-exile

Wright, Richard, *I Tried to Be A Communist*, www.theatlantic.com/magazine/archive/1944/08/richard-wright-communist/618821/

Wright, Richard, *Memories of My Grandmother*, collected with *The Man Who Lives Underground* (Vintage Classics, 2023)

Yan, Lu, *The Living Method of Turning the Light Around*, www.dailyzen.com/journal/the-living-method-of-turning-the-light-around/

Zarestsky, Robert, *The Logic of the Rebel: On Simone Weil and Albert Camus*, https://lareviewofbooks.org/article/logic-rebel-simone-weil-albert-camus/

Index

Absurdism 92
Aristotle 16, 132, 137, 147
Aurelius, Marcus 1–14, 132, 138, 147, 149

Barthes, Roland 124–30

Camus, Albert 91–101, 113–14, 127, 139
Cicero 15–25

De Beauvoir, Simone 97, 113,
De Pizan, Christine 40–48

Epicurus 135, 138, 146
Epicureanism 18, 69, 71,
Epictetus 4, 7, 29, 31, 132, 134, 146, 148, 156, 165–66, 168
Existentialism 113–14, 150, 155,

Kierkegaard, Soren 150

Lao Tzu 34–40

Machiavelli, Niccolo 48–61
Montaigne, de Michel 61–73, 141

Nietzsche, Friedrich 68, 160

Plato 4, 16, 58, 74, 93, 135–36, 138, 148–49, 150–51, 165–66
Plutarch 58, 64, 72, 138,

Rhetoric 5, 7, 15–18, 22 – 24, 25, 29, 42, 45, 50, 85, 124, 148
Rufus, Musonius 25–34
Ruskin, John 81–91

Satre, Jean-Paul 97–98, 100, 113–14, 127, 160
Scepticism 18, 69, 71–72, 148
Seneca 4, 29–30, 58, 72, 132,
Socrates 3, 16, 29, 32, 135, 140, 148, 165–66,
Sophistry 5, 16, 24–27
Stoicism 2–4, 7, 9, 13–14, 18, 21, 30, 69, 71, 131–34, 148, 154–55

Taoism 34–40
Truth, Sojourner 116–24

Weil, Simone 100
Wright, Richard 102–16
Wollstonecraft, Mary 73–81